PA

O

EASTER

WORLD WAR II GERMAN DEBRIEFS
PUBLISHED BY GREENHILL BOOKS

THE BATTLE OF THE BULGE: THE GERMAN VIEW
Perspectives from Hitler's High Command

FIGHTING IN HELL
The German Ordeal on the Eastern Front

FIGHTING IN NORMANDY
The German Army from D-Day to Villers-Bocage

FIGHTING THE INVASION
The German Army at D-Day

HITLER'S ARDENNES OFFENSIVE
The German View of the Battle of the Bulge

INSIDE THE AFRIKA KORPS
The Crusader Battles, 1941–1942

THE LUFTWAFFE FIGHTER FORCE
The View from the Cockpit

PANZERS
ON THE
EASTERN FRONT

General Erhard Raus and his
Panzer Divisions in Russia, 1941–1945

Edited by
Peter G. Tsouras

FRONTLINE
BOOKS

A Greenhill Book

Greenhill
Books

For Captain Lincoln D. Leibner, US Army,
who showed at the Pentagon on 11 September 2001
that we still have men of courage among us.

First published in Great Britain in 2002 by
Greenhill Books, Lionel Leventhal Limited
www.greenhillbooks.com

Reprinted in this format in 2011 by
Frontline Books

an imprint of
Pen & Sword Books Ltd
47 Church Street
Barnsley
South Yorkshire
S70 2AS

© Greenhill Books, 1996

ISBN 978 1 84832 619 4

A CIP catalogue record for this book is
available from the British Library

Printed and bound in England
by CPI

For a complete list of Pen & Sword titles please contact
PEN & SWORD BOOKS LIMITED
47 Church Street, Barnsley, South Yorkshire, S70 2AS, England
E-mail: enquiries@pen-and-sword.co.uk
Website: www.pen-and-sword.co.uk

Contents

Illustrations

7

Note: The maps on pages 48, 52, 55, 76, 78 and 82 are reproduced from original and surviving maps held in the US National Archives.

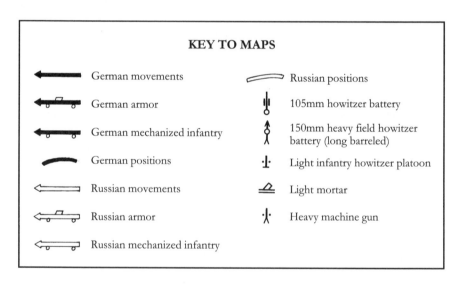

KEY TO MAPS

German movements — Russian positions

German armor — 105mm howitzer battery

German mechanized infantry — 150mm heavy field howitzer battery (long barreled)

German positions — Light infantry howitzer platoon

Russian movements — Light mortar

Russian armor — Heavy machine gun

Russian mechanized infantry

Preface

by Franz Halder
Chief of the German Army General Staff, 1938–1942

Retired General E. Raus's portrayals of extraordinary personal experiences during the Russian campaign are both exciting and instructive. The author's tactical lessons after the description of each event are to the point. Besides the study's teaching value explained in the topic leader's preliminary remarks to individual examples, its psychological value deserves to be emphasized . It becomes very clear that a strong military leader with great power of motivation is the most important factor for success.

Generaloberst (ret.) Franz Halder

Introduction

The new main-attack army, which had been detached from the troops besieging Stalingrad and had been reinforced by reserves from the eastern bank of the Volga River, assembled in the northern hills and in the valley east of Bolshaya-Vasilevka for an all-out attack against the 6th Panzer Division. Thousands of Russians filled the snowfields, slopes, and depressions of the endless steppe. No soldier had ever seen such multitudes advance on him. Their leading waves were thrown to the ground by a hail of high-explosive shells, but more and more waves followed. Any attempt on the part of the Russian masses to reach the German lines was thwarted by the fire of machine guns and guns. The frontal attack was blocked.

A few hours later, however, the Russians poured into the village from the east like a stream of lava, pushing the flank of the 4th Panzergrenadier Regiment back some 100 meters. A short time later, they pushed through the gap to the 23rd Panzer Division and rolled forward toward the rear of the troops in the bridgehead. The eastern part of the village and the vicinity of the cemetery were lost. But the division stood unshaken like a rock in the surging sea. It was only when the encirclement of the division seemed on the point of becoming complete that the Russian masses were mowed down by a sudden thunderous concentration of the German artillery and were at the same time caught in the flank by 150 tanks coming from the village, and in the rear by 42 assault guns. As a result, they were overwhelmed. Even the strongest nerves of the enemy were unequal to this eruption of fire and steel. The Russians threw their weapons away and tried like madmen to escape the infernal crossfire and the deadly armored envelopment. This was a thing which rarely happened in World War II. In mobs of several hundreds, shelled even by their own artillery and their own rocket launchers, they ran west toward the only open spot and surrendered to the German covering parties stationed there.

—Generaloberst Erhard Raus
To Liberate Stalingrad, November 1952

I first came across writings of Generaloberst Erhard Raus in early 1971 while serving as a young armor officer with the United States Army in Germany. Published as Department of the Army pamphlets, they had lain untouched in my company commander's office for ages, it seemed, from all the dust I disturbed when I pulled them out of the bookcase. Being something of a Germanophile at the time, I was fascinated by these little gems of history. As I read on, it was obvious that the distilled experiences of German generals on the Russian Front were of such immediacy to our present mission—the victors of Stalingrad, the 8th Guards Army, were just 40 kilometers east of us—that I wondered why they were so little known. After all, the Soviet Armed Forces were in the full flood of expansion, preparing for the great Theater Strategic Operation (TSO) meant to carry them to the Channel and the Pyrenees.

I was also struck by the anonymity of the authors of these pamphlets. The Army had given a brief résumé, but also added the statement that the author wished to remain anonymous. It was only years later, when I found the bible behind the pamphlets at the Army Library in the Pentagon—the *Guide to Foreign Military Studies*[1]—that I was able to unravel this mystery. This was the story of the US Army's program to capture the experience of the senior German officers (see Appendix 2 for the story of the Foreign Studies Program). Now I knew the name of the author—Erhard Raus—but, in all my reading of Eastern Front operations, the name had not stuck in my memory. Who was he? Who was this man who had so many dramatic and breathtaking stories at his fingertips?

The more I looked, the more impressed I became with one of the great unsung commanders of the twentieth century—a man who led the spearhead of the relief force that drove for the trapped Sixth Army in Stalingrad, the man who had commanded the brilliant defense in the Fourth Battle of Kharkov, the man who had led three panzer armies with distinction, and the man who was such a master of the art of war and leadership that his men coined a phrase for the saving effects of those qualities: *"Raus zieht heraus !"* (Raus pulls you through!). For a long time, the pantheon of German commanders on the Eastern Front was a murky thing at best for the Western audience. Those commanders who had fought against the Western Allies were well known—for example, Rommel and Kesselring. We had heard of Eastern Front commanders who had also gained reputations in the West—Guderian, von Manstein, von Mellenthin and von Manteuffel—and their reptuations rested not a little on the books they were able to write. But Raus wrote no book and passed away quietly in 1956.

Twenty-three years after I first blew the dust off his pamphlets, I set out to bring the writings of Erhard Raus to the attention of English-speaking readers. In 1994 Greenhill Books published the first collection of the DA Pamphlets under the title of *The Anvil of War: German Generalship in Defense on the Eastern Front.* Two of the three pamphlets included in it were Raus' *Military Improvisations During the Russian Campaign* (DA Pam 20-201, 1951) and *German Defense Tactics Against Russian Breakthroughs* (DA Pam 20-233, 1951). In 1995 Greenhill published the second volume based upon the DA Pamphlets under the title *Fighting in Hell: The German Ordeal on the Eastern Front.* Two of the four pamphlets included in it were Raus' *Russian Combat Methods* (DA Pam 20-230, 1950) and *The Effects of Climate on Combat in European Russia* (DA Pam 20-291, 1952). Fortunately, both books have been well received, helping to bring Raus's role and reputation into their proper place.

The Foreign Military Studies collection of manuscripts, however, contained even more of Raus's writings—which, if anything, were more fascinating than his published

---

[1] *Guide to Foreign Military Studies* (Historical Division, Headquarters, United States Army Europe, 1954) p. 248.

works. These manuscipts make up this book and include *The Pomeranian Battle and the Command in the East* (D-189, 1947) and *Small Unit Tactics—Unusual Situations* (P-060g, Part I [1952], Part II [1952], Part III [1953], and Part IV [1954]).

The original purpose as devised by then Colonel S. L. A. Marshall, Army Historical Section, was simple. In order to write the history of the US Army in the European Theater of Operations, the Army needed to know what was going on "on the other side of the hill." A new purpose emerged as the Cold War heated up and finally exploded in Korea—to exploit the German lessons learned in fighting the Soviets.

This, then, is the story of the German Army in adversity. Although the Army was ultimately doomed to defeat, its retreat from Russia was conducted with skill and heroism against incredible odds. Upon his return to Moscow by car after the Potsdam Conference, a senior American diplomat noted that his route followed the retreat of one of the main German armies and was littered with the debris of war. But repeatedly he would see the same scene—one or two burnt-out German tanks in defensive positions with arcs of twenty to thirty destroyed Soviet tanks arrayed around them. The author fought through this very ground. Only in 1990, in the full glare of *glasnost*, did the Soviet General Staff announce its true military losses of the war—an incredible 8,668,400 dead and eighteen million wounded, grim testimony to the achievements of the German soldier in both the offense and defense.[2]

However, it was not the purpose of the US Army to write the history of the German Army. Most of the German studies covered the events after Stalingrad when the Soviets had become the hammer and the Germans the anvil, a parallel the US Army was seeing as a very real possibility for itself. Accordingly, the manuscripts were not written with an orderly history in mind; they were written to impart lessons learned. Threading these lessons together chronologically, though, does create an historical narrative of incredible power.

Raus's works incoporated into *The Anvil of War* and *Fighting in Hell* were thematic treaments on various subjects of interest to the US Army, although historical narratives were interspersed throughout. Raus's works in this current book, *Panzers on the Eastern Front*, are straight combat narratives that each tell the story of a particular military operation. Together, they tell much of Raus's experience from the invasion of the Soviet Union on 22 June 1941 through August 1943 when he brilliantly led the defense of Kharkov. They add remarkably to the historical record and are first-rate military historical prose.

In a letter of 4 February 1951, Raus discusses the collaboration that led to the manuscripts in this book. Addressed to the chief of the Operational History Branch, Lieutenant-Colonel Nawrocky, Raus explains:

> According to your wish and my letter of 8 January 1951 I pictured as first example unusual small events out of my experience in the Eastern Campaign . . .The events I want to

---

[2] General M. A. Moiseyev, Chief of the General Staff, *Voyenno-istoricheskiy zhurnal*, No 3, March 1990.

describe took place in the entire eastern area through all the years of war and during all seasons. Each example will be different from the other and therefore has its own particular features.[3]

Chapter 1, "Barbarossa Begins," covers the 6th Panzer Division in the opening battles on the frontier with Army Group North. Chapter 2, "Raus Pulls Them Through," continues the story of the incredible series of bold actions by the 6th Panzer Division in the drive on Leningrad. The narrative then takes the division to the desperate situations in early 1942 in the face of the Russian winter and the Soviet Moscow Offensive operation that nearly doomed the German Army. Chapter 3, "To Liberate Stalingrad!," is the high drama of the attempted relief of the trapped 6th Army in Stalingrad by the 6th Panzer Division rushed from the comfort of France to face echeloned Soviet armies, not to mention the enemy's camel corps, determined not to give up their prize in the beleaguered city. Chapter 4, "Struggle Along the Donets," tells of aspects of the desperate and tenacious defense of Kharkov after the German retreat following the battle of Kursk. Finally, Chapter 5, "The Pomeranian Battle and the Command in the East," offers one of the most telling glimpses into history of any of the German manuscripts – the detailed and revealing conversations with Reichsfürher Heinrich Himmler on the military situation in February 1945 and Raus's catastrophic briefing with Hitler himself. The author uses his opportunity to expound on the nature of modern war and the tactical and leadership concepts of the German Army in the introduction to Chapter 1:

> Proper combat education and training for officers and soldiers are of vital importance to victory. The increase of their skill and efficiency to a maximum is the objective of peacetime training. This aim may be considered reached if every soldier completely masters his weapons in times of emergency and if every commander masters the tasks with which he is faced. The less commanders and soldiers have to learn in actual combat, the better has been their training for war.

Here, as at most fronts, it was also a question of dealing with new weapons and a mass commitment of enemy troops and equipment which threatened to crush everything. These events, which first appeared in the later course of the war, placed commanders and troops in unusual situations where tactical measures had to be taken which were neither prescribed in regulations nor taught. Nothing but an officer corps educated to take full responsibility and to act independently, plus the resolve of courageous soldiers, made it possible for solutions to be found to all unusual problems. An army relying on mass drilling and mass effect alone would have failed under such conditions or would have suffered heavy losses.

Chapters 1–4 comprise the four manuscripts in *Small Unit Tactics—Unusual Situations* (P-060g, Parts I–IV); Chapter 5 is *The Pomeranian Battle and the Command in the East* (D-189,

---

[3] Letter from Erhard Raus to Lt-Col M. Nawrocky dated 4 February 1951, contained in the documents associated with MS # 060g, "Small Unit Actions—Unusual Situations," Foreign Military Studies, National Archives, College Park, MD.

1947). In order to provide the reader with sufficient background, I have added Appendix 1: "The 6th Panzer Division: Its History and Order of Battle." The story of the Foreign Military Studies Program is at Appendix 2 and has been revised from the introduction to *The Anvil of War*. Additionally, I have significantly expanded the original modest notes in the manuscripts to provide the necessary context. As an illustration, the notes in Chapter 3 provide the reader with a correction to the faulty Soviet order of battle upon which Raus had to rely at Stalingrad from German intelligence, and give an accurate picture of what he faced: for example, Raus persisted in believing that he faced only the 3rd Tank Army when, in actuality, he faced the strongly reinforced 2nd Guards and 51st Armies.

I also have found it necessary to change the American military terminology in the translation back into the original German terms to describe German military organizations and concepts where those terms are more familiar to the English-speaking readership interested in German military affairs. This provides a much more precise military lexicon, bestows a sense of authenticity and accuracy, and is thoroughly explained in the notes as well. For example, the manuscript's "4th Infantry Regiment," although a direct translation of *Schützenregiment*, is somewhat misleading since the formation was motorized; the more common and descriptive term for this in English would be "4th Motorized Infantry Regiment." This term in German went out of use in July 1942 when all such regiments in panzer divisions were redesignated *Panzergrenadier*—hence the "4th Panzergrenadier Regiment." Similarly, while "battle group" is a literal translation of the German *Kampfgruppe*, it lacks the punch and imagery of the German. A particularly crude translation of the word for the average German infantrymen was "Doughboy"! I have replaced it with the correct term, *Landser*. If I have been inconsistent, it has been for the sake of clarity and usage. I have also left German ranks in the original form; translations all too often confuse the issue. For example, *Generalmajor* in German means "brigadier-

TABLE OF EQUIVALENT SENIOR RANKS

German Army	Red Army	US Army
Generalfeldmarschall	Marshal of the Soviet Union	General of the Army
Generaloberst	General of the Army	General
General der Infanterie	General-Colonel	Lieutenant-General
General der Kavallerie	General-Colonel	Lieutenant-General
General der Artillerie	General-Colonel	Lieutenant-General
General der Pioniere	General-Colonel	Lieutenant-General
General der Panzertruppen	General-Colonel	Lieutenant-General
General der Nachrichten-truppen	General-Colonel	Lieutenant-General
Generalleutnant	General-Lieutenant	Major-General
Generalmajor	General-Major	Brigadier-General
Oberst	Colonel	Colonel

general" in English and is often mistranslated as "major-general." Finally, for clarity, all Soviet units have been italicized.

The reader will notice a variation in the spelling of the author's name in a number of historical works. The correct spelling is "Raus," seemingly a simple name, but one which is consistently misspelled by both Germans and Americans as "Rauss," to include this editor in *The Anvil of War* and *Fighting in Hell.* I humbly beg the reader's pardon for the error. I have been in good company, however, since all of the German generals— von Manstein, von Mellenthin, and Guderian—who referred to him in their books and knew him personally misspelled it as well.

I would like to express my appreciation to Jayne C. Shelton for her invaluable assistance in preparing such a clean and accurate transcript of these chapters from the often barely legible originals.

Erhard Raus

> The right appreciation of their opponents... the audacity to leave for a short space of time, a small force only before them, energy in forced marches, boldness in sudden attacks, the intensified activity which great souls acquire in the moment of danger—these are the ground of such victories.

Clausewitz surely would have recognized Erhard Raus in his description of a great captain in his masterpiece *On War*.[4]

Erhard Franz-Josef Raus was born on 8 January 1889 at Wolfamitz in Austria. After his education at the Brünn Cadet School (in what is now Brno in Slovakia) in 1905–09, he received his commission as a Second Lieutenant in the Austrian Army on 1 May 1912. In World War I he served on the Russian and Italian fronts and commanded mountain troops. After the war, until 1937 he served in a number of assignments in Vienna, especially as an instructor in the military school system. On 1 December 1936 he was promoted to Colonel (Oberst). In 1938 he served as Austria's military attaché in Rome.[5]

In his formative experiences as a junior and field grade officer can be seen the great general of World War II. Like Rommel's, his service with mountain troops demanded the most of independence, initiative, innovation, and leadership. Mountain operations are by their nature independent, where the skills and abilities—especially the quick-thinking, aggressiveness, and boldness of the junior leader—are vital. Secondly, his extensive experience as an instructor developed one of the traits that must be second nature to a great general—that of teacher and trainer.

Upon the annexation of Austria in 1938, the Austrian Army was incorporated directly into the German Army, and, as with the rest of the Austrian officer corps, Raus, as a professional officer, simply changed uniforms. He was obviously well thought of

---

[4] Carl von Clausewitz, *On War*, tr. Michael Howard and Peter Paret (Princeton, NJ: Princeton University Press, 1976).
[5] Brief biography of Erhard Raus contained in the documents associated with MS # 060g, "Small Unit Actions—Unusual Situations".

enough to be appointed commander of Military Area XVII, which included Vienna, the ancient Hapsburg capital, and served there from 1939 to 1940. From 1939 to 1940 he served as chief of staff of XVII Corps.

In 1939 he began a long and distinguished association with the division with which he was to serve through some of the most dramatic moments of the war when he received command of the 4th Motorized Infantry Regiment (Schützenregiment 4), 1st Light Division (1st Leichte Division, later converted to 6th Panzer Division—see Appendix 1 for the history of the 6th Panzer Division). He commanded the regiment in the 1940 campaign in the West in which the 6th Panzer Division was commanded by Generalmajor (Brigadier General) Werner Kempf. The division, for the first time, was subordinated to XLI Panzer Corps commanded by Generaloberst (General) Georg Hans Reinhardt as part of Panzer Group Von Kleist, the vanguard of Army Group A. Raus's regiment was part of the great mass of panzer divisions that closed on the British pocket at Dunkirk from the south. A victorious 6th Panzer Division returned to garrison duty in East Prussia, now subordinated to the Eighteenth Army. In 1941 Raus received command of the 6th Motorized Brigade (Schützenbrigade 6) which included his old regiment, the newly added 114th Motorized Infantry Regiment, and the 6th Motorcycle Battalion (Kradschutz Abteilung 6).

The invasion of the Soviet Union in Operation "Barbarossa," on 22 June 1941, passed without enemy contact for the 6th Panzer Division and Colonel Raus. Only on the morning of the next day did things change. "Far to the front, clouds of dust appeared on the horizon. 'The enemy after all,' many a man thought, and speed picked up." Fighting its way through ambushes and delaying efforts of Soviet units, the Kampfgruppe led by Raus seized the bridge over the Dubysa River. The Soviets counterattacked with tanks, including the first appearance of the huge KV-1 and KV-2 models, the existence of which the Germans were completely ignorant of. Their 50mm antitank guns were useless, and the infantry were suddenly at great risk. It was here that Raus's quick thinking dominated the situation. Instinctively he employed combined arms. He wrote: "All branches of the combat arms were brought forward to participate in the antitank defense. The rumor of the invincibility of the superheavy enemy tanks had already been destroyed..." He also understood that German success in the face of technological surprise was simply not in a specific tactic.

> As always in critical situations, in this case also: the iron discipline of the soldiers, and the spirit and morale of the battle-tried, well-trained commanders and subordinate commanders decided the issue. They were not dependent on outmoded rules and instructions but knew how to act in a situation unprovided for by regulations and personal experience. Their success confirmed the suitability of the measures taken. The troops lived through this experience with unbroken courage and few losses, and again proved their excellent spirit in the engagements which followed. (Chapter 1).

In the drive on Leningrad, Kampfgruppe Raus was always one step ahead of the enemy. On 6 July it was the first German unit to break through the three-kilometer deep belt of fortifications of the Stalin Line just across the Dvina River. On 11 July the XLI Corps commander personally ordered Raus to seize the two bridges over the Luga River. Three days later he did just that, seizing both bridges intact in a daring *coup de main*, assisted by a special operations detachment from the Brandenberger Lehr Regiment. For the next week, Raus held both bridgeheads against heavy and repeated counterattacks by Soviet forces frantic to wipe out this German foothold so near to Leningrad. His Kampfgruppe numbered barely 1,500 men and was completely surrounded by up to two Soviet divisions, yet by means of skilled mobile defense and high-quality personal leadership he defeated every Soviet attempt to crush his force. Raus identified the reasons for German success in such a difficult tactical position against such odds: psychological factors, high-training, the personal presence of commanders in a crisis, and combined arms.

> The intelligent German soldier wanted to know what he was fighting for and what significance the mission of his respective unit had; only then was he capable of doing his utmost. He was an independent, individualistic fighter and felt far superior to the Russian soldier, who was trained for mass commitment. It is therefore important to make sure that these and similar psychological influences not be overlooked, even during the soldier's peacetime education and training. It is absolutely essential to imbue each man with an awareness of surpassing skill and self-confidence, and the extent of this feeling depended on how well he had been trained in the use of weapons and the utilization of terrain. To earn the confidence of the troops required exemplary conduct, sound knowledge and education and concern for the welfare of men on the part of their superior. Furthermore, it was important for each commander to appear at crucial points so as to be able to offer advice and assistance or make immediate decisions. It was his implicit duty to be present in critical situations. Of great importance, too, was the bond of comradeship which existed between the various arms and which considerably facilitated the coordination of all weapons. (Chapter 2).

Raus's ability was recognized by a promotion to Generalmajor (Brigadier-General) on 1 September. That ability would again be tested almost immediately as XLI Panzer Corps approached the outer defenses of Leningrad—the Leningrad Line—early that same month. These defenses were six miles in depth and consisted of sophisticated system of antitank ditches, earth and concrete bunkers, pillboxes with armored cupolas with machine guns and cannon that could be raised and lowered. Immediately south of the Leningrad Line, the area of Krasnogvardyesk had been converted into an outlying fortress complex and had successfully held up several German infantry corps. The 6th Panzer Division attacked from the west, penetrating the Leningrad Line and getting into the rear of Krasnogvardyesk, triggering a mass withdrawal of Soviet forces which the Germans savaged. They also broke a tank counterattack. Still, the fortress of Krasnogvardyesk had to be reduced. Raus's panzergrenadiers attacked the bunker system from the rear, engaging in savage fighting in subterranean chambers to root out the defenders. With the fall of the complex, the last major defenses of Leningrad had fallen. As Raus recounted, "Within a week, the 6th Panzer had to break through and roll up twelve positions, repel several counterattacks, and take more than 300 heavily fortified bunkers."[6]

Having broken every barrier, and having overcome every attempt at defense, the 6th Panzer Division had Leningrad in its grasp. Then they lost it. Shortly after the victory at Krasnogvardyesk, Hitler ordered XLI Panzer Corps south to assist Army Group Center in the drive on Moscow. In Operation "Typhoon" on 10 October, the 6th Panzer Division made the initial deep penetration in Russian lines that led to the encirclement of 600,000 Soviet troops at Vyazma.

On 25 November Raus assumed command of the 6th Panzer Division as the drive to Moscow took the division almost to the suburbs of the Soviet capital. But the frost had preceded him on the night of the 6th/7th. Two days after Raus took over, the division was directly north of Moscow near Yakroma when the temperature plunged to –40°C. The offensive slowed as Moscow seemed barely a hand's grasp away. Then the Soviets unleashed their Moscow counteroffensive fueled by fresh Siberian divisions. Now Raus found himself with the task of saving an exhausted division. He lost his last tank on 10 December. Hitler ordered the army to stand fast and fight it out in the freezing cold. By early January, without armored vehicles , with a skyrocketing frostbite rate, and in the face of a savage Soviet counterattack, the 6th Panzer Division faced destruction. Raus saved it. He ordered emplacements blown out of the frozen ground, covered with lumber, and heated with wood fires; the frostbite rate fell. He intercepted stragglers, formed reaction teams, and kept the shrunken division in the line. It was here that Raus acquired his epithet among the troops. According to Generalmajor Hellmuth Reinhardt, "Although the author at the end of the war was an army group commander, he attained that rank because of his reputation as a fighting commander of smaller units. He was especially skillful in extricating troops from desperate situations, and thus acquired the sobriquet '*Raus zieht heraus*,' roughly translated as 'Raus pulls them through.' "(Chapter 2).

Raus found himself holding the vital Rzhev–Vyazma road, upon which the German Ninth Army depended for its survival. But the Soviets were still dangerously close to that road. His only solution was to assume the offensive, despite the enemy's superiority. He counterattacked at the beginning of February in what he called the "Snail Offensive," a rolling series of small-unit actions aimed at driving the Russians from one village after another until he had pushed them back 10–20 miles and appropriated their vital winter quarters for his own men. The following month he initiated the "Scorpion Offensive." Once again, Raus's ability as a tactician and leader became critical.

> The available forces and material were still inadequate for an offensive in the conventional manner, and once again it became necessary to improvise tactics. Only successive surprise attacks with limited objectives plus close coordination of all arms had any chance of success. Free choice of time and place for each intended thrust was another prerequisite

---

[6] Erhard Rauss, Hans von Greiffenberg and Waldemar Erfurth, *Fighting in Hell: The German Ordeal on the Eastern Front*, edited by Peter G. Tsouras (London: Greenhill Books, 1995), pp. 78–82. For an explanation of the inconsistent spelling of Raus's name, see above, p. 16.

since the issue would be in doubt if the enemy recognized the Germans' intentions and took countermeasures. Whenever the element of surprise was lost, the objective had to be changed and the blow delivered at some distant vulnerable point. All this had to be achieved with a relatively weak striking force which was to be shifted to a different sector of the front immediately after every thrust. The tactics to be employed thus consisted of a well-coordinated but flexible system of limited objective attacks. They could best be compared to a series of paralyzing stings a scorpion would inflict in a life-and-death struggle against a physically superior opponent.7

Again the Red Army staggered back from the blows that Raus delivered. In the grim early months of 1942, Raus's abilities had been crucial in not only stabilizing a tottering front but in improving its situation and seizing the initiative from the enemy.

In April, the 6th Panzer Division was pulled out of Russia and transferred to the cozy warmth of northern France to be rebuilt. It was in July that an important fighting team was formed when Colonel Walter von Hünersdorff was assigned as commander of the 11th Panzer Regiment. If the survivors of "Barbarossa" and the replacements thought France would be a easy tour, they were quickly disabused. Raus trained the 6th Panzer Division hard for the next six months. Then, in early November, the Eastern Front beckoned again: the German Sixth Army had been encircled at Stalingrad, and Hitler ordered 6th Panzer east to joint the relief attempt.

Raus's hard training paid off immediately. As his forward regiment was unloading from its train at Kotelnikovo near the front, it was suddenly attacked by Soviet cavalry. The Germans instinctively counterattacked and smashed the enemy's 81st Cavalry Division, driving it from the town. This was only the first in a series of punishing blows Raus would rain down on the Soviet *51st Army* whose duty it was to form the outer ring of the forces encircling Stalingrad. In the next few days, Raus savaged the *4th Cavalry Corps* attempts to take Kotelnikovo and crushed it at Pokhlebin. (Chapter 3).

Assigned to LVII Panzer Corps, Raus's division formed its most powerful element. The ensuing attempt to break into the Stalingrad pocket would be the task of the 6th Panzer Divison. On 12 December Raus attacked and breached the first barrier of the Aksay River. He hammered the *51st Army* back, kilometer after kilometer, leaving a trail of wrecked Soviet tanks in his wake. He had a masterful subordinate in von Hünersdorff, and the two of them thrust the division closer and closer to the pocket, grinding up every Soviet reserve thrown in their path. The situation had become so desperate for the Soviets that Stalin himself was personally involved in the attempt to stop Raus. Stalin called from Moscow to his front commanders, "You will hold out—we are getting reserves down to you," he commanded menacingly. "I'm sending you the *Second Guards Army*—the best unit I've left."8

Even the *2nd Guards* were not enough. Raus broke them in a final battle on 20 December. Having exhausted their armor, they resorted to mass infantry attacks:

---

7 Erhard Rauss and Oldwig von Natzmer, *The Anvil of War: German Generalship in Defense on the Eastern Front*, edited by Peter G. Tsouras (London: Greenhill Books, 1994), p. 40.

8 Paul Carrell, *Hitler Moves East, 1941–1943* (London and Boston, 1963) p. 605.

The Red riflemen surged forward in multitudes never before encountered. Attack wave followed attack wave without regard for losses. Each was annihilated by a terrific hail of fire without gaining so much as a foot of ground. Therefore, the Russians went around the two flanks of the German division in order to encircle it. In the course of this maneuver they came between the German artillery position and the panzer regiment. Firing from all barrels, 150 tanks and self-propelled assault guns attacked the Russian masses form the rear when they tried to escape the fire from the artillery. In their desperate situation many Russians threw down their weapons and surrendered. Succeeding elements flowed back . . . The Russian mass assault had collapsed.[9]

Barely 35 kilometers remained on the way to Stalingrad. The men of the 6th Panzer Divison could even hear the sound of gunfire from the beleagured Sixth Army, but its commander would not defy Hitler and order a breakout. Had he done that, the chances are that Raus would have been able to meet his forces halfway. That was not to be. The Sixth Army stayed put, and the Soviets attacked elsewhere, throwing the front into crisis. Raus' division was pulled out of its bridgehead and ordered north to put out the new fire.

The Army Group Commander, Field Marshal Erich von Manstein, was later to write:

The very versatility of our armour and the superiority of our tank crews were brilliantly demonstrated in this period, as were the bravery of the panzergrenadiers and the skill of our anti-tank units. At the same time it was seen what an experienced old armoured division like 6 Panzer could achieve under its admirable commander General Rauss [sic] . . . when it went into action with its full complement of armoured vehicles and assault guns.[10]

After the Soviets frustrated the relief of the Sixth Army, they launched a major attack westwards to drive the Germans further out of reach of the doomed forces in Stalingrad. The spearhead of the *1st Tank Army* overran the great supply and communications centre at Tatsinskaya, a bare 130 kilometers from Rostov; if it should lunge that much further the whole German position in the southern Soviet Union would collapse. Raus and the 6th Panzer rode to the rescue and snapped the spearhead of the *1st Tank Army*, destroying its lead corps and recovering Tatsinskaya. Paul Carrell describes Raus's night attack:

And now General Raus opened the nocturnal tank battle between Maryevka and Romanov. The enemy, held up frontally, was attacked from both flanks and in the rear. The Russians were taken by surprise and reacted confusedly and nervously. Raus, on the other hand, calmly conducted the battle like a game of chess.[11]

It was no accident that Raus was promoted to Generalleutnant (Major-General) on 1 January 1943.

In the confusion of the collapse of the German front after Stalingrad fell in January and Kharkov in early February, Manstein became desperate for talented senior officers.

[9] Rauss, *Fighting in Hell*, pp. 86–7.

[10] Erich von Manstein, *Lost Victories* (London and New York, 1958; London and Novato, CA, 1982) p. 330.

[11] Paul Carrell, *Scorched Earth: The Russian-German War, 1943–1945* (Boston, 1966) pp. 118-123. UK title: *Hitler's War on Russia* (London, 1966).

On 6 February 1943, he reassigned Raus to command what became known as Provisional Corps Raus—three infantry divisions, Panzergrenadier Division Grossdeutschland, and the Führer Escort Brigade. His mission was to stop the drive of the *3rd Tank Army* toward the bend of the Dnieper and cover the arrival of a panzer reserve. Once the reserve had arrived, Raus's corps formed the left flank of the attack by 1st SS Panzer Corps on Kharkov, smashing or driving away every Soviet unit in his path. In its attacks north of Kharkov, Grossdeutschland achieved a first:

> It was in this action that Tiger tanks engaged the Russian T-34s for the first time; the results were more than gratifying for the Germans. For instance, two Tigers, acting as an armored point, destroyed a pack of T-34s. Normally the Russian tanks would stand in ambush at the hitherto safe distance of 1,350 yards and wait for the German tanks to expose themselves upon their exit form a village. They would then take the German tanks under fire while the Panthers [*sic*; "Tigers" is meant] were still outranged. Until now, these tactics had been foolproof. This time, however, the Russians had miscalculated. Instead of leaving the village, the Tigers took up well-camouflaged positions and made full use of their longer range. Within a short time they knocked out sixteen T-34s which were sitting in open terrain and, when the others turned about, the Tigers pursued the fleeing Russians and destroyed eighteen more tanks. It was observed that the 88-mm armor-piercing shells had such terrific impact that they ripped off the turrets of the T-34s and hurled them several yards. The German soldiers' immediate reaction was to coin the phrase, "The T-34 raises its hat whenever it meets a Tiger." The performance of the new German tanks was a great morale-booster.[12]

After the recapture of Kharkov, Provisional Corps Raus was redesignated XI Corps with four infantry divisions, and Raus was promoted to General der Panzertruppen (Lieutenant-General) on 1 May. By this time, he was training his corps for the upcoming Operation "Citadel," the Battle of Kursk. Raus paid particular attention to the problem of crossing the dense Russian minefields. His divisions were rotated to the rear for intensive training in how to identify the emplacement of enemy mines. They were also taught how to survive tanks running over their foxholes. The Luftwaffe's 7th Flak Division was attached to XI Corps because it would have the mission of protecting the flank of Army Group Kempf's main attack force, III Panzer Corps (which contained Raus's old division, the 6th Panzer).

In the 5 July German assault, the infantry of his corps penetrated the minefields with almost no loss and roved several miles into the Soviet defenses. Raus skillfully improvised tactics for the flak division to support the attack of his infantry which was fighting its way through the enemy's dense field fortifications with hand grenades and bayonets. He also quickly organized the flak to crush serious tank counterattacks that penetrated his infantry defenses, utterly destroying two tank brigades.[13]

As the Germans retreated after Kursk, the role of fighting the tough delaying actions was left to Raus and XI Corps. In the grim fighting around Belgorod in early August

[12] Rauss, *The Anvil of War*, p. 139.
[13] *Ibid.*, pp. 48–9.

1943, during which he successfully employed the technique of delay on successive positions, he offered a self-portrait, during the crisis of the battle when Soviet penetrations had begun to panic XI Corps:

> Every experienced commander is familiar with this sort of panic which, in a critical situation, may seize an entire body of troops. Mass hysteria of this type can be overcome only by energetic actions and a display of perfect composure. The example set by a true leader can have miraculous effects. He must stay with his troops, remain cool, issue precise orders, and inspire confidence by his behavior. Good soldiers never desert such a leader. News of the presence of high-ranking commanders up front travels like wildfire along the entire front line, bolstering everyone's morale. It means a sudden change from gloom to hope, from imminent defeat to victory. . . . This is exactly what happened.[14]

Shortly after Belgorod, Raus found himself in another desperate defensive operation as he withdrew to the Donets River north of Kharkov for the epic struggle that would be called the 4th Battle of Kharkov. With originally five divisions spread in an arc around that city, XI Corps was attacked by four Soviet armies, including the *5th Guards Tank Army* fresh from its triumphs at Kursk. For eight days Raus slowly fell back to the outer defenses of Kharkov, in a dogged delaying action in the scorching late Russian summer. His old 6th Panzer Division had become detached from its corps and retreated through Raus's front. Raus immediately put it under his command and placed it on his open left flank.

A new crisis emerged when it was discovered that the 168th Infantry Division had disappeared from the line. The 6th Panzer extended its line to fill the gap while Raus personally hunted down the missing division to find it 40 kilometers in the rear, where the commander had taken it after suffering a loss of nerve. Raus dealt with the commander and plugged the division back into line. Then the Soviets penetrated the Donets line and threw a tank force into Kharkov. Raus ordered the 6th Panzer to clean it up while he looked to the main blow that was building.

While holding off the *53th*, *67th*, and *7th Guards Armies* to the north with his depleted infantry divisions, he had to face an open left flank. It was here that the *5th Guards Tank Army*, commanded by the redoubtable Pavel Rotmistrov, the victor of Prokhorovka, struck at the bottleneck of the German salient around Kharkov. But Raus was quicker—and luckier.[15] He concentrated the tanks from the attached 3rd Panzer Division and 2nd

---

[14] Rauss, *The Anvil of War*, p. 192.

[15] Carrell, *Scorched Earth*, pp. 305–6. Raus was also lucky. The *5th Guards Tank Army* ran into the German Army Group South supply dump at Feski northwest of Kharkov crammed with two months' supply of everything necessary to support two armies for three months. That included liquor. At Feski was an entire year's production of the French spirits industry as well as liquor looted from all of conquered Europe. There was so much vodka that it was stored in carboys. The German quartermaster threw open the dumps to any German unit that had transportation. Within two days it had been cleaned out except for the vodka. None was touched: with French cognac, Spanish port, and Italian Chianti to choose from, who would want vodka? It was then that the *5th Guards Tank Army* overran Feski—and did not move for three days. When the Russians had drunk the last carboy dry and recovered from their hangovers, they discovered that SS Panzer Division Wiking had reinforced Raus's defense and occupied the high ground in front of them.

SS Panzer Divison "Das Reich" just at that point. Repeated hammer blows of the *5th Guards* eventually shattered on the anvil of XI Corps' defense in a dramatic night battle:

> Many tanks and several farm buildings went up in flames. The plateau on which this great night tank duel was fought was illuminated by their pale light. This made it possible to recognize the contours of Red tanks at a distance of more than 100 yards, and to shell them. The thunderous roll turned into a din like the crescendo of kettledrums as the two main tank forces clashed. Gun flashes from all around ripped the darkness of the night throughout the extensive area. For miles, armor-piercing projectiles whizzed into the night in all directions. Gradually the pandemonium of the tank battle shifted to the north. However, flashes also appeared farther and farther behind the German font, and fiery torches stood out against the night sky. Not until two or three hours later was calm restored in the depth of the German front.

The *5th Guards Tank Army* lost 420 tanks in three days' fighting. Raus had left it a burnt-out husk. It was the second drubbing Raus had delivered to Rotmistrov, having bled his *7th Tank Corps* white outside of Stalingrad.[16]

Although Kharkov was eventually ordered to be abandoned by higher headquarters, Raus had covered himself with renown. The day before the city was abandoned, Hitler awarded Raus the Oak Leaves to the Knight's Cross, the 280th such award of 890 given out in the war. With his brilliant defensive operations at Belgorod and Kharkov, Raus had saved Army Group South from one disaster after another. The Army Group South commander, General Erich von Manstein, showed his regard for Raus by bringing him on his own initiative to a conference called by Hitler at Vinnitsa in late August. He proved himself the right man in a crisis. And suddenly a great new crisis fell upon the Germans. The Soviets had torn open the front west of Kiev in November and were preparing to exploit the opening and conduct a major envelopment of major parts of the army group. The disaster was the result of Hitler's decisions, but he needed a scapegoat and he relieved Generaloberst Hoth, commander of the Fourth Panzer Army. Raus, who had served briefly as commander of XLVII Panzer Corps (4–25 November), seemed the ideal man to take over the 4th Panzer.

It was just in time. He assumed command on 26 November 1943 near Ternopol. Within a week of his assumption of command, Raus seized the initiative. He said that "the situation demanded immediate action" and launched a major spoiling attack with the three panzer divisions of XLVIII Panzer Corps against the *1st Ukrainian Front.* The Soviets were taken completely by surprise, and the front's artillery completely was overrun and lost. It was a classic operation that employed deception and imagination. After savaging the *1st Ukrainian Front,* Raus restored the German front with infantry and withdrew XLVIII Panzer Corps into reserve, ready for the next blow. Raus's spoiling attack

> . . . achieved the dual purpose of relieving an encircled corps and enabling the Germans to build up a continuous front where previously there had been a wide gap. The

---

[16] Rauss, *Fighting in Hell,* pp. 69–1.

annihilation of strong enemy forces was an incidental, though important, result of this operation.

The enemy's strategy had been dealt a severe setback, and his losses had been severe—200 tanks destroyed and 800 guns captured.[17]

Shortly thereafter Raus employed a different technique—delaying and blocking actions—to blunt the Soviet Christmas offensive west of Kiev. The Soviet armies thrust and hammered at the Fourth Panzer Army to break through, but succeeded only in moving it about 100 kilometers west in five weeks of sustained operations despite a superiority in tanks of 1,200 to 200. Generalleutnant F. W. von Mellenthin, XLVIII Corps Chief of Staff in these battles, was to write:

> The calm and able leadership of Colonel General Rauss [sic], the commander of Fourth Panzer Army, had succeeded in overcoming a dangerous crisis. It is true that the Russians captured Zhitomir on 31 December, and on 3 January had the satisfaction of crossing the 1939 frontier of Poland. But in fact their offensive power had been worn down, the German front in Western Ukraine was still relatively intact, and the fighting spirit of our troops remained unbroken.[18]

Raus continued to command the Fourth Panzer Army through the fighting retreat of Army Group North from the Ukraine to the Carpathian Mountains. In April of 1944, he conducted a masterful zone defense against a major Soviet breakthrough attempt in the area of Lvov, in western Ukraine. He then launched sharp attack into the flank of the opposing Soviet forces that allowed the First Panzer Army trapped behind Soviet lines to break out.

On 18 May Raus succeeded the brilliant Generaloberst Hans Hube as commander of the First Panzer Army (Army Group South) after the latter had been killed in an air crash on his way to receive the Diamonds to the Knight's Cross personally from Hitler. On 15 August Raus was promoted to Generaloberst (General). On 16 August 1944 he was transferred to Army Group Center and command of the Third Panzer Army, badly mauled in the catastrophe of the destruction of Army Group Center in June. He commanded this army in the long, nightmarish retreat through Lithuania, East Prussia, and Pomerania. In East Prussia in December 1944, he was able to repeat the success of the zone defense against a Russian breakthrough for an entire month. In this operation, the Third Panzer Army consisted of nine weak divisions with 50 tanks, 400 guns, and insignificant air support; the Soviet front opposed to it consisted of the *3rd Belorussian Front*'s 44 divisions with 800 tanks, 3000 guns, and strong air support.[19]

Building on the experiences in the zone defense operations around Lvov, Raus constructed a defensive system 50 miles in depth in East Prussia: "Everyone, from corps commander to private, made strenuous efforts to improve the defense system." With the fine touch of a master, Raus had constructed the forward positions with their sudden

---

[17] Rauss, *The Anvil of War*, p. 145–9.
[18] F. W. von Mellenthin, *Panzer Battles* (Norman, OK: Oklahoma University Press, 1971) pp. 269–70.
[19] Rauss, *The Anvil of War*, pp. 164.

evacuation in mind, just before the main Soviet attack. This succeeded completely, and the Russian bombardment fell upon empty German positions. When the infantry hit the real main defense line, they were stopped cold. But their mass of armor overwhelmed the German antitank defenses and kept moving deeper into the defenses. At this point, Raus struck at the Soviet flanks and rear with his tank and assault gun reserves. The head of the Soviet column finally bogged down in the depth of the German defenses.

> The German infantry, supported by assault guns, tore gaps in the Russian attack columns which had been weakened by heavy artillery and rocket fire. Before long the entire enemy attack force wavered and fell back in confusion. During the evening, the former main line of resistance was reoccupied by the German infantry. The booty was rich, aside from 122 burned-out tanks piled up on the slopes near Kussen. Improvised zone defense had saved the German forces from being annihilated and had stopped all enemy breakthrough attempts.[20]

On 8–12 February Raus was relieved of his command in East Prussia and transferred with his Third Panzer Army staff to Army Group Weichsel in Eastern Pomerania. The army group commander was Reichsführer Heinrich Himmler. Raus immediately requested an interview since he had been given no duties as yet, and on 13 February Himmler received him. Raus was frank and to the point, despite Himmler's brutal reputation. The Reichsführer listened intently, and, to Raus's surprise, agreed with him completely. Himmler may have had no military qualifications, but he had enough wit to see that Germany was collapsing around his ears and the broad reasons for it. Nothing seemed to come of the meeting, however, as Raus's eight weak divisions with barely 70 tanks held a 150-mile front on the Oder River around Küstrin some forty miles east of Berlin. He had argued strenuously with Himmler against the attack of the Eleventh SS Panzer Army ordered by Hitler. It failed, just as he predicted. He was ordered to relieve its commander and on 21 February take over the front to stabilize the situation in the face of the massive Soviet counterattack. A second interview on 7 March, this time ordered by the Reichsführer, led to Himmler's recommendation that the general brief Hitler himself the next day.

Raus was stunned by the physical appearance of Hitler:

> I faced a physically broken-down, embittered and suspicious man whom I scarcely recognized. The knowledge that Adolf Hitler—now only a human wreck—held the fate of the German people in his hands alone was a deep shock to me.

Generaloberst Heinz Guderian, Chief of OKH (Oberkommando des Heeres, or Army High Command), was present at the meeting and recorded Hitler's surreal conduct:

> Rauss [sic] began by outlining the general situation. Hitler interrupted him: "I'm already in the picture so far as the general situation goes. What I want from you is a detailed exposition of the combat ability of your divisions." Rauss now gave an exact description which showed that he knew every yard of his front and was capable of judging the value

---

[20] Rauss, *The Anvil of War*, p. 167.

of every unit under his command. I was present while he spoke and found his exposition outstandingly lucid.[21]

Hitler's treatment of Raus was typical of his wildly erratic and bizarre behavior in the last weeks of the war. He was to turn on the general when he could not achieve miracles, just as he, in the his last hours, would condemn the German people as unworthy. Guderian went on:

> When he had finished, Hitler dismissed him without comment. Raus had scarcely left the Chancellery shelter, where the conference had taken place, before Hitler turned to Keitel, Jodl, and myself and shouted: "What a miserable speech! The man talked of nothing but details. Judging by the way he speaks, he must be a Berliner or an East Prussian. He must be relieved of his appointment at once.!" I replied: "Colonel-General Raus is one of our most capable panzer generals. You, my Führer, interrupted him yourself when he was trying to tell you about the general situation, and you ordered him to give you a detailed exposition of the state of his divisions. And as for his origin, Raus is an Austrian and therefore a compatriot of yours, my Führer."[22]

Then Jodl and Hitler argued whether Raus was really an Austrian. Guderian resumed his pleading for Raus:

> Please let me urge you, before you make any decisions, to remember that Colonel-General Raus showed an exact knowledge of all his front, that he was able to give a personal evaluation of every division under his command, that throughout a long war he has consistently fought with great distinction, and that finally—as I already said—he is one of our best panzer generals.[23]

Guderian had argued in vain. As usual, Hitler clung tightly to his worst decisions. Raus was to refer to the end of his career wryly: "My successor arrived the next day at my headquarters in Stettin with a Führer order and in accordance, I had to turn over command of the Army to him and was transferred to the officers' reserve pool. *That was the end of my 40-year tour of service.*"[24]

Raus' record in command, especially after the middle of 1943, is a remarkable saga of a skillful fighting retreat against an enemy flood-tide which he repeatedly delayed, halted, or drove back with a variety of deadly ripostes and improvisations. Raus was a man who could "quickly grasp" a situation and then act decisively, employing "speed" and "shock," the troika of qualities of the great commander, as defined by the great Russian commander of the eighteenth century, Aleksandr Suvorov. He was also an extremely cool-headed officer—a characteristic much remarked upon by subordinates

---

[21] Heinz Guderian, *Panzer Leader* (London: MacDonald and Jane's, 1952; London and New York: Ballantine Books, 1987), pp. 348–9.

[22] Guderian, *ibid.*, pp. 348–9.

[23] Guderian, *ibid.*, p. 349.

[24] Raus's replacement was General der Panzertruppen Hasso von Manteuffel, who had ridden to well-deserved fame as commander of the German Army's elite Panzergrenadier Division Grossdeutschland. Himmler's replacement was Generaloberst Gotthard Heinrici, an extremely capable officer.—Editor.

and superiors alike. Above all, he was the ultimate professional—a man who played the bad hands well.

Epilogue

Hitler's relief of Raus probably saved his life. He surrendered to US forces. Had he continued in command in Pomerania he may well have fallen into captivity by the Soviets, at whose hands he could have expected a show trial in revenge for all the harm he had done them. At best had he would have seen more than ten years' imprisonment.

His American captivity led to a final professional contribution—the manuscripts embodied in this book and the two that were incorporated into *The Anvil of War* and *Fighting in Hell*. Together with most of his colleagues in S. L. A. Marhall's program, he was released from captivity in 1948. He continued to write for the Americans and produced most of his work from 1950 to 1952. He died at Bad Gastein on 13 April 1956 and is buried in his native Vienna.

Peter G. Tsouras
Lieutenant-Colonel, USAR (ret.)
Alexandria, Virginia
2001

Chapter 1

Barbarossa Begins

Preface

Proper combat education and training for officers and soldiers are of vital importance to victory. The increase of their skill and efficiency to a maximum is the objective of peacetime training. This aim may be considered reached if every soldier completely masters his weapons in times of emergency and if every commander masters the tasks with which he is faced. The less commanders and soldiers have to learn in actual combat, the better has been their training for war.

Every tactician and instructor recognizes these principles and tries to impress them as deeply as possible upon his officers and soldiers. Yet the best-trained troops had to learn many new things at the beginning of the war or after a change of theater of operation and were faced with tasks for which they were not prepared. In fact, it even happened sometimes during the war that troops were compelled, in unusual situations, to contravene certain regulations that had not yet been canceled or brought up to date.

The above, in itself, points out the difficulty in preparing officers and men to meet an opponent whose way of thinking and acting is so fundamentally different from their own that it often cannot be understood at all. In addition, there are the peculiarities of a theater of war which place troops in situations for which there is apparently no solution. Much embarrassment was caused the German soldier by the combat tactics of the opponent—tactics with which he was not familiar. Deceptions and tricks cost the German Army much blood. An acclimatization of several months was often necessary before a unit transferred to the East became a match for the combat conditions existing there.

Thus, it happened at times that a division at full strength but in action on the Eastern Front for the first time either failed to perform or only succeeded at great loss in performing a difficult mission which was easily handled by a division experienced in Eastern conditions, even if the latter had been bled white in previous combat. This fact alone was proof enough of the necessity to disseminate the experiences gained in the East to the units of the German Army employed in other theaters of war in order to protect them from heavy setbacks and heavy casualties in the event of commitment in the East.

Here, as at most fronts, it was also a question of dealing with new weapons and a mass commitment of enemy troops and equipment which threatened to crush everything. These events, which first appeared in the later course of the war, placed commanders and troops in unusual situations where tactical measures had to be taken which were neither prescribed in regulations nor taught. Nothing but an officer corps educated to take full responsibility and to act independently, plus the resolve of courageous soldiers, made it possible for solutions to be found to all unusual problems. An army relying on mass drilling and mass effect alone would have failed under such conditions or would have suffered heavy losses.

The above remarks will now be substantiated by a number of small examples drawn from the personal experience of the author during four years of campaign in the East, indicating why unusual situations occurred and how they were overcome in each individual case. In order to allow better judgment of the events, the examples will be retold as they occurred.

The Author

Example 1: The Surprise Attack at Paislinis, 23 June 1941

It was the second day of combat in the East. After the deep breakthrough at the frontier on 22 June, the tank formations quickly pushed on to the east in order to prevent the enemy from taking up positions in the heights of Rossienie and to reach the important Dubysa sector. The 6th Panzer Division (see Appendix A for division organization[1]) was assigned the task of occupying the Lithuanian town of Rossienie and then pushing quickly on to the east to capture the two vehicular bridges across the Dubysa River east of the town. Split up into two columns,[2] the division had been proceeding in the direction of Rossienie since dawn of 23 June. The enemy infantry, which had been far overtaken the day before, had entirely disappeared. Steadily advancing German troops were on all roads and highways. Tank and artillery columns rolled powerfully ahead, threatening to crush everything opposing them. Far to the front, clouds of dust appeared on the horizon. "The enemy after all," many a man thought, and speed picked up.

Up to this point no shot was fired. Fighter planes circled peacefully in the sky by themselves; not a single enemy aircraft was to be seen. Nature was still peacefully spread out in the soft light of the morning sun. The large-scale troop movement resembled a peaceful march to the starting position of a maneuver.

Suddenly, the air was torn by a heavy barrage. Where the dust clouds were still visible on the horizon, black earth now spouted high into the air. Machine guns began to chatter

---

[1] In Operation "Barbarossa", the 6th Panzer Division formed part of XLI Panzer Corps, along with the 1st Panzer Division and the 36th Motorized Division. XLI Panzer Corps was commanded by General Georg Hans Reinhardt. XLI Panzer Corps with LVI Panzer Corps, commanded by General der Infanterie Erich von Manstein, formed the 4th Panzergruppe, commanded by Generaloberst Erich Höpner. The Panzergruppe was subordinated to Army Group North commanded by Generaloberst Erich von Leeb. The Panzergruppe was an armored force the size of an army, but operating in conjunction with an army. The Panzergruppen were redesignated Panzer Armies on 1 January 1942.—Editor.

[2] The two columns represented "Kampfgruppen R und S" (literally, "Battle Groups R and S"). A Kampfgruppe was a German term loosely applied to improvised combat units of various sizes, named usually after their commanders. In this case, the "R" stands for Raus, who, as commander of the 6th Motorized Rifle Brigade, was the natural commander of the Kampfgruppe, making up half of the division.—Editor.

and their fire penetrated the sound of the increasing barrage. The "Landser,"[3] covered with dust, wondered what could be happening up front. The column commanders already knew the answer.

A long time before, the advance detachment, the cause of the dust clouds which had been observed, had radioed that strong enemy forces had occupied the heights south of Rossienie. They were lying near the route of advance of the southern column and were spread out in front of the town like a protecting bulwark.

From the distance, the community's highest point crowned by a chapel could already be discerned. All rear echelons advanced steadily and without hesitation, as it was their mission to support the advance guard and overcome enemy resistance as quickly as possible. The advance guards had already attacked the enemy but were too weak to defeat him. The 6th Reconnaissance Battalion, assigned to the motorcycle battalion, had quickly reconnoitered the local situation. Shortly thereafter, the bulk of the southern column, which was ahead of the northern one, entered the engagement. Under the protection of friendly artillery fire, the 114th (Schützenregiment) Motorized Rifle Regiment and the panzer battalion assigned to it moved into position and attacked the hills where the ground had been thoroughly plowed up by our own shells.[4]

After a severe struggle, an advanced ridge was seized from the strong enemy, but the enemy, who had built up his main effort behind this ridge, did not intend to give up the key point in his defense. The struggle lasted over two hours without a decision having been reached. The completely open terrain made attacking difficult. *In addition, the artillery lacked ammunition and the tanks had to find a way through swamps and forests in order to attack the enemy in his flanks and rear and thus force him to give up his resistance.*

It was therefore all the more important for the northern column—which had started out on the same road as the southern column but which had left the road at Erzwilkas in order to make its way to Rossienie by the shortest route—to arrive before Rossienie in time to seize that town in a coordinated attack with the forces of the southern column.[5] The last part of the narrow dirt trail led along Slyna Brook through a partly marshy forest area difficult to view as a whole, which, east of Paislinis, changed into open meadowland covered with large fruit trees.

Up to this point, Kampfgruppe "R" had not met any enemy resistance, but no sooner had its leading company moved into the open country than its left flank came under rifle

---

[3] "Landser" was the German equivalent of "GI" or "Tommy" for the Americans and British.—Editor.

[4] Each of the Kampfgruppen was built around one of the two Schützenregiments, literally "Rifle Regiments" but in effect motorized or mechanized infantry regiments as opposed to foot Infanterieregiment. In addition to the Schützenregiment, each Kampfgruppe included a battalion from the panzer regiment, plus artillery and engineers and other support. The 4th Schützenregiment was the core of Kampfgruppe "R" and the 114th Schützenregiment was assigned to Kampfgruppe "S." In July 1942, every Schützenregiment in panzer divisions was redesignated as Panzergrenadier.—Editor.

[5] Colonel Helmut Ritgen, who was at the time adjutant of the 2nd Battalion, 11th Panzer Regiment, wrote: "On 23 June we continued our attack dowards the Dubyss River with the two battle groups abreast: Group Seckendorff on the right, and Group Raus on the left." Ritgen, "6th Panzer Division Operations," *The Initial Period of War on the Eastern Front, 22 June–August 1941*, David M. Glantz, ed. (London: Frank Cass, 1993), p. 113.

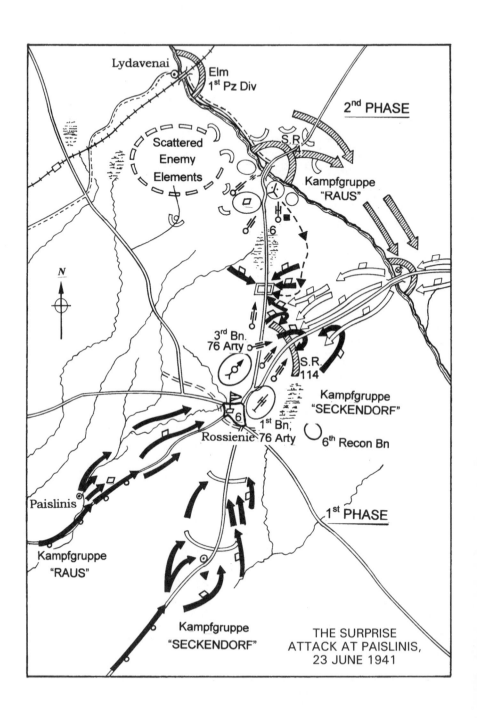

THE SURPRISE
ATTACK AT PAISLINIS,
23 JUNE 1941

and machine-gun fire delivered at very close range. The first victim of the surprise attack was the company commander, who was driving at the head of the column and who was shot through the forehead by an enemy sniper from a distance of approximately 100 meters before he had time to give an order. The company automatically dismounted with lightning speed and returned the fire. The tanks assigned to the leading company advanced immediately, firing into the thicket and holding down the enemy. The leading tank soon received a direct hit from an antitank gun and dropped out. Shortly thereafter, the two following companies of the advance guard penetrated the forest and attacked the enemy in his flank and rear with small arms. The latter's destruction seemed certain, but the storming riflemen made little headway in the thicket of the young forest and were not able to cut off the enemy's retreat to the north.

Although it was of only company strength, the enemy force escaped. As he was in full cover, the enemy's losses were small. Several weapons were captured, among them a 37mm antitank gun of German origin. It was probably this gun which had damaged our own tank from a distance of about 50 meters and the crew of which had been killed in flight by the fire from the other tanks.

Though the situation of the leading elements, caught by the surprise attack in the open terrain, had looked critical at first, casualties were light, consisting only of a few wounded and the very capable company commander who had unfortunately been killed. The casualties were not caused by the massed surprise fire from the thicket, which fire was unsteady and whizzed over our heads, but almost exclusively by snipers hidden in the tops of fruit trees and aiming at their victims at close quarters. They remained in their hiding places looking for worthwhile targets—primarily officers—even after some of the tanks stopped underneath the trees and began to fire into the fringe of the forest.

As long as the snipers fired during the height of the battle, they remained unnoticed. It was not until they continued firing after the noise had died away that they were discovered and brought down by machine-gun fire. The last of them tried vainly to flee. Immediately recognized in the open terrain, they were killed by the fire of the nearest machine gun before they were able to reach the cover of the forest. Snipers in the trees of a forest were no novelty for the troops, but here for the first time they had been found in fruit trees in the open terrain where no one expected them. Though doomed, they had executed their mission. They had carried it out regardless of the fact that their lives were being forfeited. That was the new experience in the surprise attack at Paislinis.

The enemy unmistakably had intended to delay the rapid advance of the strong Kampfgruppe "R" by a systematically planned surprise attack, since the Kampfgruppe's appearance at Rossienie not only threatened the town but also the rear of the strong Russian forces fighting in the hilly area to the south of the town. The location of the surprise attack had been skillfully chosen. It was immediately adjacent to the German route of advance which all the enemy weapons dominated from the flank. It allowed the placing of snipers in the trees, offered full protection against early discovery, made a quick envelopment difficult, and enabled the enemy forces to withdraw from the attack unobserved. The plan to eliminate the German officers by sharpshooters was clever. The numerically weak enemy unit could be proud of its success. It forced the German advance elements to interrupt their rapid motorized progress and caused a delay of more than half an hour in addition to the losses mentioned above.

On the other hand, on the basis of the situation, Kampfgruppe "R" was correct in trying to use the vehicles as long as possible in order to bring about a quick decision at Rossienie. The risk of a minor surprise attack had to be taken. Dismounting at that time and looking in the strips of woods for small enemy units or stragglers would have led to a loss of time far out of proportion to the success obtained. The actual loss of time was not too important because the leading elements had already reached the assembly area for the planned attack on Rossienie, and the bulk of the Kampfgruppe followed without delay.

The danger that several commanders might have simultaneously fallen victim to the surprise attack was prevented by previous training and repeated orders that officers should not form groups. As usual, the officers endeavored to be as far to the front as possible in order to be able to orient themselves quickly at the beginning of the engagement and to receive or to issue orders. Including the commander, they had joined the advance column, but were distributed in such a manner that they could take matters in hand immediately but could not drop out simultaneously.

Example 2: A Regiment's Position is Overrun by Superheavy Tanks

The incident at Paislinis concerned only a small unit and had no psychological repercussions. All eyes were on Rossienie, lying on the ridge in the bright noonday sun like a fortress dominating the surrounding country. Here and in the countryside in front of the town, the enemy had dug in to try to stop both the tanks, which were already approaching, and the 4th Motorized Infantry Regiment echeloned in depth, which was following closely behind. The friendly batteries were already hammering at the enemy positions which had been located and were battering the reserves which were coming to his aid.

Simultaneously, Kampfgruppe "S," which was engaged in a hard fight on the heights south of the town, prepared for a decisive action. Its tanks penetrated the enemy position and joined other German tanks at Rossienie. Soon after, the two Kampfgruppen cleaned out the town and the surrounding heights. Enemy resistance collapsed after a short time in the face of concentric attacks by all forces of the division. Some courageous enemy battalions still tried to stop Kampfgruppe "R," which had immediately initiated an advance toward the bridge on the road to Siluva, but they were overrun by tanks and dispersed by riflemen. Individual pockets of resistance were stormed by the riflemen and after a short struggle were eliminated.

In the first hours of the afternoon, the two Kampfgruppen reached their objectives—the two bridges across the Dubysa—which were occupied after minor resistance had been overcome. The bridges were somewhat beyond Rossienie and lay 50 meters below the level of the surrounding country. The northern bridge was crossed by riflemen who formed a bridgehead on the heights beyond. The tanks had traversed the river first by the aid of the derelict bridge, leaving reserve units in the bridgehead, defenses for which were immediately prepared. A few hours later, the southern Kampfgruppe, too, had dislodged the enemy rearguards and had occupied the eastern bank of the Dubysa with the 6th Motorcycle Battalion.

After having covered 55 kilometers and after several hours of combat, the 6th Panzer Division had achieved the day's objectives. The setting sun cast a rosy glow, and quiet prevailed even before twilight fell. The steaming field kitchens appeared, and everyone not occupied with guard duty assembled around them to take a well-deserved hot meal, bringing to a happy conclusion a successful day. The officers discussed combat events and made preparations for the next day. But the commanders reflected upon the accomplishment of the enemy, too, and verbally expressed their astonishment that the same infantry which had faced them the day before south of Tauroggen and which already had been overrun at noon and left far behind could have covered 75 kilometers on foot within twenty-four hours and, in the absence of proper roads, could have again prepared immediately for defensive operations and could have fought as stubbornly as the day's events proved without any rest. This fact put a damper on their joy, for it made it apparent that this stubborn opponent might well lose ground but he would never admit his defeat. The following day was to prove the correctness of these thoughts.

During the night the two bridgeheads were widened and improved without incident in order to facilitate continuation of the offensive.[6] Dawn came, but no order was issued to resume the advance. It was still possible that it would arrive, for it was only necessary to press a button and the war machinery would start running within a few minutes. Perhaps enemy intentions had become known which had upset the plans of our own High Command? To all appearances, the latter assumption was hardly to be adopted.

The sun was sending forth its first rays when suddenly, in the south, the roar of artillery became audible. The fire increased; volley after volley of shells burst in the southern bridgehead area and even made houses in Rossienie tremble and window panes rattle. The sound of the firing and the roar of the shells made it clear that the enemy was preparing to attack. The area was too flat and too overgrown to make it possible to observe what was going on in the adjacent bridgehead six kilometers distant. The southern Kampfgruppe's artillery also became active. The noise of the battle had lasted only twenty minutes when it was steadily increased by the heavy sounds of guns and

---

[6] Raus does not mention an incident of that night reported by General Kilmansegg of the West German Army in 1987. At the time Kilmansegg was a division staff officer. He referred to Raus's bridgehead, which "was not given up in the night. In it were about two platoons and these were overrun by a Soviet attack during the night. The next day we found all the personnel shot, that is, murdered, and atrociously mutilated. Eyes had been put out, genitals cut off and other cruelties inflicted. This was our first such experience, but not the last. On the evening of these first two days, I said to my general, 'Sir, this will be a very different war from the one in Poland and France.' " Glantz, *ibid.*

machine-gun fire. The trained ear of the soldier with war experience immediately recognized that tank fighting was going on.

It slowly shifted to the west—not at all a good sign. An inquiry at the division confirmed this fear. It was later discovered that it was the Russian *XIV Tank Corps* which had counterattacked. Evidently its objective was to recapture Rossienie and to dislodge the 6th Panzer Division from the plateau. That placed Kampfgruppe "S" in a very difficult position.[7] It was not so much the numerical superiority of the enemy which made the situation precarious for our command and troops, but the totally unexpected appearance of colossal tanks for which German tanks and antitank weapons appeared to be no match. The tanks were of the superheavy Russian model KV-1, the most dangerous they possessed until the end of the war (later improved and called KV-2).[8]

Soon after the beginning of the heavy artillery fire, they attacked and pierced the positions of the 6th Motorcycle Battalion, which was committed to the bridgehead, running over and crushing numerous motorcycles and even the serious casualties of a company. Under the overwhelming pressure of the enemy, the battalion had to withdraw to the western bank of the river. Covered by the bulk of Kampfgruppe "S" at the fringes of the forest, it again offered stubborn resistance.

There was still hope of holding the western bank when suddenly the giant tanks traversed the Dubysa without difficulty and reappeared. Even the concentrated fire of the artillery and all other heavy weapons of the Kampfgruppe was not able to keep off the steel pachyderms. Though enveloped in fire and smoke, they immediately started attacking and crushed everything in their paths. Untroubled by the shower of heavy howitzer shells and earth falling down upon them, they attacked road block 121 in spite of the flanking fire of the antitank guns from the wooded areas, rolled over the antitank guns dug in there and broke into the artillery area.

About one hundred friendly tanks, one-third of which were Panzer IVs, now assembled for a counterattack. Some of them faced the enemy in front, but the bulk made an assault from the flanks. From three sides, their shells hammered against the steel giants, but the effort to destroy them was in vain. On the other hand, very soon we had

---

[7] According to Colonel Ritgen, "These unknown Soviet tanks created a crisis in Battle Group Seckendorff, since apparently no weapon of the division was able to penetrate their armor. All rounds simply bounced off the Soviet tanks. 88mm flak guns were not yet available. In the face of the assault some riflemen panicked. The super-heavy Soviet KV tanks advanced against our tanks, which concentrated their fire on them without visible effect. The command tank of the company was rammed an turned over by a KV and the commander injured. I suppose the Soviet tank crews had no time to familiarize themselves with guns of their tanks or zero them in, since their fire was very inaccuarate. Furthermore, the Soviets were very poorly led. Nevertheless, the appearance of these heavy tanks was dramatic." Glantz, *ibid.*, p. 114.

[8] The author is referring to the tank designed by the team lead by Lt-Col Zh. Kotin at the Kirovskiy Factory in Leningrad. The two models were the KV-1 heavy tank and the KV-2 heavy artillery tank. The KV-1 had crew of five, weighed 43 tons and had a 76.2mm gun as its main armament. The KV-2 was armed with a 152mm howitzer in a much larger turret; it was dubbed "Dreadnought" by its crews. The paper strength of a Soviet tank division in July 1941 included 210 medium T-34, 102 T-26 or BT light tanks, and 63 KV model heavy tanks. Steven Zaloga and James Grandsen, *Soviet Tanks and Combat Vehicles of World War Two* (London: Arms and Armour Press, 1984), pp. 115–19.

casualties ourselves. After a long struggle with the Russian giants, the German armored units had to withdraw into covering terrain to escape destruction by the enemy. In addition, the rifle battalions, which for a long time defended the wooded areas west of the Dubysa bridge against the pursuing enemy infantry and its escort of tanks and which suffered heavily from the fire of the heavy enemy artillery, finally had to withdraw. By utilizing all means of cover, they gradually regrouped to the west.

More and more enemy forces pressed on from the rear and particularly put to a severe test the riflemen and motorcyclists fighting on both sides of the road. New enemy tanks pressed from the east in pursuit, and west of these stood the bulk of the supertanks following their breakthrough under the steady fire of the German artillery and tanks. To get out of this dilemma, the only solution was to let the enemy tanks run over the German forces once more, whereupon the latter could escape on the sides and make contact again with the 114th Schützenregiment, which one hoped to find there.

Squatting in small trench positions, under road bridges and culverts and in grain fields, the Germans awaited the approach of the second wave of heavy enemy tanks. Waiting became hell as the long arm of the friendly artillery now also reached these tanks, wounding the riflemen as well in the process. Envied were those comrades who had succeeded in hiding underneath bridges and in passageways and who were able to observe the events at a close distance unnoticed by the enemy. Nearer and nearer came the giant tanks echeloned in width and depth. One of them encountered a marshy pool in which a German tank was stuck. Without hesitating, the black monster rolled over the tank. The same happened to a German 150mm howitzer which had not been able to get away in time. When the heavy enemy tanks approached, the howitzer fired directly at them without causing any reaction at all. One of the tanks drove straight for the howitzer which fired a direct shot at it at a distance of 100 meters, hitting it in the middle of its front armor. A glare of fire and simultaneously a thunder clap of the bursting shell followed, and the tank stopped as if hit by lightning. That's the end of that, thought the gunners as they took a deep breath. "Yes, that fellow has had enough," said the chief of the section. Their faces dropped, however, when suddenly one of them exclaimed, "It is moving again." And indeed, it advanced again, its tracks rattling loudly, moved the gun like a toy, pressed it into the ground and ran over it with ease, as if it were an everyday affair. The heavy howitzer was finished, but the crew escaped unharmed.

The bulk of the enemy tanks had scarcely suffered from the counterattack of the German 11th Panzer Regiment, but it had been stopped and dispersed, thus losing impetus of attack and enabling Kampfgruppe "S" to fall back and occupy a new defense position around Height 106 and reorganize the defense. All branches of the combat arms were brought forward to participate in the antitank defense. The rumor of the invincibility of the superheavy enemy tanks had already been destroyed by the 100mm battery, which succeeded in the same way as the 88mm antiaircraft in finishing off some of the monsters. As a result of this, the latter began to be more cautious and correspondingly less dangerous—a fact which was a great aid to the defense.

Once again the enemy concentrated his entire formations in wooded areas and grain fields and started a decisive drive with his tanks in mass formation against Hill 106. No sooner had the giant tanks left their shelter than they were met by volleys of armor-piercing shells from all guns of the 88mm antiaircraft battalion which, with the 100mm gun battery, well camouflaged in staggered positions, destroyed a number of the heavy tanks and brought their attack to a standstill. Columns of smoke rising to the sky from burning tanks spread signs of the German defense victory far and wide. Later, disconnected attempts of the enemy to pierce or outflank the defense positions also met with the same fate. Nor could the local attacks of the enemy infantry which followed turn the tide; for it was weakened and exhausted by the steady fighting and marches and no longer able to effect a decisive breakthrough. It was, after all, the same infantry which had faced the 6th Panzer Division on the day of the outbreak of war and which was not trained to work in conjunction with armored formations.

The 6th Motorcycle Battalion and 114th Motorized Infantry Regiment were particularly severely tested in the above engagement. To be attacked by surprise by unusually heavy tanks, and to be twice penetrated and overrun without having any weapons able to halt or destroy the enemy, demands more than can be expected of even battle-tested soldiers. The behavior of the troops must be prized even more highly when one realizes that they had never before been overrun by enemy tanks. In later stages of the Eastern campaign, rifle formations, which had become an integral part of tank divisions, were no longer confronted with the problem of being run over in shelter holes by tanks. As always in critical situations, in this case also, the iron discipline of the soldiers, the spirit and morale of the battle-tried, well-trained commanders and subordinate commanders decided the issue. They were not dependent on outmoded rules and instructions but knew how to act in a situation unprovided for by regulations and personal experience. Their success confirmed the suitability of the measures taken. The troops lived through this experience with unbroken courage and few losses, and again proved their excellent spirit in the engagements which followed.

Example 3: A Superheavy Tank Blocks a Reinforced Regiment

The reader of the preceding example may ask what happened to Kampfgruppe "R" during this difficult situation. Why did it not come to the aid of the other group? Let us first take up the first question.

Nothing of any great importance took place in the Kampfgruppe "R" sector. The troops improved their positions, reconnoitered in the direction of Siluva and on the eastern bank of the Dubysa in both directions and chiefly tried to find out what was happening in the area south of the bridge. They also made contact with Kampfgruppe "S" and the bridgehead of the 1st Panzer Division at Lydavenai. Only scattered enemy units were encountered. Upon cleaning out the wooded area west of the friendly bridgehead, units of our riflemen encountered stronger enemy infantry which still held two places on the western bank of the river.

Contrary to procedure, captured prisoners during these local operations, among them a Russian first lieutenant, had been transported to the rear by motor vehicle in a group under the guard of a single noncommissioned officer. Halfway to Rossienie, the driver suddenly saw an enemy tank on the road and stopped. At the same moment the Russian prisoners, about twenty in number, unexpectedly attacked the driver and the noncommissioned officer, who was standing next to the driver facing the prisoners, and tried to take their weapons from them. The Russian first lieutenant had already reached for the noncommissioned officer's submachine gun when the latter succeeded in freeing one arm and in striking such a heavy blow on the chest of the officer that he staggered back, dragging with him the prisoners who were closest to him. Before the prisoners, coming from two sides, were able to tackle the noncommissioned officer again, he had, with the power of an athlete, torn away his left arm, still held by three men, so that he had both arms free for a moment. With lightning speed he pressed his submachine gun against his hip and fired into the mutinous crowd. The effect of the burst was disastrous. None but the wounded officer and a few others succeeded in jumping off the vehicle and escaping into the forest; all the rest had been mown down by the burst. The vehicle, now empty, turned around and reached the bridgehead again in spite of the fire from the tank.

This little drama was the first indication to the bridgehead garrison that their only supply route had been blocked by a superheavy tank (KV-1), which succeeded, moreover, in severing the telephone connection to the division. The intentions of the enemy were not yet clear. Kampfgruppe "R" expected an enemy attack against the rear of the bridgehead. The antitank battery was immediately brought into position near a flat hilltop in the vicinity of the command post of the 6th Motorized Infantry Brigade (Schützenbrigade,) a spot which was at the same time Kampfgruppe headquarters. In order to reinforce the antitank defense, a field howitzer battery stationed in the vicinity turned its gun tubes 180 degrees to the south, and the engineer company was directed to block the road and the surrounding country by prepared mines if necessary. The tank battalion, stationed as it was in the forest, was also to regroup so that it could launch a counterattack at any given moment.

Hours passed, but the enemy tank hardly moved. Now and then it fired in the direction of Rossienie. Scouts sent out to reconnoiter the vicinity of the giant tank could, at noon on 24 June, observe the KV-1 but could not make out any concentration of forces which might lead one to expect an impending tank attack. The commander drew the conclusion that they were tied up in the tank battle described in the second example. Steps would have to be taken at once, however, to destroy the annoying tank on the road or at least to drive it off. Its fire had already set ablaze twelve motor vehicles on their way from Rossienie with necessary supplies for the troops. It was not possible to remove the wounded to the medical aid stations after the fighting around the bridgehead, so that several severely wounded men, among them a young lieutenant who had received a point-blank shot in the abdomen, died in the ambulance because an operation to save his life could not be carried out in time. All attempts to drive around the tank proved a failure. Either the vehicles got stuck in the mud or, in making a wide detour, they fell into the hands of the enemy, many of whom were still in the woods.

The new 50mm antitank battery, therefore, had been ordered that very forenoon to work its way along to within effective range of the tank and to destroy it. The company commander and his brave soldiers had beamed with joy at this honorable mission and had gone to work full of confidence that they would be able to carry it out speedily. Their progress from hollow to hollow could be exactly observed from the brigade command post. They were followed from roofs, piles of wood and tops of trees by the eyes of numerous comrades awaiting with rapt attention the outcome of the mission. By this time, some of the guns had approached to within 1,000 meters of the tank, which stood plainly visible in the middle of the road and which did not seem to have observed them. Other guns had been out of sight for some time, when suddenly they emerged from the last hollow in front of the tank and, well-camouflaged, prepared for their mission. Half an hour later, the whole battery had joined them there.

The conjecture was advanced that the tank might have been damaged and left by its crew since it stood motionless on the road, a perfect target. The ridicule from one's fellows which would result from finishing off a dead tank would just have to be chanced. The first shot flashed forth from the antitank guns. The traced trajectory pointed like a silver ray directly into the target. In no time, it had covered the intervening 600 meters. A glare of fire appeared, followed by a violent impact. The tank received a direct hit. A second and third shot followed.

The spectators cheered and shouted like onlookers at a shooting match. "A hit! Bravo! The tank has been polished off." The tank did not move. It did not discover the firing battery until it received the eighth hit. Now it took aim and silenced the battery with a few 80mm shells.[9] Two antitank guns were shot to pieces and the remainder damaged. The battery suffered dead and wounded and had to withdraw the balance of the personnel into safe cover in order to avoid further losses. Only after night had fallen could the guns be recovered. The enemy tank was undamaged, the operation a failure. Deeply depressed, the battery commander returned to the bridgehead with his soldiers. His newly introduced weapon, in which he had absolute confidence, had proved inadequate in fighting the monster tank. Disappointment was great and general. A new way to master the situation had to be found.

Only the 88mm antiaircraft guns, with their heavy armor-piercing shells, could manage the task. On the same afternoon, an antiaircraft gun was withdrawn from the fighting near Rossienie and cautiously advanced from the south toward the tank, which still faced north—the direction from which it had previously been attacked. The long-barrel gun approached to within two kilometers of the tank, a range at which satisfactory results could be guaranteed. Unfortunately, some burned-out motor vehicles, victims of

---

[9] The author's recollection is in error: the KV-1 was armed with a 76mm gun.

the monster tank, were still lying at the side of the road obstructing visibility. On the other hand, they offered camouflage behind which the target could be more closely approached. Having been adapted to the surroundings by the fastening of numerous tree branches to its exterior, the gun was moved forward cautiously, in order not to warn the stationary tank. Eventually the fringe of the forest, which offered a good firing position and good visibility, was reached. The distance to the tank was only 800 meters. The first shot, therefore, was bound to be a direct hit and to destroy the tank. The gun was moved into position.

The tank had not moved since its first encounter, but its crew was alert and the men had good nerves. They observed the approaching gun without interfering with its task, since, as long as the gun was in motion, it could not endanger the tank. The nearer it came, the more easily it could be destroyed. The critical moment for both parties arrived when the gun crew made preparations to take up firing positions. Immediate action was then imperative. Under extreme mental strain, the crew of the antiaircraft gun prepared to fire, but at the same moment the tank swung its turret around and opened fire. Every shot hit the mark. Heavily damaged, the antiaircraft gun was knocked into the ditch, where it was left by its crew. The crew also had casualties. Machine-gun fire from the tank prevented the recovery of the gun and the dead gunners. The failure of the second attempt, which began under such good conditions, was bad news. Now the hopes of its crew had been lost together with the gun.

On this day, the Kampfgruppe had to depend on canned food, as the only supply road could not be opened. A much greater anxiety, however, had been temporarily removed. The enemy attack on Rossienie had been repelled by Kampfgruppe "S." Its troops had been able to hold the positions on Hill 106. The danger that the bulk of the enemy tank corps might wheel around to the rear of Kampfgruppe "R" and surround it was thus removed. Only the smaller but annoying matter of driving the monster tank off the supply route remained. What could not be done by day had to be accomplished by night. In the forenoon, the staff of the Kampfgruppe[10] discussed all possibilities of destroying the tank, and preparations were made for attempting different solutions to the problem.

The third solution consisted of having engineers blow up the tank. The night of 24/25 June was selected for this purpose. The engineers were the only ones who inwardly relished the fact that the qualified weapons had not succeeded in destroying the tank, for now they had a chance of doing just that. When the commander of the 3rd Company of the 57th Engineer Battalion wanted to select twelve volunteers by a raising of hands, all 120 hands went up. In order not to offend anyone, every tenth man was chosen. The twelve lucky ones could hardly wait for night to come. Explosives and all necessary equipment had already been prepared. The men were now oriented in detail about the operation, rules of conduct were given, and every man was made familiar with his

---

[10] The Kampfgruppe staff was surely the staff of Raus's own 6th Schützenbrigade.

mission. Headed by the commander of the company, who personally led the operation, the team marched off after nightfall. The road led to the east past Hill 123 on a little-used sandy path to a projecting tip of the strip of woods in which the tank was located, then through this sparsely-wooded region to the assembly area.

The stars twinkled in the sky. Their pale light was sufficient to show the contours of the nearest trees, the road, and the tank. Avoiding any noise which might betray them, barefooted scouts crept to the edge of the road and observed the tank from close quarters and also how best to approach it. It stood at the same place with its turret shut. Complete calm reigned far and wide. Only now and then a short flash of light cut the air, followed by a dull thundering. At times an enemy shell whizzed past, bursting in the area near the fork of the road north of Rossienie. It was the last rumbling of a hard combat day. About midnight, the harassing fire ceased altogether.

Suddenly there was a cracking and snapping in the forest on the other side of the road. Whispering, ghostlike figures moved toward the tank. Had its crew gotten out? There followed knocks against the turret, whereupon its cover was lifted and something was passed upward. Judging from the soft clicking noise, it must have been bowls of food. The company commander was immediately informed and simultaneously besieged with questions: "Shall we rush them and capture them? They seem to be civilians." The temptation was great and probably would have been an easy matter. The crew of the tank was still in the turret, however, and the attack would have alarmed them and perhaps wrecked the whole enterprise. Therefore, it was out of the question. As a result of the unexpected episode, another hour of waiting had to pass until the armed civilians (partisans) had withdrawn.

In the meantime, the tank and its surroundings were reconnoitered. It was one o'clock before the engineers could get to work. The crew of the tank slept in the turret and had no idea what was going on around it. After an explosive charge had been fixed to the caterpillar track and the tank's thick side, the patrol withdrew and lit the fuse. A loud explosion tore the air. The mission had been carried out and the success seemed decisive. No sooner had the echo of the explosion died out, however, when the machine gun of the tank burst into action, its fire covering the near vicinity again and again. The tank itself did not move. Its caterpillar track seemed to have been destroyed. An examination of the damage was not possible as long as the tank shot wildly in every direction. The patrol, therefore, returned to the bridgehead quite dejectedly, not too sure of its success, and made its report, adding that one man was missing. Attempts to find him in the darkness would have proven useless. Shortly before dawn, a second, though smaller, explosion was heard in the area of the tank, an explanation for which no one could give. The machine gun of the tank again swept the surrounding terrain. Then everything was calm.

Soon afterward, the day began to dawn in the east. The rays of the golden morning sun bathed forests and fields in their light. Thousands of dewdrops glittered on flowers and grasses. The first birds began to sing. The soldiers stretched their limbs in their tents and rubbed the sleep from their eyes. A new day had come. The sun was high in the sky when a barefooted soldier with his boots hanging from his arm went past the brigade combat post. The watchful eye of the commander saw him. A sharp summons was issued and the wanderer stood anxiously facing his superior officer, who in clear language asked for an explanation of the reason for the morning walk in that strange attire. Was he a passionate follower of Kneip?[11] Such enthusiasm was certainly out of place here.

Very embarrassed, the solitary walker confessed the reason for his guilt. Every word of this taciturn delinquent had to be extracted by severe questioning. As the answers were given, however, the officer's face brightened. After some ten minutes of such questioning, the solitary stranger was offered a morning cigarette, which he accepted in an embarrassed way. Finally, with a smile, the colonel patted him on the shoulder and even shook his hand in parting. A strange turn, thought the curious onlookers, who had only been able to observe what was going on without hearing what had been said. What had the barefooted boy done to have found favor so quickly? It could not have been a triviality. Their curiosity was not satisfied, however, until they learned in the order of the day an extract of the report which the young engineer had given. The report follows:

> I was listening sentry and lay in a ditch close to the Russian tank. When everything was ready, I and the commander of the company attached a demolition charge which was twice as strong as regulations provided to the caterpillar track of the tank, returned to the ditch and lit the fuse. Since the ditch was deep enough to offer protection against splinters, I waited there to see the effect of the explosion. The tank, however, repeatedly covered the fringe of the forest and the ditch with its fire after the explosion, and more than an hour went by before things were calm again. I then crept to the tank and examined its caterpillar track at the place where I had attached the charge. Hardly half of its width had been destroyed. I could not find any other damage done to the tank.
>
> When I returned to the assembly point of the combat patrol, it had departed already. When looking for my shoes, which I had left there, I found another demolition charge that had been left behind. I took it, returned to the tank, climbed on it barefooted and fastened the charge to the gun barrel in the hope of at least destroying this. It was not large enough to do any greater damage. I crept under the tank and detonated the charge. Upon the explosion, the tank immediately covered the forest fringe and ditches with its fire again. The fire did not cease until dawn and not until then could I crawl out from underneath the tank. Inspecting the effect of the demolition, I saw to my regret that the charge I had found had been too small. The gun was only slightly damaged. On arrival at the assembly point I tried to put on the boots, but they were too small and did not belong to me. One of my comrades had changed boots by mistake. This is why I returned barefooted and too late.

This is truly the tale of the brave man.

The tank was still blocking the road, however, and fired and moved about as if nothing had happened. The fourth solution, set for the morning of 25 June—to have dive-bombers attack the tank—was not carried out because the latter were urgently

---

[11] Father Kneip, the nineteenth-century leader of a "back to nature" movement for physical health, icy baths, sleep under the stars, etc.

needed elsewhere. Whether they would have succeeded in destroying the tank by a direct hit remains an open question. The stubborn occupants of the tank would never have been chased away by mere close bomb hits. Under any circumstances, the tank had to be eliminated, as the fighting power of the bridgehead garrison would have been seriously endangered if the road had remained blocked.

Therefore, the fifth plan had to be put into effect—a plan which involved the loss of men, tanks and other weapons to an extent not yet known. The intention, however, was to mislead the enemy and thus reduce losses to a minimum. It was planned to divert the attention of the Russian KV-1 through a feint attack by a friendly tank formation and, in the meantime, to bring another 88mm antiaircraft gun into position to destroy the tank. The terrain was very suitable for the purpose, making possible a close approach to the tank and observation of it from the higher wooded area to the east of the road. Since the forest was sparse and consisted only of small trees, tanks could be moved in various directions.

The tank formation soon arrived and started hammering at the KV-1 from three sides. The crew of the giant tank was visibly nervous. Its turret repeatedly swung around to catch one or the other of the German tanks with its gun as they slipped past, firing at it through narrow gaps in the wood. It was always too late: no sooner had the German tank been located than it had already disappeared. The KV-1 crew knew that their tank's thick armor, which resembled elephant hide, would resist the German shells, but the crew had ambitions of destroying the annoying tormentors without leaving the road unguarded.

Fortunately for the Germans, in its eagerness the crew overlooked securing the rear, from which direction disaster was approaching. The antiaircraft gun had already taken up a position beside the one which had been hit on the preceding day. Its powerful tube pointed at the tank and the first shot thundered away. The wounded tank giant still tried to swing its turret to the rear, but a second and third shot hit the target in the meantime. The tank could not carry out its intention, but it was not set on fire as expected. It no longer reacted to the fire of the Germans, but it seemed too early to be certain of success. Four additional heavy armor-piercing shells from the 88mm antiaircraft gun were necessary to dispatch the tank. Its gun, which had been hit eight times, rose into the air and the tank stood motionless on the road as if it meant, even now, not to give up the blockade.

The witnesses of this exciting duel were now anxious to ascertain the effect of their fire. Great was their surprise when they found that only two shots had pierced the armor, and five other shots of the antiaircraft gun had only made deep dents. They further found eight blue spots made by the new 50mm antitank guns. The result of the attack of the engineer patrol consisted of damage to the caterpillar track and a slight dent on the gun barrel. No traces of the fire from the German tanks could be found. Driven by curiosity, the small "Davids," climbing up on the fallen "Goliath," in vain tried to open the lid of the turret. In spite of drawing, pushing and hammering, they did not succeed.

Suddenly the gun barrel started to move again and they dispersed in amazement. Quickly, engineers took hand grenades and pushed them into the hole produced by the hit at the lower part of the turret. A dull explosion followed and the lid opened. In the interior of the turret lay the bodies of the brave crew, which before had only fainted. Deeply moved by such heroism, we buried the dead with all honors. Their fight to the last breath was a small heroic drama on the part of the enemy.

After having been blockaded for forty-eight hours by a single tank, the road was now open again and motor vehicles started shuttling to the bridgehead, bringing ample supplies for further combat. The troops had full freedom of action again and could come to the aid of Kampfgruppe "S." It would have been a mistake to have intervened with insufficient means in that battle and to have used up the last rounds of ammunition without having been able to bring about a decision unless it had been absolutely necessary. One could not run the risk of facing further enemy attacks completely defenseless. This answers the second question at the beginning of this example.

The fact that the German command kept its nerve and that Kampfgruppe "S" held out bravely during the critical situation was rewarded on the following day when the entire Kampfgruppe "R," reinforced by units of the 1st Panzer Division, broke forth from its bridgehead and pushed on to the south in a spirited attack along the eastern bank of the Dubysa, in order to cut off the retreat of the enemy corps. Only a precipitous retreat with large losses of equipment saved the corps from destruction. The three-day battle with all its surprises had come to an end. It was crowned by a German victory. The blitzkrieg went on.[12]

---

[12] John Erickson writes of the Soviet forces engaged in this fighting: "The Soviet 2nd Tank Division (3rd Mechanized Corps) moved at night toward its operational area, the Tilsit–Shauliya highway; this blow came from the south-east and was aimed at the 6th Panzer Division, whose units the Russians caught on the march. The Soviet war diary reads: 'Tk. Div. 3 MC fought tank action in region of Skaudvila, destroying 100th Mot. Regt., up to 40 tanks, 40 guns, in the evening entered Rasienai are without fuel.' The 2nd Tank Division lay immobilized for much of 24 June for want of fuel. During these whirling tank-battles, which spanned the three days from 23–26 June, some 250 Soviet tanks went into action, many of them the older, flimsier machines but suported by 'armoured giants', the formidably massive KV-1s and KV-2s . . . On 26 June, however, as 1st and 6th Panzer Divisions cut through the Russian units and linked up, the 3rd Mechanized Corps was blown to pieces by German guns on the high ground; the 12th Mechanized Corps pulled out of the trap with the remnants of 2nd Tank Division, by now spent in fuel and ammunition. The first sustained crisis had come and gone." John Erickson, *The Road to Stalingrad: Stalin's War with Germany*, Vol.1 (New York: Harper & Row, 1974), p. 143.

Chapter 2

"Raus Pulls Them Through"

Introduction

by Hellmuth Reinhardt, Generalmajor a.D.[1]

The introduction to the German basic tactical manual entitled 'Conduct of Field Operations" (Army Manual No 300/1) contains the following two sentences:

> The variety of situations arising during wartime is boundless.
> The rules of warfare cannot be summarized comprehensively in manuals. The principles outlined in these manuals have to be applied in accordance with the prevailing situation.

These precepts are illustrated by means of the examples given below which have been compiled by Generaloberst a.D. Raus on the basis of his experience during the 1941–42 Eastern campaign; they constitute Part IV of his study entitled "Unusual Situations."[2] It is not the solution arrived at for each particular situation which makes these examples valuable for purposes of training and as object lessons, but rather the manner in which the respective solution was reached and put into effect. For instance, Example 1, entitled "The Gateway to Leningrad"—which depicts, as part of the offensive launched in the summer of 1941 by Army Group North against Leningrad, the capture and defense of a bridgehead far in advance of the bulk of the German forces—can by no means be regarded as a standard example of a bridgehead defensive. It demonstrates, however, how, on the basis of evaluation of our manpower and equipment, of the likely course of action on the part of the enemy, and of the terrain conditions, the overall plan was developed which made possible the fulfillment of our mission. The utilization of this example for training purposes furthermore gains in importance by reason of the fact that it describes how this plan was put into practice. It shows how carefully the unit adapted its actions to this plan to such an extent that during the course of battle even the subordinate commanders were able at any time to take appropriate action in conformity

---

[1] The term "a.D." stands for "ausser Dienst" (Retired).

[2] Generalmajor Reinhard refers to the original manuscript, from which this chapter was taken, in the Foreign Military Studies collection now held at the National Archives (College Park, MD). For the sake of clarity, in the flow of this book the manuscript parts have been reordered to fit the historical sequence of the operations described. Manuscript P-060g, Part IV, was converted into Chapter 2 of this collection of all four of Generaloberst Raus's four manuscripts. Part I becomes Chapter 1, Part II become Chapter 4, and Part III becomes Chapter 3. A fifth manuscript, D-189, becomes Chapter 5, *Guide to Foreign Military Studies 1945–1954*, Historical Division, Headquarters, United States Army, Europe, 1954.

with the overall plan without having received any orders or just on the basis of brief instructions; and how, thanks to their training in tactics, they exercised sound judgment.

Examples 2 and 3, which are concerned with the same period and tactical problems, deal with the bitter fighting during the winter of 1941/42 in the sector of Army Group Center. They are typical of winter combat and in that respect also supplement excellently the examples cited in MS # P-060d, Part II (*Small Unit Tactics—Winter Combat of Infantry Troops in Russia*).[3] However, here too their main value as object lessons lies elsewhere.

Example 2, entitled "Ski Battalions and Tanks in an Attack on Ice Bunker Positions," again places emphasis on correct evaluation of the situation—that is, the appraisal of our strength, of the enemy, and of the terrain and weather conditions as the basis of our mode of procedure. At the same time, however, the example also points out quite distinctly that independent action according to the prevailing situation is not the same as failure to pay attention to tactical principles, but that, on the contrary, it is necessary to apply such rules of tactics. In doing so, however, we must always be guided by circumstances and never by a prescribed formula. Therein lies this art: the German Army, while training its men in tactics, made use of the applicatory method whereby the principles laid down in the manuals always were conveyed solely by means of practical examples.

Example 3, entitled "Combined-Arms Attack Utilized as a Training Medium," deals with one of those rare situations where it was possible to use the applicatory method to such an extent that a major battle also served as a lesson in tactics. In fact the arrival of fresh enemy troops even made it possible to pose an interesting problem in making decisions. The educational value of this example lies chiefly in the fact that it demonstrates how the proper appraisal of the enemy served as a basis for our action and that, in addition, it illustrates how, through the proper conduct of operations, it was possible to achieve coordination between various weapons and the separately attacking groups along the lines of the overall plan.

Although the author, at the end of the war, was an army group commander, he attained that rank because of his reputation as a fighting commander of smaller units. He was especially skillful in extricating troops from desperate situations, and thus acquired the sobriquet "*Raus zieht heraus*," roughly translated as "Raus pulls them through." He is admirably qualified to write combat studies dealing with minor as well as major tactics.

Example 1:
The Gateway to Leningrad: Events from 11 to 20 July 1941[4]

I. Lessons

The following example describes the actions of a German combined-arms task force which, far behind the Russian front, captured two strategic bridges which it held for days

---

[3] This manuscript was written by Generalmajor Reinhardt in 1951.
[4] Raus also discusses this operation in Rauss, *Fighting in Hell*, pp. 57–9.

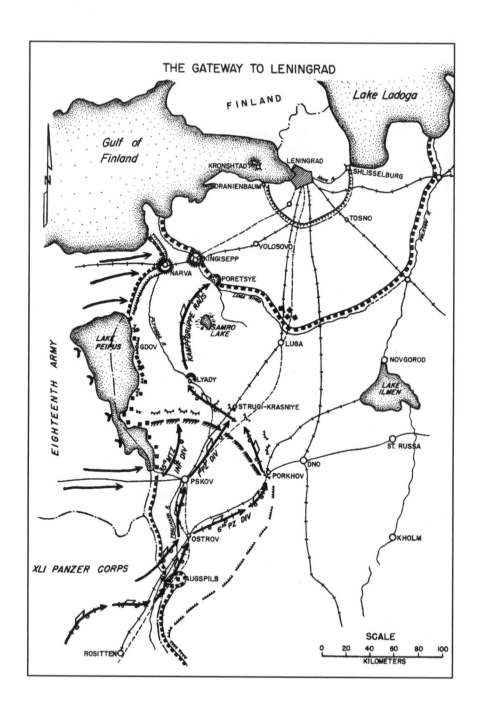

THE GATEWAY TO LENINGRAD

against vastly superior enemy forces until the bulk of the German forces was able to arrive.

Such a difficult mission could only have been carried out by a unit imbued with exceptional courage and under the able leadership of commanders and subordinate commanders who had been trained to take the initiative in keeping with the task assigned. The unit in question fulfilled these requirements. In addition, this remarkable operation is a perfect example demonstrating when and how orders should be issued. In this particular case neither the commander of the combined-arms task force nor any of his subordinate officers ever received or issued even one single written order. The uniqueness of the situation, with its constant surprises and fluctuating battles, made it impossible to follow the customary procedure of issuing commands. The circumstances offered neither the time to draw up any written orders nor the possibility to get them safely through all the turmoil of battle to the subordinate commanders. This principle of encouraging "all levels of command to act on their own initiative" and of issuing orders by word of mouth is an absolute necessity particularly for conducting operations with mobile troops. This example illustrates in detail and helps to evaluate the effects produced by putting this method into practice.

II. History and Situation in General

1. Terrain and Weather Conditions. In order to comprehend the difficulties this extraordinary operation entailed and to be able to properly understand the situation faced by the unit and evaluate its achievements, it is necessary first of all to take into consideration the terrain and weather conditions which prevailed.

During the previous thrust launched by the armored units of the XLI Panzer Corps (of which the 6th Panzer Division also was a part) the troops, while passing through the southern part of the Baltic states which was rich in forests, still managed to find roads on which the endless motor transport columns were able to travel at a more or less swift pace. However, as soon as they entered Russian territory and had to leave the few roads which were passable, conditions unmistakably changed for the worse. The march of Kampfgruppe Raus of the 6th Panzer Division became an incredibly difficult task as soon as the unit was compelled to discontinue its drive on Porkhov and suddenly had to wheel northward at a 90-degree angle, continuing in a straight line in the general direction of the advance of the 4th Panzergruppe, moving on sandy and swampy roads which from time immemorial had never been used by any motor vehicles. Moreover, the roads shown on our maps frequently ended in swampland which, had we attempted to cross it, would have led to disaster. The occupants of the wretched huts which we came across here and there also were bewildered when we requested them to make a circle around the swampy area and lead us to a village which was marked on our obsolete maps as being located on our route of march.

These people were not familiar with the name the village was called on our maps because it was decades since this name had been changed. In many cases only the compass and our instincts made it possible for us to get out of perilous situations such as those where a vehicle, trying to pull another out of the swamp, would get hopelessly bogged down. At some points it happened that dozens of tanks which had been brought to the rescue were stuck fast in the mire until finally a twenty-ton prime mover with supersize tracks would extricate them from the swamps. There were two extensive swampy forest areas in particular which taxed troops and vehicles to an incredible degree. Finally, exerting their last remaining strength, the troops succeeded in making their way through these areas, moving at a pace of one and a half kilometers per hour. One of these areas was located around Lake Samro and the other stretched south of the Pskov–Leningrad *Rollbahn*.[5] The region between these areas consisted of sand dunes which were in part sparsely overgrown with coniferous trees. The march unit, using the method of following in the tracks of the preceding vehicle, was able in spite of all difficulties to traverse this area at the rate of ten kilometers per hour. Every river and brook was a veritable marsh and could not be forded. All bridges in the swampy areas were dilapidated and collapsed under the load of the heavy motor vehicles. The measures taken to remedy the situation are described below.

In the daytime, the endless swampy and sandy regions sweltered under the broiling sun. Throughout the entire operation, the usual weather of the northern midsummer prevailed: skies forever blue, long hot days, and short cool nights. The warm dry weather made it possible to camp in the open throughout the entire period. There were only a few village wells, some of which were up to 30 meters deep. These wells, the bottoms of which were still covered with ice, provided excellent drinking water, of which there was a shortage at many places. The entire region was thinly populated and poor in natural resources.

2. The Advance. After the troops had crossed the Dvina River and had breached the Stalin Line, whose concrete pillboxes extended three kilometers in depth (Kampfgruppe Raus being the first unit which had penetrated the enemy positions on 6 July 1941 after two days of fighting), the 4th Panzergruppe continued its lightning-like advance on Leningrad. On 11 July, shortly before reaching Porkhov, the Kampfgruppe suddenly had to wheel northwestward at a 90-degree angle in order to come to the assistance of the 1st Panzer Division (XLI Panzer Corps), which was locked in desperate fighting on the Leningrad *Rollbahn*, and then had to establish a bridgehead at Lyady. After extremely difficult and time-consuming marches and battles, it was possible, by launching a sudden attack, to capture the bridge over the Plyussa River and occupy Lyady.

This surprise raid was carried out by a first lieutenant without orders. This first lieutenant, after he and his advance party had routed one enemy engineer unit in a fierce forest battle a few kilometers south of the river, got into his cross-country command car, shouting at his troops nothing but the brief order "Follow me!" Then, driving over sandy

---

[5] A *Rollbahn* was a road designated as a main axis of motorized transportation from which all animal transport and marching columns were normally barred.

roads and through brushwood, he rushed toward the bridge as fast as he could so as to be able to reach it ahead of the enemy engineers. His troops followed him, recklessly unmindful of the fact that the enemy had resumed firing. Thus they succeeded in capturing the enemy troops guarding the bridge, who were taken completely by surprise, before they could be alerted and reinforced. Through this action the bridge, which was 150 meters long and 10 meters high, fell into our hands without a fight.

However, no sooner had the Russian engineers and partisans been driven from the village when I received from the commander of the XLI Panzer Corps (Generaloberst Georg Hans Reinhardt), who was himself driving ahead to Lyady, verbal orders to continue immediately advancing northward to capture the two bridges which crossed the Luga River at Poretsye and thus to open the gateway to Leningrad. Without delay I dispatched the motorcycle messengers, who had been left at my headquarters by the units, to summon the respective commanders, and I passed these instructions on to them, giving them the necessary information regarding the point of departure and the route and organization of march. Some of the commanders made notes of certain particulars and asked questions, while others discussed ways of rendering mutual assistance, how to make the assigned engineers, tanks, radio trucks, artillery and other heavy weapons an integral part of the organization, as well as problems of supply. All these instructions, too, including the minutest details, were issued by word of mouth only. Throughout the march I stayed with the advance guard battalion and at times also with the advance party or with those elements of the column who were bogged down in the rear and with whom radio contact was maintained. The rallying cry of the corps commander, like an electric spark, kindled a flame in the hearts of the soldiers. All weariness was immediately forgotten. Dusk had not yet fallen when the engines which had only just stopped began to hum again. Unit after unit kept rolling along smoothly in duly protected march formation. We were beginning to hope that it would be possible to reach the goal, which was still 100 kilometers away, in a few hours.

However, as soon as we reached the swampy region of Lake Samro, the road suddenly changed into marshland of the worst kind. Tanks and guns bogged down and the prime movers and other emergency vehicles suffered the same fate. Only after hours of laborious effort on the part of all officers and troops, who, tormented by thousands of mosquitoes, kept on dragging beams, planks, logs, brushwood and the brush mats they had brought along to the necessary places, was it possible to get out of this marshy terrain and to surmount this handicap as well as the obstacles of still more swampy spots to follow. It was only after a night-long struggle through sand and mud that the unit managed to reach a road that was passable. After marching past a village set afire by the enemy, and extinguishing the fire of a burning bridge, the troops moved at a quick pace toward the desired goal. This time it was the commander of the engineer platoon attached to the advance party who, without orders, at once drove with utmost speed across the burning Dolgaya bridge so as to be able to begin extinguishing the blaze at the other side of the river where the fire had broken out first. The engineers succeeded in

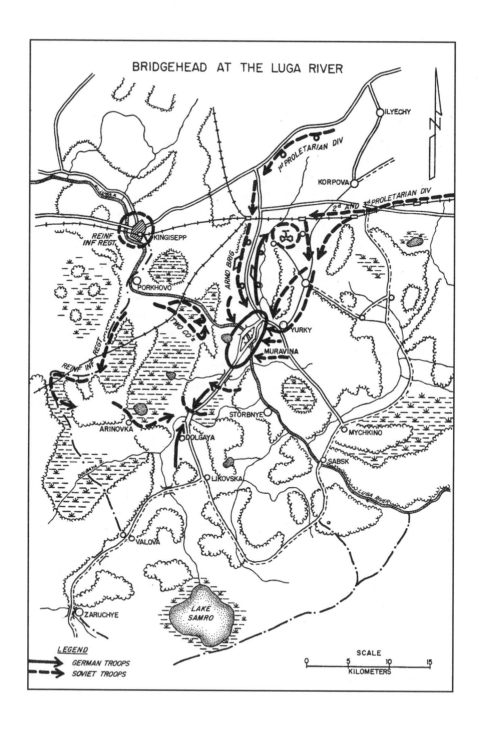

BRIDGEHEAD AT THE LUGA RIVER

putting out the fire with sand and water so rapidly that the load capacity of the charred bridge was still sufficient to carry even the heaviest weight. The loss of this bridge would have been highly detrimental because it was neither possible to ford the deep river nor cross the adjacent terrain, which was swampy throughout. If the column had been held up for any length of time at this point, which was under observation of the enemy air force, the operation might have ended in failure. Thanks to the initiative of the young lieutenant, this danger was dispelled. Shouts of "Enemy planes!" were suddenly heard. However, they flew over the column without attacking. Returning, they flashed light signals and dropped slips of paper. These Russian notes, translated by the interpreter, read: "Identify yourself or we shoot!" However, the column calmly continued its march and did not halt even when the challenge was repeated. Finally the planes dropped out of sight. Their uncertainty was well-founded because, after all, the column, moving in the direction of Leningrad, had been driving for many kilometers behind the Russian lines at Lake Peipus. The unconcerned manner in which the units maintained their course seemed to have reassured the Russian fliers, who probably were convinced that such behavior could be ascribed only to Russian columns.

Shortly before reaching the Verza bridge, the column was ordered to halt in a high forest in which it was hidden from the view of the enemy. This was done in order to provide the chance to close up from the rear and to issue instructions concerning the capture of the Luga River crossings as well as the establishment and defense of the bridgehead. The order which, on the basis of an obsolete map (scale 1:300,000), was given to the commanders by word of mouth was phrased approximately as follows:

> The enemy in all probability has not yet recognized the Kampfgruppe as a German unit. It is of paramount importance to seize the Luga bridges quickly and intact. To this end the advance guard will make a surprise attack on the enemy guards on the bridge and eliminate them. Following this, the accompanying engineer company will immediately remove all mines and take charge of securing the bridges. The main body of the Kampfgruppe will follow close behind. It will advance without delay across the bridges toward Ivanovskoye, occupy the road fork there, and conduct reconnaissance by way of Yurky and Srednoye. The artillery will provide fire support for the Kampfgruppe from a position at the southern shore of the Luga River. Distribution of heavy weapons remains the same as heretofore. The 6th (Mechanized Infantry) Company of the 114th Motorized Infantry Regiment will place itself at my disposal and hold itself in readiness in the forest area south of the bridges. At this point, too, the troops will park all supply vehicles and repair to the auxiliary station. Each unit will be responsible for its own security. The flak battalion will provide air raid protection in the area south of the bridges. My command post will be established close to the southern end of the new bridge. I expect the attack to be carried out with determination and vigor, and I look forward to a complete victory.

There were no further questions or regroupings, so that only ten minutes later the column again continued to roll, organized as heretofore. If our assumption that the units had not yet been recognized by the enemy was correct, any attempt to reconnoiter the bridge area had to be avoided because this might have seriously jeopardized the operation, whose success depended on maintaining the surprise element. It was therefore decided to effect a quasi "peacetime march." Spearheaded by a tank company, the advance guard arrived at Muravina. The column, advancing through the forest and the village located in front of the approaches to the bridge, reached the river crossings without being seen. Not until then did the Russian guards on the bridges realize their mistake. Since they had neither antitank guns nor other tank-destroying weapons at their disposal, they fled panic-stricken to their bunkers, from where the pursuing engineers drove them without a fight and captured them. The tanks, in the meantime, had been rolling across the two bridges and also cleaned out the large log bunkers at the other side of the river.

3. Arrival on 14 July. Half an hour later the unit, in accordance with orders, had seized without a fight not only the two Luga bridges but the road fork at Ivanovskoye as well.[6] The security guards who had been taken completely by surprise were in our hands.[7] Kampfgruppe Raus, after three days and nights of incessant struggle with the hardships of nature, advanced 200 kilometers and on 14 July at 1000 had reached a point 105 kilometers from the city in the "gateway to Leningrad."

The previous challenge of the enemy planes—"Identify yourself!"—was finally answered in unmistakable manner through an attack launched by several German tanks on the nearby Russian airfield of Yastrebina. This again was a secondary operation which resulted from the initiative taken by a young officer. The officer in question was a panzer unit lieutenant who captured a Russian aircraft observer at the church tower of Ivanovskoye. From this Russian observer the lieutenant found out that the Russian airfield of Yastrebina, which was barely ten kilometers away and to which he, the observer, was assigned, was occupied by strong forces. Making a quick decision, the lieutenant requested permission to pay the Russian airfield a visit together with his platoon consisting of five tanks. "Permission granted, but make sure you come back soon!" This was the reply to his request—a request which was all the more remarkable in view of the fact that for three days and nights the unit had been unable to rest and therefore was completely exhausted. The enemy lost no time in paying us a return visit.

Meanwhile it was necessary to report the arrival at our destination and the establishment of the bridgehead. However, the radio transmitters, hampered in their operations by the extensive swampy forests,[8] were unable to overcome the difficulties

---

[6] "The two bridges fell undamaged into the hands of a special detachment of the "Brandenberger" Regiment—so much was the enemy taken by surprise." Paul Carrell, *Hitler Moves East 1941–1943* (Boston: Little, Brown and Co., 1963) p. 226. The regiment was Brandenberg Lehr (Brandenberger Training Regiment), a cover name for the German Army's special operations force. Raus does not mention their presence.—Editor.

[7] The Soviets claimed that the Germans were able to "overcome the resistance of the cadets from the Leningrad Infantry School named for S. M. Kirov and the soldiers of the 2nd Leningrad Militia Division, who occupied defensive positions there. They forced the Luga with a rush . . ." *History of the Great Patriotic War. Volume II: The Repulse by the Soviet People of the Treacherous Attack by Fascist Germany on the USSR, Creating Conditions for a Radical Turn in the War* (June 1941–November 1942) (Moscow: Voyenizdat, 1961), p. 53.

[8] This confirms US experience that radio communication is hampered by the presence of coniferous forests.

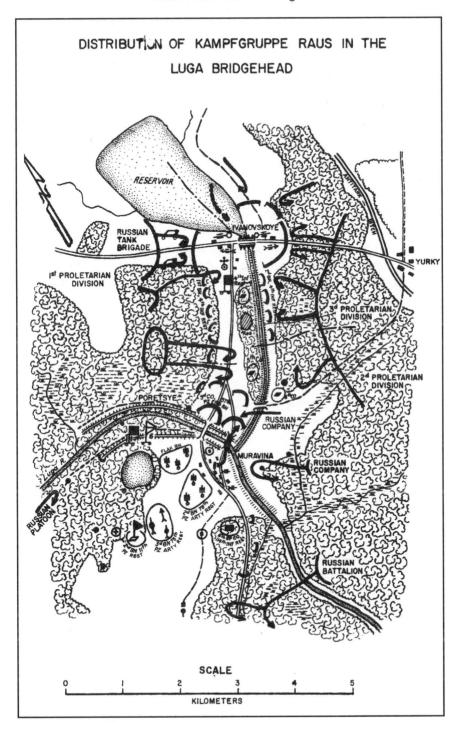

DISTRIBUTION OF KAMPFGRUPPE RAUS IN THE LUGA BRIDGEHEAD

of the immense distance. Not until a radio truck was sent 60 kilometers to the rear did we succeed in dispatching our message to the corps over the airwaves. This message was worded as follows: "Bridges captured intact at 1000 and secured through bridgehead. 14 July. Kampfgruppe Raus." The radio truck had only just returned when the road was blocked by an enemy regiment. The five tanks, too, soon returned from their raid gratified with their success. Driving through the hangars and over the planes standing about on the ground had been a rare treat for them. The operation of these five tanks proved to be more effective than any bombing attack we might have made. The field, which they had left a heap of ruins, was ablaze. Flames and dark clouds of smoke lit up the sky and could be seen from afar. All airfields in the Leningrad area—and there were quite a number of them—were alerted. Hardly an hour had passed when the completely worn-out troops who had only just arrived in their respectively assigned sectors were roughly jolted out of sleep. Out of a clear sky, the villages, farms, roads, and adjacent fringes of forest were subjected to a veritable downpour of bombs of considerable intensity. A particularly large share was meted out to the villages of Muravina and Poretsye situated on both sides of the bridges. My headquarters, located in the village of Muravina, was deprived of shelter—suffering the same fate as the troop units—and had to take refuge in the nearby forest.

This was enough of a warning signal for us. Without delay, foxholes for protection against tanks and air raids were dug everywhere, and these foxholes, provided with a thick protective covering, were interconnected until they formed a narrow zigzag system of trenches. Waves of enemy wing formations then attacked in succession until the day drew to a close. Unfortunately, so far north, darkness was quite late in coming. However, the enemy air force abandoned its practice of conducting low-level flights, which were virtually demonstration flights, as soon as the quickly organized antiaircraft defense began to inflict serious losses. The Luftwaffe was not likely to come to our aid very soon because its ground organizations were unable to keep pace with the rapid advance of the armored units.

4. The Enemy's Advance. The first short night passed quietly. However, there was no doubt that the enemy would do his utmost to eliminate immediately the danger threatening Leningrad. The effects of his countermeasures were bound to make themselves felt in a short while. Infantry forces in large numbers, artillery and tanks were moving up on all railroads and highways. The Russian forces consisted of three alerted Leningrad proletarian divisions[9] and one tank brigade. It was their mission to annihilate the German unit which had rushed forward to the Luga River and to recapture the two bridges.

---

[9] Proletarian divisions were born of the Soviet Northern Front's trained manpower shortage. By late June, the city of Leningrad began forming 'militia divisions' (*Divizii narodnovo oplcheniya*, or DNO). "On 30 June, a preliminary organization for the 'Leningrad National Militia Army' (*Leningradskoi armii narodnovo opolcheniya*: LANO) was formed, with Military Soviet, staff and political sections to supervise the recruitment and training of the militia divisions. At its second meeting on 4 July, the militia army Military Soviet decided to speed

The German defense forces, however, were determined to resist any enemy superiority and to hold out until help could arrive. The commanders were aware of the fact that an extremely critical situation would arise in case the main body of the division, which was following behind and with which contact was no longer maintained, did not arrive in time.

5. Organizational Structure. Kampfgruppe Raus was made up of the following:

The headquarters staff of the 6th Motorized Infantry Brigade (Schützenbrigade)

The 4th Motorized Infantry Regiment (Schützenregiment) (two battalions)

The 6th Company, 114th Motorized Infantry Regiment (Schützenregiment) (on half-track armored personnel carriers)

The 2nd Battalion, 11th Panzer Regiment (consisting of staff headquarters and three companies and equipped with sixty tanks)

The 2nd and 3rd Battalions, 76th Panzer Artillery Regiment (equipped with three light and three heavy batteries)

The 3rd Company, 57th Panzer Engineer Battalion

One antitank company (equipped with nine 50mm antitank guns)

One flak battalion (equipped with twelve 88 mm flak and thirty-six 20mm flak)

One ambulance column and one supply echelon

This made a total of:

Seven infantry companies, including 1,500 riflemen

Two machine gun companies, including 230 machine guns

One infantry howitzer company, including 12 infantry howitzers

One engineer company

Sixty tanks

Twenty-four guns

Nine antitank guns (50mm)

Forty-eight flak

---

matters up, to cut the original plan of forming fifteen divisions and to prepare instead three DNO formations for the Luga defence line by 7 July. The men—students, workers, professional people, sometimes whole families—volunteered readily enough, and formed up within city districts or particular factories; the regiments took their designations from them. Early in July, DNO-1, DNO-2, and DNO-3, simply kitted up but without heavy weapons, with a tiny cadre of regular troops but in general barely trained, and wished on as gallant men (which they were) by friends and relatives, moved off for the Luga battle-lines." John Erickson, *The Road to Stalingrad: Stalin's War with Germany*, Vol. 1 (New York: Harper & Row, 1974) pp. 148–9. The Soviet *Military Encyclopedic Dictionary* describes these formations as made up of volunteers not subject to mobilization. Such divisions were "close in strength level to a Soviet Army rifle division. The senior command slots were manned primarily by regular officers, while the remainder were filled with miltarily-trained Home Guard specialists. Subsequently the People's Home Guard divisions were redesignated regular rifle divisions." MSU N. V. Ogarkov, Chairman of the Editorial Board, *Voyennyy entsiklopedicheskiy slovar* (Moscow: Voyenizdat, 1983). "From just one university, volunteers including 2,500 students, aspirants, and teachers went to the front. As in the Civil War, the nucleus of the volunteers was the skilled workers of the Leningrad factories. Communists and Young Communists composed from 20 to 46% of the personnel in the militia divisions and commando regiments." *History of the Great Patriotic War*, p. 55.

III. German Objectives And Measures

1. Defense Plan. The enemy's armored strength was equal to ours; however, he possessed a twelve-fold superiority in infantry forces. Bearing this factor in mind, it was necessary for us to achieve the closest possible concentration of our forces and the most advantageous utilization of the terrain. It was obvious from the outset that our forces would not be sufficient to enable us to set up an unbroken defense ring around the bridges and the equally important road junction of Ivanovskoye. All the same, it was imperative that these two strategic areas as well as the intermediate terrain remain in our hands if, in conformity with our mission, the bridgehead was to become the gateway to Leningrad.

If we were to establish just a small bridgehead, abandoning the road junction to the enemy, this major prerequisite for success could not have been achieved because in that case the concentration of strong forces would have been out of the question. Consequently, in order to defend this corridor—which was five kilometers in length and not more than several hundred meters wide—it was necessary to employ the kind of tactics whereby the bridges and the road junction would remain in our hands at any price and it would be possible for us to repeatedly mop up the intermediate terrain. Under the circumstances, a rigid defense of the cardinal points was called for, to be conducted hand in hand with a mobile defense of the intervening terrain. The road junction obviously was the crucial point because its possession also was of decisive importance for the control of the bridges. Moreover, the terrain and vegetation favored this choice of tactics. The bridgehead was protected in the north by a reservoir 15 meters in depth and in the east by a 6 to 10-meter deep ditch with steep banks. Both the reservoir and the ditch constituted a perfect antitank obstacle which the Russian infantry too would find difficult to cross. In the west, a swampy forest region reached close up to the road. Although it was impossible for tanks to drive on this road, several sections of it were passable for infantry forces. South of the bridgehead there were extensive swampy forest areas which at certain spots were passable for smaller units and light weapons. Here it was sufficient to employ one security detachment and small tactical reserves. Major enemy units of all types which might have seriously endangered the bridgehead were forced to use the supply route where we were able to fight them with tanks. Therefore, owing to terrain conditions, the enemy's armored attacks everywhere were confined to the roads. Only at the western outskirts of Ivanovskoye and within the bridgehead area was it possible for tanks to move along a narrow terrain sector on both sides of the road. In addition, the bridgehead was in a favorable position by reason of the fact that it was not open to enemy view from any side so that the enemy artillery would be able to fire only according to the map or with the assistance of aerial observation. At that time the Russians were not as yet familiar with the latter method, while they barely had had the opportunity to make use of the former. Owing to these facts, the forces occupying the bridgehead could be seriously endangered only if the Russians with their vast superiority in numbers were to launch their attacks under coordinated command and simultaneously from all sides, or if the Kampfgruppe were to be without supplies for more than a week. Neither of these contingencies was likely to arise.

2. Distribution of Forces. These factors constituted the psychological precept on which the defense was based. Accordingly, the road junction became the focal point of defense, and it was there that the main body of the 4th Motorized Infantry Regiment was committed, with one battalion each facing east and west respectively. It was the task of the regiment to block the two approach roads and protect the adjacent open flanks. For defense against superheavy tanks (Type 1) it was assigned some 88mm flak and 100mm high-velocity guns. As reserves, the regiment had one infantry company and one tank company each at its disposal. Responsibility for the immediate protection of the bridges devolved on the engineer commander, to whom, in addition to his unit, a number of small antiaircraft guns had been assigned. The 6th Company of the 114th Motorized Infantry Regiment was in charge of guarding and securing the area south of the Luga River. In case of emergency, the company also was able to make use of the personnel of all supply trains stationed in the area which could be organized quickly and committed as alarm-type units. Every headquarters was responsible for its own safety. All artillery, antiaircraft, and antitank elements had to be ready at all times to repulse the enemy troops in close combat with their respective weapons or to be committed as infantry for launching counterthrusts. The artillery commander and the tank commander, with two tank companies, which had been earmarked for mobile action on both sides of the Luga, remained under the immediate control of the brigade commander. These units were charged with the responsibility to attack, without waiting for orders, any and all enemy troops trying to pass the road and to rout them. Several tanks attached to headquarters were detailed to remain at all times at the southern banks of the Luga and in case of need to come without delay to the aid of the 6th Company, 114th Motorized Infantry Regiment. It was planned to concentrate the artillery fire primarily on the area on both sides of the strongpoint on the road. Consequently, the artillery commander was dependent on direct cooperation with the 4th Motorized Infantry Regiment. The constant personal contact maintained between the brigade commander and the unit assured the coordinated action of all weapons and eliminated all possibilities for misunderstandings.

3. Issuing of Orders and Preparation of Defensive Positions. These ideas are in meaning, and practically even in wording, identical with the verbal order given to the commanders of the 4th Motorized Infantry Regiment, the 2nd Battalion of the 11th Panzer Regiment and the 76th Panzer Artillery Regiment. The issuing of commands was preceded by a joint reconnaissance and evaluation of the terrain which conveyed a picture at variance with the map. In view of the fact that all enemy security detachments had been captured and the partisans had fled as soon as the first of our units had arrived, we were not troubled by any enemy action for more than twenty-four hours, with the exception of the enemy air force; however, the nearby forest offered protection against its effects. This was highly advantageous and facilitated not only our reconnaissance operations but also the preparation of the position in every respect. The opportunity was given to inspect the constructions from all sides, including the angle from which the enemy would view them. Above all, this made it possible to emplace our antitank weapons to the best advantage and to camouflage them to perfection. Important also was the fact that we were able to reconnoiter thoroughly the forest regions which extended close up to the road on both sides and to ascertain the location of some narrow trails leading across the swamps. These paths were guarded constantly so that we could not be taken by surprise by enemy troops attacking from the forest. Not until much later did it become possible to have the inaccurate maps replaced by aerial photographs and prints of captured Russian maps (scale 1:100,000) which were up-to-date and which also could be utilized for map firing.

At all those spots where the terrain made possible the commitment of armored troops, the telephone lines were installed on tall, sturdy trees, or, if there were no trees, in shallow, dry road ditches which were covered with a layer of sand or earth and camouflaged with grass. In this way they were hidden from enemy view and remained intact even while tanks passed across these spots. This procedure proved quite effective. The planning of such and similar details was not the task of the tactical commander but fell within the province of properly trained special units. The tactical commander merely had to make sure whether or not the measures taken by these units were expedient, and he was required to take action only if this was not the case or if something of importance had been overlooked.

IV. Course of Action

1. Events on 15 July 1941.

a. *Enemy Air Raids.* On the second day (15 July), the enemy air forces, as expected, again appeared on the scene early in the morning. They were amazed at the completely changed picture. There was no sign of any German soldier or weapons or vehicles nor of any constructions. Everything had been buried in the ground or camouflaged. The familiar landscape lay peaceful and serene before them. Was it possible (they probably wondered) that the Germans had withdrawn after destroying the Yastrebina airfield? However, any such hope the Russians might have held was crushed the moment their leading bomber wing approached the Luga bridges, at which point the planes were scattered by a shower of large- and small-caliber shells fired by our flak battalion. The enemy bombs missed their target. Two trails of smoke in the blue sky indicated that the antiaircraft fire had hit the mark. During their low- level flights, the enemy fighter plane escorts too suffered losses due to machine-gun fire which struck from various directions. Nevertheless, the Russians time and again and at short intervals attacked the bridges and suspected troop concentrations which they wanted to crush before the first of the Russian infantry and tank units, which were moving up, would arrive.

b. *Attack of the 1st Proletarian Division.* These forces made their appearance during the course of the morning and briskly advanced on Ivanovskoye on both sides of the road leading up to it from the west. Their mission was to capture the Luga bridges that same day. Suddenly they were attacked by the German batteries whose concentrated fire forced the Russian infantry forces to take cover. Although the enemy tanks had stopped, they soon continued to roll by fits and starts. The Russian infantry troops, pushed forward by their officers and commissars with pistol in hand, followed in small groups and brief spurts. The Russian tanks, setting the pace and advancing in wedge formation, were already approaching the German line in order to break through when they were attacked from ambush gun emplacements by the fire of our 88mm flak and 100mm guns at a distance of barely 500 meters. Every burst of fire was followed by a cloud of smoke. The ranks of the Russian infantry, too, had grown considerably thinner as a result of our artillery and machine-gun fire. The attack was coming to a standstill. More Russian infantry units were thrown into battle for the purpose of giving the attack new impetus. These units too had been hit hard, particularly by the fire of the heavy batteries. This was a disastrous baptism of fire for these troops who had never been engaged in battle before. Their irresolute rushing about in all directions and the withdrawal of their tanks, of which a dozen already had been put out of action, were unmistakable signs of a crisis. At that moment thirty German tanks, firing from all guns, burst forth with a roar and launched a counterattack, disabling additional Russian tanks and scattering the Russian infantry. The enemy attack, during which the Russians had suffered heavy casualties, ended in failure. After brief pursuit of the enemy, our tanks were ordered to return. The troops of the Proletarian Division, struck to their very marrow by this serious defeat, moved with more caution. It was impossible for them to repeat the attack that same day, which as a rule the Russians were wont to do several times.

It was the commander of the tank company attached to the 4th Motorized Infantry Regiment who had taken the initiative in this counterattack. He was observing the course of events from the church tower of Ivanovskoye and was the first to recognize the crisis which had arisen in the enemy situation. He rushed to the nearby command post of the regiment and recommended the counterthrust. This action was approved by the artillery commander, and, with the effective support of the artillery, ended in victory.

c. *Attack of the 3rd Proletarian Division.* In the meantime the 3rd Proletarian Division, advancing by way of Yurky, had assembled for action at the fringes of a thick forest of saplings east of Ivanovskoye. Their attack, launched without fire support, was carried out during the early afternoon in several closely spaced waves, the troops advancing on both sides of the road and moving toward the dam across the completely open terrain. The German artillery, which earlier had been covering the assembly area with fire, laid down a barrage from flanking positions on the brown-clad masses. In addition, the fire from numerous machine guns, tanks and other heavy weapons broke loose, covering the area with telling effect. The attack broke down in a few minutes. A field of carnage was the result of this senseless action.

Nevertheless, the attack was repeated three more times that day, ending in failure each time. The German infantrymen, who were fighting from foxholes and embrasures established along the embankment of the brook flowing from the reservoir, suffered only minor losses.

2. Events of 16 and 17 July 1941: Recurrence of Enemy Attacks. The next two days were characterized by heavy artillery fire which always started at 0600 hours in the form of intense bombardment and which repeated prior to every attack launched by the enemy along the same lines and alternately in those sectors where fighting had raged the day before. These attacks, through which the Russians did not gain even one inch of ground, resulted in their suffering very heavy losses. Although the concentrated fire of the enemy artillery and the constant air raids did cause disagreeable breakdowns and losses, they did not have the power to impair the overall structure of the German defense.[10]

3. Events on 18 July 1941.

a. *New Enemy Tactics.* Not until that day did the Russians finally realize the futility of their endeavor and try to gain a victory by changing tactics. They began to set up defensive positions on both sides of Ivanovskoye for the purpose of making available the forces necessary to carry out their new plans. To this end, they withdrew their western front somewhat and began to dig in. In the eastern sector they came to a standstill immediately in front of the forest of saplings, the troops remaining in the open. As cover they used their dead, whose bodies filled the air with a pestilential smell, piling them up at night by the hundreds and covering them with sand and earth.

The enemy's primary objective now was the capture of the two 200-meter long Luga bridges, which thus far had been damaged only slightly and which could be repaired quickly. The Russians attempted to seize these bridges by means of attacks converging from all directions. However, here too the coordination of the Russian units failed. Their plan had been a sound though hazardous one, but its chance for successful execution was frittered away in isolated actions which were not coordinated with regard to time and space. At first the Russians attempted to seize the bridges by means of a surprise raid.

b. *Surprise Raid.* During the night of 18 July, one company of the 2nd Proletarian Division sneaked across the brook north of the old bridge. At dawn these troops suddenly fell upon the weak German security detachment, occupied the bridge and then pushed on toward Muravina in order to capture the new bridge as well. However, at this point the company encountered German machine-gun units, who

---

[10] Raus elaborated on this situation in *Fighting in Hell*, p. 58: "The Russians . . . had no visibility because the edges of the woods were in German hands. Russian artillery fired 20 times as many rounds per day as did the German batteries. It pounded the bridges and the edges of the woods. In unobserved fire the Russians sent more than 2,000 medium shells a day in the direction of the bridges without ever hitting them. Enemy aircraft roared all day above the narrow corridor of the bridgehead and inflicted serious losses. Soon, therefore, the road was lined with a long row of German soldiers' graves, marked with birchwood crosses."

had been committed to secure the southern banks of the Luga, and was stopped by them. Almost immediately the 6th Company of the 114th Motorized Infantry Regiment, which had been standing by, appeared on the scene. This company, on its armored vehicles, attacked the Russian company precisely at the moment when the troops, prompted by the noise of the approaching German tanks, were attempting to make their escape across the old bridge. The Russian company was wiped out to the last man. Thus the Russians' audacious action miscarried so completely that they lost all desire to repeat it. One thrust against Muravina, launched immediately afterward by one Russian company at the opposite shore of the Luga River, had probably been intended to aid the company which had met with disaster. However, this attack came too late and was easily repulsed by the machine gun detachment.

This night surprise attack had been prepared and executed by the enemy with great skill and had considerably endangered the bridges. The action of the German company commander required no special orders since it was his main task to come to the aid of the guards on the bridges in case these crossings were threatened by the enemy. Even if this had not been his mission, he would have had to act the same way since his company was stationed in the immediate vicinity of the spot where the raid had occurred, and in accordance with the situation and regulations he was duty-bound to render assistance on his own initiative. However, credit was due him owing to the fact that his exemplary action in attacking rapidly and vigorously promptly eliminated the danger threatening these very strategic bridges.

c. *Friendly Planes Attacked by German Machine-Gunners.* During the morning, one fighter squadron was sighted flying low over the forest at the very spot where Russian Rata planes were wont to approach Muravina. Our machine guns (as usual) immediately fired on these planes. However, this time they were German planes, namely, the first German fighter squadron which had reached us. Unfortunately, the machine-gunners who were well-trained had immediately shot down the plane in the lead which, however, still managed to make an emergency landing in friendly territory. The squadron commander who had been flying this plane was only slightly wounded. Staying as guest at brigade headquarters, he soon recuperated; however, he found life in the encircled bridgehead highly disagreeable.

d. *Attacks Launched Against the Road.* Throughout the day, several Russian battalions in succession, coming from west and east, advanced from the swampy forests in the direction of the road. Those coming from the east were repulsed by the security detachments of the 2nd Battalion, 4th Motorized Infantry Regiment, who were stationed along the shore and supported by tanks. The enemy forces attacking from the west succeeded time and again in breaking through as far as the road. However, each time this happened they were simultaneously enveloped by German tank companies from the north and south respectively, and driven back into the forest. At night the field kitchens and maintenance vehicles as usual kept rolling without interference across the bridges to the troops.

The actions of the German tank companies, too, were always carried out, in conformity with the overall plan, without waiting for orders, because any order issued by the Kampfgruppe commander or the commandant of the sector (4th Motorized Infantry Regiment) would have come too late in view of the rapidity with which the Russians effected their breakthrough and the short distances they had to cover. The tank battalion commander directed the coordinated action of the tank companies by means of voice radio transmitters with which each tank was equipped.[11] During combat, it would have been suicidal, either during the day or at night, for any troops or vehicles other than armored to move on or on both sides of the road. It was, therefore, also impossible to dispatch messengers to units engaged in battle. For the reasons cited above, it was necessary for those reserves not armored to stand by, organized for battle, so as to be able to make a counterthrust. In any event, the only orders given were brief instructions issued by word of mouth through the telephones or radio.

e. *Local Operations.* In the Ivanovskoye area, only some isolated local actions took place. One attempt, made by weak Russian forces advancing from the north to push along the reservoir up to the bridge at the lock, was easily repelled. However, the effects of one surprise attack, launched from the forest by a Russian infantry unit which advanced from the west accompanied by one superheavy tank, were more distressing. This attack was aimed at paralyzing the German operational control which, as the Russians presumed, was centered in the vicinity of the church. Although, through a counterthrust, we were able to quickly drive back the Russian infantry troops who had broken through our security line, the superheavy tank emerged from the forest and drove with such speed and so close past the well-camouflaged 100mm gun that there was no possibility to fire it. The tank circled the church and crushed everything which appeared suspicious, including our regimental headquarters. Our tanks were powerless because their fire had no effect on this monster. At long last, one particularly plucky noncommissioned officer put an end to this critical situation. He jumped on the tank and kept firing his pistol into the driver's vision slot. The latter, wounded by bullet spatter and his vision obstructed, was compelled to turn back in an attempt by crossing the Russian lines to force his troublesome passenger to abandon his ingeniously chosen position. Shouting and swearing, the driver of the tank again passed the 100mm gun. Not until the moment they were just about to cross the German lines did the noncommissioned officer jump off the tank, leaving the giant-size vehicle to its fate. Thus the smallest weapon had put to flight the heaviest tank. However, no sooner had the tank reached no man's land when it burst into flames, struck by a direct hit from the 100mm gun.

---

[11] Soviet tanks at this time were not equipped with radios save those of platoon and company commanders. This gave an immense advantage to the Germans, who were able to coordinate actions much more quickly and precisely.—Editor.

That same morning, one Russian company, moving along swampy roads, made its way to the rear of the bridgehead for the purpose of attacking the artillery positions while assault detachments sneaking along the Luga River were to eliminate the brigade headquarters. Both of these operations ended in failure owing to the vigilance of the German security detachment. They were recognized in time and repelled by the local reserves.

However, more menacing was another assault carried out about noon by one Russian battalion. This thrust, launched from the swampy forest at the southern banks of the Luga, was aimed at the supply trains which had been parked in a pine forest. This attack, which came as a surprise, started off some wild and aimless firing which created great confusion. The Russians succeeded in crossing the road and pillaging a number of trucks. The enemy assault finally broke down in front of an ordnance repair shop which contained several new machine guns and a large amount of ammunition. The Russians were just attempting to regroup so as to continue the thrust with renewed vigor when they were attacked from the rear and overwhelmed by the 6th Company, 114th Motorized Infantry Regiment, which had quickly appeared on the scene. The remnants of the Russian battalion scattered in headlong flight, leaving behind their entire loot. Soon thereafter the site of this raid was marked by a grave on which a cross carried the inscription: "Here lie 157 Russians who died in battle."

During this action, the 6th Company, 114th Motorized Infantry Regiment, in keeping with the overall combat mission, immediately and without waiting for orders, joined in the forest battle which raged in its rear. Through its attack launched on the road, the troops of this company separated the forces of the Russian battalion and threw them into confusion; firing from their vehicles, they inflicted heavy losses upon the Russian troops. It goes without saying that, in all instances where it was still possible, the Kampfgruppe commander was notified in advance, so that in case of need he would still be able to take action and issue additional instructions. In cases such as the raids on the bridgehead, where this was impossible, the Kampfgruppe commander had to be advised the quickest way possible at the start of the battle or immediately thereafter.

f. *New Artillery Tactics.* The enemy artillery, too, changed its method of fighting. They discontinued the ineffectual firing on the bridgehead and began to concentrate on bombarding the bridges. After that, more than 1,000 shells droned daily across the woods toward this target. However, owing to the fact that observation was impossible for the Russians, they never succeeded in hitting the mark with any telling effects.

g. *Shortage of Ammunition.* The enemy planes struck like swarms of hornets at our batteries and any other target they identified. It had not taken them long to realize that our flak fire was becoming weaker owing to the increasing shortage of ammunition. By the afternoon, our antiaircraft guns were compelled to cease firing altogether. The few shells still available had to be reserved for antitank defense. Our machine guns too had to confine themselves to attacking only particularly troublesome low-flying airplanes. Even the artillery was forced to curtail considerably its consumption of ammunition so that at least in critical situations it would still be able to play a decisive part.

The ammunition problem to an ever-increasing degree became the chief source of anxiety for the German command. However, as long as the infantry and armored troops had sufficient ammunition at their disposal, the bridgehead was in no danger. Yet these quantities, too, were apt to be depleted rapidly should we be called upon to repulse large-scale assaults. Fortunately, the Russians, owing to their costly attacks, had become worn out to such an extent that, for the moment, they were unable to summon sufficient strength for major operations. Nevertheless, in just a few days they might again be able to bring their depleted units up to full strength, and pandemonium would break loose again. It was extremely doubtful whether the Kampfgruppe would be able without sufficient ammunition to resist such assaults. And still there was no sign of life from the main body of the panzer corps which was following behind. Had these troops been held up or even committed elsewhere? These were the questions everyone discussed anxiously.

h. *Surprise Raid across the Reservoir.* One night event came as the conclusion of the fifth day of encirclement which we had weathered successfully. Shortly before midnight, the security detachments who were guarding the embankment of the reservoir reported hearing sounds made by the oars of rowboats which were slowly moving toward the floodgate. Owing to the prevailing dead silence, these sounds were clearly audible. The operational command, however, had been expecting the Russians to make an attempt at destroying this strategic installation and had taken the necessary precautions to prevent such a catastrophe. The floodgate was protected by wire nets and floating minefields which were mean to stop the Russians from reaching the target and were designed to alert the machine-gun nests, which were equipped with searchlights, in case the approach of enemy troops was not heard or observed. In this case the Russians had failed to make sure that the sound made by the oars was drowned out by the noise of battle, although we had expected them to do so. Consequently, German forces were waiting for them in front of the target with machine guns ready to fire, and when they arrived the area was illuminated by searchlights, and the Russians were annihilated. The operation had failed miserably and we escaped the danger of being swept away by roaring floods.

4. Events on 19 July 1941. Arrival of Reinforcements (3rd Battalion, 118th Motorized Infantry Regiment). At break of day on 19 July we suddenly heard the boom of guns from the south. Soon thereafter we were informed that the 3rd Battalion, 118th Motorized Infantry Regiment, of the 36th Motorized Infantry Division (XLI Panzer Corps) was approaching. This battalion had turned off at Shabsk, where the 1st Panzer Division had established an additional bridgehead and, assigned as reinforcements, was pushing its way forward along the southern banks of the Luga River. The battalion had orders to rest in the forest south of Muravina throughout the day and to wait until nighttime before reinforcing the western front of the bridgehead. This delay was absolutely essential to avoid exposing the troops to the danger of being attacked by enemy planes and heavy artillery fire while crossing the bridges, which might have resulted in their annihilation. On that day it was necessary, therefore, for the present occupants of the bridgehead to keep on fighting alone and holding out at all costs. Unfortunately, the battalion commander, devoted to his duty, attempted to reconnoiter the front sector assigned to him in the daytime, and he as well as all the personnel accompanying him were killed while on the way there. The battalion itself, without incurring any losses, reached its sector during the night and, supported by one tank company in the rear, held this sector against all subsequent attacks.

As much as we welcomed this increase in strength, it did not alter the fact that the ammunition shortage was critical. Since the battalion had been compelled to travel on foot on the road from Shabsk, which led through swampy forests, the troops had been able to take along only as much as they could carry and whatever could be loaded on a few Panje wagons.[12] We were now apprised of the fact that the main body of the corps had been stranded for days on the road which had been completely destroyed by the Kampfgruppe, and, in order to get out of the swamps, it had been necessary for them to construct a corduroy road many kilometers long parallel to the march route. Their arrival was expected in the near future. On the whole, the sixth day of encirclement, except for lively air and artillery activity, passed relatively peacefully.

5. Events on 20 July 1941.

a. *Vehement Tank Battle.* During the night of 20 July, the Russians were busy removing the wrecked tanks, as was evident from the sounds of towing audible nearby. This indicated that they were planning new assaults. In fact, soon after dawn newly arrived superheavy tanks (KV-1s) attacked Ivanovskoye from both sides and rolled over the foremost lines and some machine-gun positions before they could be put out of commission by our 100mm guns. These were new tanks which came straight from the factory and they were driven by civilian assembly mechanics. Then a furious fire duel broke out between the flock of smaller-type tanks which were following the superheavy tanks, and the German tanks; this battle resulted in losses on both sides. The tank duel, which was brought to a conclusion by a thrust our tanks made through the gap the Russians had created by moving the wrecked tanks, ended in a Russian defeat.

b. *Renewed Mass Assault.* As a next move, the Russians, by using newly arrived infantry forces which had been trained but briefly and were ruthlessly being pushed into battle in large numbers by commissars, attempted to accomplish the objective wherein the tanks had failed. First these troops tried to storm the dam, but the attack

---

[12] Russian peasant carts.

collapsed under the fire of automatic weapons of all types. Thus they suffered the same fate as those Russians who had attacked previously and across whose piled-up bodies they had just advanced. Following this battle, their bodies too were used as building material for the reinforcement of positions. The attack launched subsequently from the west was just as unsuccessful, and, even before the Russians reached their goal, they were overrun and scattered by our tanks, which were again rushing into battle.[13]

Another enemy attempt, made soon thereafter, to seize the bridges through a mass assault was frustrated like the one that took place the day before.

c. *Critical Ammunition Shortage.* These victories were very gratifying; however, not only did they use up the ammunition dropped by the Luftwaffe in the artillery positions area that day and the day before, but they also consumed the last remaining supplies of cartridges of all types. The ammunition crisis was at its height. Although additional supplies via aerial delivery might bring relief, they could not end the shortage.

d. *Threatened by Annihilation.* Just then a German single-engine fighter plane dropped the following message: "Enemy regiment with artillery advancing on Muravina; has started out at 0930 hours at Dolgaya bridge." This was very bad news. It meant that, within three hours, the Russians might be in the rear of the bridgehead. We knew that if they launched attacks simultaneously at this point and on the two flanks, then our last hour had struck, for, without ammunition, even the bravest unit will be doomed. However, as the proverb says, "God is nearest when the need is greatest."

It was imperative that we take quick action, but the question was how? Should we throw all our tanks into battle against these fresh enemy troops? That would mean losing the bridgehead in case the Russians launched their attacks with the same intensity as those made earlier that day. For only the armored troops still had sufficient ammunition at their disposal; hence they constituted the backbone of our defense. Taking such a step might amount to suicide by the Kampfgruppe. We therefore dared not weaken the bridgehead by depriving it of any men or weapons whatsoever. Thus nothing else remained but to have the troops stationed at the southern shore of the Luga carry out defensive measures. A passive defense would have resulted in confining the Kampfgruppe to a narrow space, and would have evoked the danger of being crushed by the enemy's superior strength. We knew that only a bold decision would make it possible to dispel all danger. It was the decision to attack.

e. *The Attack which Saved the Kampfgruppe.* Without delay the 6th Company, 114th Motorized Infantry Regiment, was alerted and reinforced by three tanks taken from

---

[13] Unbeknownst to the Germans holding the brigdehead, the defending troops were personally visited by the Minister of War, Marshal of the Soviet Union K. E. Voroshilov, "to be with the cadets and militiamen. He required not only that they stop the enemy, but that they throw him back beyond the Luga. The presence of K. E. Voroshilov in the forward positions and his simple words full of stark truth encouraged the Soviet soldiers, and they fulfilled their assignment with great honor. . . . However, at the price of great losses, th enemy was able to hold small beachheads on the right bank of the Luga." *History of the Great Patriotic War*, pp. 53–4.

headquarters. The spirited company commander was just being given his instructions, when suddenly we heard the thunder of guns and furious machine-gun fire coming from the south. This meant that our troops must have engaged in battle with the Russians, which could only relieve our own situation. "Very well, hurry and get going!"—those were the last words with which the energetic young officer was dismissed.

The issuing of orders was effected by word of mouth and did not take long. It consisted of a brief orientation of the company commander concerning the seriousness of the situation and the assignment of his mission. The company commander repeated the instructions and explained in a few words how, on the whole, he proposed to carry them out. Since the officer concerned had proved his mettle and was widely experienced, it would have been advisable to lay down any rules or even prescribe his method of procedure, all of which would have to depend on the local situation, which could not be observed from the bridgehead. Before their departure, I addressed the troops of his company and said a few words in appreciation of their previous achievements. Their eyes radiated absolute confidence, and the decisive victory which was attained proved how justified they had been.

No sooner had the company commander left when we received a radio message from our motorcycle battalion informing us that, while advancing toward the bridgehead accompanied by one supply column, they had become engaged in bitter fighting at the Dolgaya River with vastly superior enemy forces; they requested our aid. Our brief radio reply "Reinforcements are on the way" was promptly acknowledged. The 6th Company, 114th Motorized Infantry Regiment, too, had listened in on both radio messages by means of the radio equipment it had been assigned.

Barely twenty minutes after the troops had departed, we heard the muffled sounds of tank and raging machine-gun fire. The armored unit had assaulted the enemy regiment, which was engaged in combat with the attacking motorcycle battalion, from the rear, striking at its batteries and heavy weapons. Thereupon it pushed forward on the road, firing from all its guns, and joined forces with the motorcycle battalion.

The Russian regiment, panic-stricken by this surprise attack on its rear, suffered heavy casualties and lost its entire heavy equipment. By noon, the motorcycle riflemen and the armored company were already arriving south of Muravina. They had scored a total victory. The route of march had been cleared and thus the danger threatening the bridgehead eliminated.

f. *Outcome.* The unusual situation, with all its hardships and distress, had come to an end. Numerous sacrifices had been required, as vividly evidenced by the battlefield, which looked like a huge cemetery. Graves of German soldiers, decorated with crosses made of birchwood, lined each side of the road. In the back thereof were mass graves in which were buried Russian soldiers numbering fifteen times as many as the German dead, and the wrecks of 78 tanks which had tried to storm the German stronghold at the Luga.[14]

Several days later, the remaining portions of the 6th Panzer Division also arrived. They were followed by the 1st Infantry Division and other units. They rolled up the enemy positions toward both flanks. The gateway to Leningrad was open; the blitzkrieg continued.

V. Evaluation

Many lessons may be learned from the above example in the field of psychology, tactics, command technique and training. It would be difficult to single out any one category in particular, because these aspects entered into the picture in all situations and were closely interwoven. I shall, nevertheless, attempt to discuss separately and in greater detail the facts pertaining to command technique as the principal theme. However, first I briefly wish to deal with experiences which pertain to the more important spheres.

1. Psychological Factors. What was the incentive which prompted the exemplary behavior of the troops who, after enduring extraordinary physical hardships and faced by an almost hopeless situation, successfully resisted enemy forces who were vastly superior in number and *matériel?* It was the high aim which the troops looked upon as their mission, the awareness of their superior ability, and their unshakable trust in their commanders and comrades. It is therefore evident that the decisive factors where psychological in nature. The intelligent German soldier wanted to know what he was fighting for and what significance the mission of his respective unit had. Only then was he capable of doing his utmost. He was an independent, individualistic fighter and felt far superior to the Russian soldier who was trained for mass commitment. It is therefore important to make sure that these and similar psychological influences not be overlooked, even during the soldier's peacetime education and training. It is absolutely essential to imbue each man with an awareness of surpassing skill and self-confidence, and the extent of this feeling depends on how well he has been trained in the use of weapons and the utilization of terrain. To earn the confidence of the troops requires exemplary conduct, sound knowledge and education, and concern for the welfare of his men on the part of their superior. Furthermore, it is important for each commander to appear at crucial points so as to be able to offer advice and assistance or make immediate decisions. It is his implicit duty to be present in critical situations. Of great importance, too, was the bond of comradeship which existed between the various arms and which considerably facilitated the coordination of all weapons. For example, the Kampfgruppe, during the actions described in this example, was composed of combined-arms and other units which had fought side by side several times in the past and therefore knew each other. A fine feeling of comradeship existed between the commanders, and this was highly beneficial for the mutual assistance they rendered each other. Consequently, the striking

---

[14] According to Raus, "The Germans counted more than 2,000 dead Russians." Rauss, *Fighting in Hell*, p. 58.

power of a unit is ruined whenever its component forces are separated, the sick and wounded not returned to their organic units, or the supporting arms changed without cogent reason. Experience has proven that a unit which has been welded together over a long period through comradeship possesses a far superior striking power than that of a unit which is equally strong but whose troops and commander hardly know each other.

2. Tactics. The operations in connection with the establishment and defense of bridgeheads were among the most important tasks of the Eastern campaign, and these duties were assigned quite frequently, particularly to the mobile troops. During the course of this campaign I, myself, together with the troops subordinated to me, have fought in various sectors and more than sixty bridgeheads, not even two of which were alike in character. Each one constituted an individual structure, conditioned by its mission, the terrain, the situation, the forces holding it and their equipment. Not one of these bridgeheads even remotely resembled the one at the Luga River, which even my subordinate commanders at first considered to be untenable. The units which arrived subsequently regarded the setup of this bridgehead as absurd, and were quite astonished that it had been possible to hold it under such difficult circumstances. Yet there was no one who, even after careful reflection and being apprised of preceding events, was able to specify how the measures taken might have been improved. The victory gained verified the advisability of the tactics applied. It would have been impossible for infantry forces alone to hold the bridgehead, even if they had been equal in strength to all other available forces, but it would have been even more difficult for merely armored units without infantry. The organized harmonious teamwork of all arms, combining rigid and mobile defense tactics, was the only possible procedure under the circumstances.

The tactics applied within this restricted area were particularly characterized by the necessity to grant the subordinate commanders much more freedom to act on their own initiative than would usually be the case. It is essential that such commanders are taught and trained to do this already during peacetime. The German commanders and subordinate commanders of all ranks to a high degree had been trained to act independently, and the victories achieved for the most part may be attributed to this fact.

It was curious to note that the Russians almost never attacked simultaneously on both fronts, which considerably facilitated our defensive task. This was due not so much to their inefficiency in coordinating the operations of adjacent units as to the exceptional firing conditions occasioned by the restricted area. Whenever Russian machine-gun or rifle fire broke loose at the western front, it was necessary for their troops at the eastern front to take full cover because, owing to the flat trajectory of the weapons used, the sheaves of fire which were aimed at our positions also took effect on the Russian positions in the east. Consequently, whenever the Russians attacked simultaneously from the west and the east, their respective troops were firing at each other. While the Russians, when opening fire, at the same time endangered their front on the opposite side, this handicap of being exposed to friendly fire did not affect the German troops since they were firing outwards. On the other hand, for reasons cited above, any firing done by the Russians also exposed to danger our two defensive lines, one in front and the other in the rear. This situation was remedied by erecting parapets facing both ways; the one facing the rear had to be constructed somewhat higher than the other, and was particularly well-camouflaged. Our troops soon were able to overcome the effect these unusual combat conditions had on their morale. All the more affected, however, were the troops and staffs subsequently brought up to the bridgehead, who assumed that this fire from the rear, which had covered an extremely short distance, had emanated from enemy troops who had broken through; consequently they became much concerned.

The battles which took place in the bridgehead on the Luga River may be regarded as a remarkable example of how the Russian tactics were strongly influenced by the fact that their positions were endangered by their own infantry weapons. In addition, the vegetation within the bridgehead area and its narrowness obstructed the Russians' view and impaired the effectiveness of their numerically vastly superior artillery and airplanes, which possessed complete mastery in the air. Only the consideration of these factors makes it possible to understand why our losses had been moderate, even though this was the only time, never again repeated, that the enemy air force concentrated its operations to such a degree and for so long a period as it had done in the case of this isolated bridgehead which they were determined to crush at any cost.

3. Issuance of Orders. This study contains numerous specific illustrations providing details about issuing commands by word of mouth. In some examples, the text of the orders is also quoted verbatim. At this point I wish to add some basic rules concerning oral commands and describe the manner in which this was carried out.

The smaller the unit, the more frequently were orders issued orally. From platoon level down the orders given were in general never written. There were some exceptions in the case of isolated small groups with independent missions. However, as the war continued, the practice of issuing oral commands was adopted even by medium and large units in ever-increasing measure. Almost invariably, the oral order consisted of a brief summary of the conclusions reached during a conference held with the subordinate commanders in the terrain adjoining the front, or in exceptional cases concerned the outcome of a conference held at high command level, also with the aid of a map. Such an order was binding and made it possible for the subordinate units to take all necessary measures for its execution without delay. The conference itself, which, according to expediency, was attended by those who were to execute the order, by technical assistants and arms specialists, offered the opportunity to clarify ideas concerning details in connection with the execution of the order and made it possible to consider special requests and settle any misunderstandings. The subsequently issued written order briefly summarized the most important points. It served primarily as a reminder and in most cases ended up as a supplement in the war diary. The procedure described above proved quite successful wherever sufficient time and the possibility were given to make use of it, and as a rule this was the case. Consequently, this practice became the established rule, and corresponded to the principle of command according to front conditions. What mattered most was not the proximity of headquarters with its frequently large staff, numerous vehicles, and abundant equipment, but the presence of the commander, who was the only one to give orders, make decisions and take full responsibility. Therefore, the written order, which was customary at the beginning of the war, more and more gave way to the above-described policy of maintaining direct personal contact with the front. Tactical orders, as a rule, were not transmitted by telephone or radio, with the exception of operational orders to armored and other mobile units on the march or in combat, which were issued if the enemy's interception of our radio messages was not likely to have any detrimental effects due to the rapidly changing situation. By placing radio trucks at least at the head, the center and at the end of each column, it was possible constantly to control the movement of troops and effect changes of direction during the march. In this way, it was possible, even during the long march to the Luga, to determine quickly the exact point of and reason for any road jams, and to remedy the situation. Without this expedient, the column would have been scattered and would not have been able to arrive at its destination in time, if at all, and not at full fighting strength.

I also wish to add a few words with regard to the technique of giving verbal commands. Every order, including the one given verbally, should be brief and explicit. It should convey only essential information and must be comprehensible to everyone. Verbosity should be avoided just as much as speaking too briefly. Furthermore, it is necessary to discriminate and take into account the fact whether the order is being given to an intelligent, well-spoken individual or an inexperienced plain soldier. As a matter of principle, every verbal order, or at least the gist of it, should be repeated by the person to whom it is given. Important verbal orders should afterward also be set down in writing and subsequently transmitted to the one to whom it has been given by word of mouth. The person issuing the order must know exactly what he intends to say and whether his order can be carried out.

Map entries or simple sketches are valuable aids in connection with written as well as verbal orders. They quickly enable the person receiving the order to understand the situation, help him visualize his task, and make it unnecessary to use many words. Therefore, this method proved particularly effective whenever we were called upon to commit immediately a newly arrived unit, and this was frequently the case, especially as far as mobile units were concerned.

4. Factors Concerning Training. By no means of least importance was the question of training, and the fact that it played an important part in the above-described victory. At every opportunity as far back as during the peacetime training of officers and enlisted men, emphasis was placed on the fact that difficult situations in particular could only be mastered by practicing determination and initiative. Numerous examples in connection with the most recent campaigns presented conclusive evidence to this effect. To do nothing in situations of this kind was denounced as "shameful," even in training manuals. Making an error in the choice of means was excusable, but never the failure to take action. Every soldier knew that he would be accountable for his conduct to his superior, who would recognize initiative and condemn any failure to act. Consequently, special importance was attached to the training of men to become self-reliant commanders and determined individual fighters. As a result, our troops were superior to the Russians who fought *en masse*, and this was the reason behind many of our victories.

Example 2: Ski Battalions and Tanks in an Attack on Ice Bunker Positions (February to March 1942)

I. Lessons

It is the purpose of this example to illustrate the method of attacking strongpoints in villages and bunkers during severe winter weather and to point out how the resulting difficulties were overcome. The example also helps to comprehend the great tactical significance of villages and shelters during winter combat.[15]

Emphasis has been placed on the following tactical principles:

1. It is possible to conquer an enemy superior in numbers and weapons in the winter, provided a way can be found to block his supply routes far and wide.
2. Units with winter mobility should be equipped with heavy weapons so as to be able to force a decision.
3. Piecemeal commitment of troops will lead to failure.
4. Violations of the fundamental rules of tactics will have serious consequences.

II. Situation And Objective

1. Location of Combat Area. This example deals with actions which took place six months after the period covered by Example 1, and in an area which was 500 kilometers from the region discussed in Example 1. The area in question was the source region of the largest rivers of European Russia—the Volga, the Dnieper and the Dvina. It was still severe winter, and the cold weather, with temperatures down to –62°F, threatened to annihilate the German Army just as it had once destroyed the army of Napoleon. However, by then the most critical point had been passed.

2. Situation at Army Group Center. An examination of the general situation at Army Group Center, then fighting at the focal point of the winter battles, reveals how this situation affected the front. This front had the appearance of an intricate maze such as has been practically unparalleled in history. This curious structure developed by reason of the fact that the Germans lacked sufficient forces to be able to organize and hold a compact and rigid front. Since Hitler had emphatically prohibited any retrograde movement, the unit tenaciously clung to the supply routes, the loss of which would have spelled disaster. As a result, the German troops, despite frequent disruption of supply shipments, never suffered from lack of ammunition or food. The Russians, on the other

---

[15] Raus also addresses this period at length in *The Anvil of War*, pp. 33–40.

hand, who had been pouring into the impassable and heavily wooded intermediate terrain, were compelled to eat their horses and finally even the skins of their horses to keep from starving. The Russian artillery was so short of ammunition that it was not able to fire more than five to ten shells per battery daily. This state of affairs accounts for the fact that this front which, due to its unusual irregularity, had increased from 500 to 1,800 kilometers (equal to the distance from Vienna to Madrid), could be held for many months by very weak units composed for the most part of supply elements, and that subsequently it was possible to evacuate these positions without suffering any losses. Each one of the three German armies committed at this front commanded several front sectors, the direction of which sometimes varied by as much as 180 degrees.

3. Situation at the 6th Panzer Division. The sector of my division, which at that time consisted only of three battalions and a larger number of units of other arms fighting on foot and all types of supply services, was 80 kilometers wide and constituted the western front of the Ninth Army (under General Walter Model). In the north, the division was facing one Russian Guards[16] corps and in the south one cavalry corps. Nevertheless, not only did we succeed in holding the front against vastly superior enemy forces but, by means of offensive actions, it was even possible to move ahead up to 40 kilometers.

4. Objective of the 6th Panzer Division. The following account deals with two such remarkable local actions which took place at the northern flank of my sector.

It was the purpose of the attacks with a limited objective, which were launched in succession, to drive the Russians from the railroad and the only available supply route. At this point both the railroad and the supply route passed close by the front line, and consequently movements were frequently disrupted by the enemy. The Russian attacks were all the more facilitated by the fact that in this particular sector strips of forest extended as far as the road and the railroad bridge across the Osusa River. It was therefore necessary for us to gain possession of this forest region, which was ten kilometers deep and just as wide, so as to be able once and for all to put an end to these dangerous stoppages.

5. Weather Conditions. It was still the middle of winter with temperatures around –40°F. The snow reached a depth of up to one meter in the open terrain and about half a meter in the woods. Sled tracks led to all occupied villages. The snow was shoveled off the important supply routes.

6. Terrain Conditions and Utilization of Settlements. The terrain was slightly undulating, and two-thirds of it was covered by forests. In the open areas, numerous small villages and homesteads were located which were grouped around one large main town. All villages located both on our side as well as that of the enemy were occupied by troops, and the villages near the front were prepared for all-around defense. Several

---

[16] The Soviets desperately reached into the Tsarist past of Russia in order to resurrect the term "Guards" to designate an elite formation. Those Soviet formations which distinguished themselves were redesignated "Guards" and received a new unit number from a Guards lists separate from the list for regular army formations.—Editor.

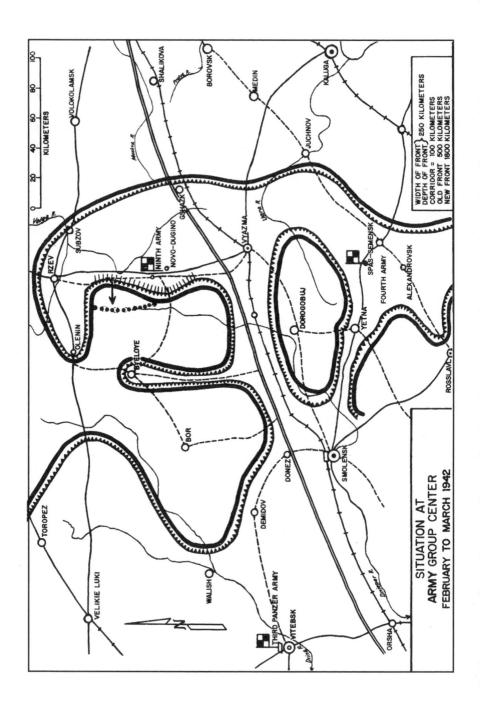

villages were organized to form a defensive system, of which the main town constituted the focal point. The defensive constructions consisted of snow barriers (parapets) and ice bunkers in large numbers. While the means available to the troops made it possible to blast several holes in the solidly frozen ground, it was impossible to dig trenches or erect parapets made of earth. The buildings themselves served as warm shelters. Therefore, only in emergencies were they utilized directly for defensive purposes. It would not have been difficult for either side, particularly the German forces, to set fire to the villages by means of airplanes and artillery, thus depriving the enemy of vitally important shelters. However, this happened only during heavy fighting. Otherwise it was to the advantage of either side to avoid such destruction, because each counted on being able to make use of these villages in the near future. In any event, there was the fear of reprisals.

The combined village strongpoints constituted the backbone of the defense. The intermediate terrain was guarded only by weak outposts stationed in isolated homesteads, and the roads were secured by patrols.

III. Course Of Action

1. Events on 16 February 1942.

a. *Advance up to Tatarinka.* The immediate objective of the German attacks was the seizure of all villages held by the Russians in the bottom of the valley on both sides of the Vasilevka–Tatarinka road. For this purpose, "Kampfgruppe Z" (comprising three battalions reinforced by some tanks, antiaircraft and antitank guns), which was made up of the remnants of the 6th Panzer Division and one infantry battalion which had lost its commander, was assembled for action in the eastern portion of Natchekino and the fringes of the forest adjoining it on both sides. After bitter close combat supported by the artillery of the entire division (24 guns) as well as several support aviation wings, the Germans also succeeded in conquering the western section of the village held by the Russians and in breaching the strong enemy defensive positions. After removing mines and obstacles, the snow was cleared from the narrow stretch of road in the erstwhile no man's land, and thus connection was established to the supply route used by the enemy. Only then was it possible for our tanks to be committed in small groups, one following the other, in pursuit of the Russians. They scattered the enemy troops, who were falling back on the road and in the stream bed, and advanced up to Vasilevka, which was the focal point of the Russian defense. The sudden appearance of our tanks prevented the commitment of the Russian reserves which were being rushed forward, so that the positions at Vasilevka were unable for long to hold out against the subsequently launched attacks of the 4th and 114th Infantry Battalions respectively;[17] and the capture of Vasilevka

---

[17] Casualties had drained away the fighting strength of the 6th Panzer's motorized infantry regiments to the point where each was consolidated into a single battalion.—Editor.

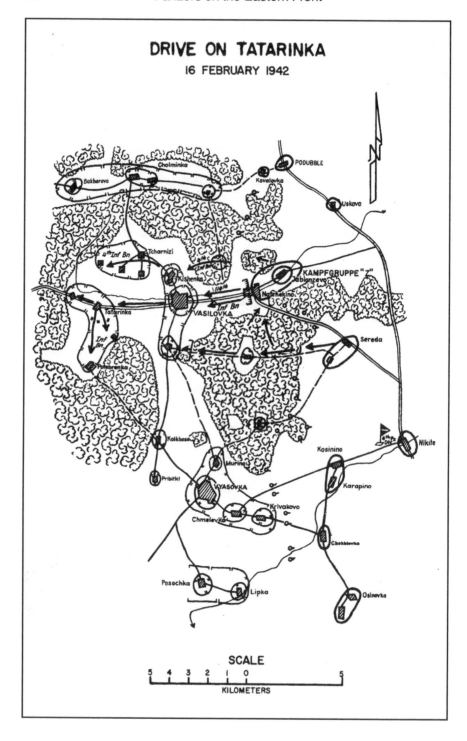

DRIVE ON TATARINKA

16 FEBRUARY 1942

SCALE

KILOMETERS

was achieved that same morning. Two battalions as well as the tanks immediately continued pushing westward and after stiff resistance occupied Tatarinka. Thus the focal point of the Russian rear defensive system also was in German hands. Operating from these two cardinal points, the Germans then captured and mopped up the remaining villages. Even before night had fallen, all villages were occupied and the Russian defensive positions converted into a German defensive system.

Destroying the ice bunkers which had been established everywhere required direct antitank, antiaircraft and tank fire. In order to drive the Russians out of the all-around defense positions and buildings, we had to engage in bitter close combat with hand grenades and submachine guns. The powerful support rendered by the numerous heavy weapons and the Luftwaffe contributed noticeably to ultimate victory and the fact that our losses remained moderate. The weak remnants of the defeated enemy regiments were driven into the adjacent forests, where they began to prepare new positions in the snow.

During these actions, the enemy's previously described weakness in the conduct of his operations became plainly evident. The Russians suffered defeat because of the absence of air force support and the fact that the assistance rendered by their artillery was inadequate. Our attack had driven a wedge 15 kilometers deep into the Russian defensive front, and this provided us with a basis for subsequent operations.

b. *Various Incidents during Battle.* After the western portion of Natchekino had been captured, the Russians launched a counterattack from log bunker positions which had been established in the forest south of the village. It was their aim to strike at the flank and rear of the German infantry troops who were already in the process of advancing westward. However, no sooner had the Russians reached the open terrain between the forest rim and the village when they were caught by the enfilade fire of the tanks just moving behind the infantry, and suffered heavy casualties. The remaining enemy elements fell back in an attempt to reach the forest positions they had abandoned and find refuge there from the devastating fire of our tanks. They were greatly shocked when suddenly they were met by machine-gun fire coming from their own positions. This fire emanated from the German southern flank detachment which had turned into the forest and had meanwhile reached and occupied the abandoned Russian bunkers. The Russians, caught between the fire from two directions, were wiped out. This disaster suffered by the Russians was due to their inadequate combat reconnaissance, which failed to discover in time either the presence of our tanks or the advance of our flank detachment in the forest. Otherwise the Russians would have realized the precariousness of their situation and would not have attempted the counterattack. In addition, they had relied on their security detachments which had been stationed at the forest edge west of Sereda but which, however, had long since been overrun by the German flank detachment. This would lead to the conclusion that liaison between the Russian forest bunker position and the above-mentioned security detachments also had not functioned properly.

Moreover, the Russian unit launching the counterattack, despite its exposed position, had taken no steps to protect itself in any direction and recklessly and in large numbers had pushed on toward a field of snow which provided no cover. These violations against the basic rules of all tactics, namely with regard to reconnaissance, security and liaison, had resulted in their destruction.

Even though the German spearhead (which, in the open terrain, was supported by all weapons on the march route) quickly succeeded in forcing its way westward, the advance of the flank detachment through the forests progressively became more difficult. Although they were able in each forest to make use of one beaten track the Russians had made, and on which they succeeded in marching single file, these detachments, just as they were about to leave the forest, each time unexpectedly were confronted by enemy positions protected by dead abatis made of tree branches. They were able neither to capture these positions by means of a frontal attack nor to bypass them through the thicket on both sides of the path, which was covered with deep snow. Moreover, the German northern flank detachment (consisting of one reinforced company) was suddenly attacked in the center of the "Africa Forest" by numerous snipers in trees and held up for a long time at that very point. Neither of the two flank detachments succeeded in capturing the Russian positions at the western edges of the forest and in reaching the open terrain. At long last, they were rescued from their unpleasant situation by units which had been detached from the main body of the German forces and detailed to attack the rear of these Russian positions.

Before the infantry battalion could to advance from Tatarinka in the afternoon and undertake the push southward, it was necessary to drive the Russians from the groups of farms and villages south of Tatarinka. Although the battalion commander had been given strict instructions to await the arrival of one tank company and one 88mm flak battery which was being brought up from Vasilevka before undertaking this operation, he attacked earlier because he had assumed that he was facing only weak enemy forces. While the companies were crossing elevated terrain just south of Tatarinka, they were suddenly caught by furious machine-gun fire which was coming from several farm buildings and forced them to fall back behind the elevated terrain. They were able to continue to attack only when it became possible to emplace the heavy antitank and antiaircraft guns, which had in the meantime arrived, and to demolish the identified enemy machine-gun bunkers by direct hits. Due to the fact that the young battalion commander had underestimated the enemy, we suffered unnecessary losses and the advance on Potebrenka was delayed. Following our capture of Potebrenka (south of Tatarinka), the battalion, which in the afternoon had been attacking at that point (at the forest rim opposite Potebrenka), came across a log bunker position which was occupied by Russian troops and also served as quarters with heating facilities. At nightfall, this position was taken by assault and, since it was not suitable for German defensive purposes, was demolished. Our destruction of such shelters compelled the enemy to fight and sleep in the open at −12°F, which considerably impaired his fighting capacity. Consequently, within a very short while, it became possible to have the German attack unit committed at that point replaced by improvised units suitable only for defense, which made the attack unit available for other offensive operations. Even more effective was the following procedure employed in one sector, which involved using a ruse we had learned from the Russians. Just before the enemy was expected to arrive, the bunkers, which had been left intact, were evacuated, leaving behind interconnected hand grenades and other demolition charges which the engineers had hidden in the twigs and straw covering the floor; these exploded at the slightest touch, and not only destroyed the bunkers but also inflicted losses upon the enemy.

2. Events on 17 February 1942: Russian Counterattacks. In spite of the enemy's weaknesses described above, we still had no reason to assume that the Russians would accept defeat with fatalistic resignation, for they still had at their disposal large numbers of armed troops, as well as fanatics whom they kept inciting. The Russian counterattacks began the very next day. Enemy reserves, which had been brought up quickly without artillery support, attacked those bunker positions which, covered by machine guns, artillery and tanks, were established in the most forward villages. These efforts, which the Russians repeated during the following days, remained unsuccessful. They increased their losses without making it possible for them to recapture even one single village. The Germans, on the other hand, by means of local raids on isolated farmsteads, even succeeded in improving their positions.

3. Events on 18 February 1942.

a. *Evaluation of the Situation.* Seen from a tactical point of view, the countermeasures taken by the Russians thus far could be regarded as ineffective. Much more troublesome, and in fact dangerous, were the effects of a pincer attack launched by strong Russian forces from their adjacent defensive sectors against the unguarded communication route from Natchekino to Vasilevka. At this point, the forest extended up to the road on both sides. This enabled the Russians to approach the road without being observed and to cut off the German spearhead, which was rushing westward, from its rear communications. Although the German command had taken this contingency into consideration, it had not seemed very likely in view of the prevailing enemy situation, with which they were familiar. In each of the two adjacent sectors, one Russian regimental combat group was stationed. These combat groups would be unable to participate in such action with large numbers, lest they themselves were to risk the danger of being smashed. Moreover, these two regimental combat groups were not attached to the same corps. The German command knew from experience that in such cases it was first necessary for the command headquarters, to which the corps was subordinated, to take action in order to coordinate the operations of the two regimental combat groups. It was also true that the southern combat group would have had to face a long and difficult march

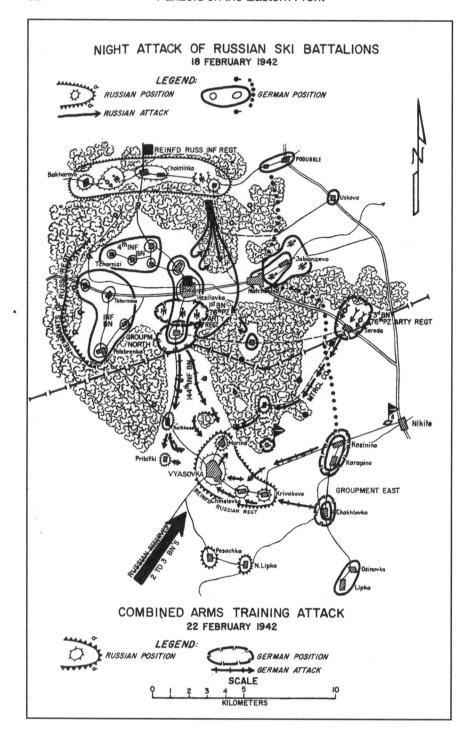

NIGHT ATTACK OF RUSSIAN SKI BATTALIONS
18 FEBRUARY 1942

COMBINED ARMS TRAINING ATTACK
22 FEBRUARY 1942

which for ten kilometers would lead through a forest region without any roads or paths and covered by deep snow. The only beaten track through the forest was blocked by German security detachments. Therefore, the only possibility left to the Russians would be a drive from the north, which, however, could be effective only if for this purpose the Russians were to detach several battalions to the Cholminka sector. In view of the overall situation prevailing at Rzhev, this was doubtful. Should this contingency nevertheless arise, then the tactical reserve which was stationed in the Natchekino–Yablonzevo area anyway would be available. This reserve was made up of one well-trained motorcycle-ski company, one engineer-ski company, several assault guns and eight armored reconnaissance cars, and these forces could effectively be supported by the bulk of the heavy artillery stationed in the same area. Arrangements had been made to assure coordination between the reserve and the "Vasilevka" defensive sector, to which the three light howitzer batteries had been moved.

b.   *Events during the Night.* The night of 18 February was bright with stars. Calm prevailed in all sectors. For reasons of security, there was no movement of vehicles on the road to Vasilevka after dark. However, at irregular intervals the road was guarded by strong patrols. Nevertheless, one Russian ski unit managed, between these intervals, to cross the road in small groups toward the south and to cut the telephone cable to the front. The sounds they made were drowned out by the rustling of the trees. One hour before dawn, one German parka-clad infantry-engineer unit equipped with skis was advancing on a forest path en route to the village south of Vasilevka for the purpose of assisting in the construction of fortifications. Some elements of a Russian ski unit, who by chance were arriving at that spot at the same time and were clad and equipped just like the German engineer platoon, joined the German platoon which was marching, at intervals, in the same direction. The German and Russian troops, with their fur-lined collars turned up and trudging along without speaking, failed to recognize each other. Not until they reached the fringe of the forest located several hundred meters ahead of the village did the Russians come to a halt in order to make preparations for their action. The German troops, disturbed by this (incomprehensible for them) stop, started a dispute which revealed the error committed on both sides. After brief hand-to-hand fighting, during which the respective opponents were recognized only when speaking, the Russians dispersed and vanished into the forest. The German forces who had remained on the road fired some bursts after them from their submachine guns which aroused the attention of all local security detachments. Then complete silence reigned again, causing the latter to think that what had occurred was a small raid, and they attached no significance to this incident. Only the German company which had settled down in the village located opposite that point was alerted by the fire suddenly bursting forth close by, and occupied its position. Soon thereafter the first engineer troops arrived all out of breath and told about the strange encounter with the Russian ski unit. After a while, the entire engineer platoon appeared and reinforced the company occupying the position.

Sounds of a brief skirmish coming from the direction of a German outpost in the forest indicated that the Russian ski unit had passed that way too.

c. *Russian Surprise Attack on Vasilevka.* Just before dawn, Russian troops suddenly appeared in front of the northeastern section of Vasilevka. The machine-gun sentries immediately opened vehement fire, and the alarm quickly spread to the entire eastern sector and the village of Kishenka adjacent to the north. The German troops had not as yet had a chance to occupy all the ice bunkers when the Russians in the lead jumped into a snow ditch connecting two bunkers. The German regimental commander and one assault detachment were just then arriving there. After brief close combat, the invading Russians were routed. The Russians thereupon also attacked from the south, where they encountered our artillery, which was firing from all guns on a Russian ski battalion which was advancing in waves. The enemy attack immediately came to a standstill, and the Russian troops tried to take off their skis which hampered them in fighting. Dawn was already beginning to break, which resulted in a visibility of from 300 to 500 meters, so that the Russians, since it was now possible to hit them with direct machine-gun fire, suffered heavy losses. This attack broke down completely. However, at practically the same time, Russian ski units made a speedy drive on the northern sector, where, heedless of the fire pouring down on them, they succeeded in penetrating at several points. Two reserve assault detachments were still engaged in retaking the respective sections when one German sergeant and his platoon rushed forth from Kishenka, where an enemy attack had just been repelled. This sergeant had recognized the danger threatening the northern sector and, acting on his own initiative, he and his platoon attacked the Russian ski unit in the rear and forced it to retreat. Thus the critical phase of the enemy surprise attack was overcome.

d. *Attack Launched by Russian Ski Troops.* While these actions were taking place, the noise of heavy battles could also be heard in the south, where one Russian ski company was unsuccessfully launching an attack on the small village located on a hill, which was occupied by weak forces. This was the Russian ski unit which during the night had marched in one column with the German troops and, because of this incident, had not been able to reach its destination until daylight.

Another day was beginning to dawn. The snow-covered slope which from Vasilevka rose to the forest and was 1,000 meters wide sparkled in the first rays of the rising sun. The edge of the "Africa Forest"—so called because of its shape— began to be visible, looking as if strewn with diamonds and dipped in gold. New Russian ski units suddenly emerged from the southern tip of the "Africa Forest," called "the Cape," and set out in the direction of Vasilevka. They were charged with the mission to carry along in their advance the Russian battalions pinned down in front of the village and attempt in a daytime attack in force to achieve the victory wherein the night raid had failed, namely, the capture of Vasilevka and the blocking of our supplies. They presented a spectacle which the German defenders were watching as though it were a sporting event. Not until the echeloned lines were coming ever closer and some already had reached the road did the German troops realize that they had to prevent the "finish" of these Russian ski troops. Concentrated fire from all weapons hurled the Russian skiers into the snow even before they were able to reach the lines of their comrades. Hundreds of scarcely visible dots denoted the area where the valiant skiers had disappeared with lightning speed. Their run was ended. Although they still tried to continue on foot, this was impossible due to the deep snow. The sight of any large-sized target was sufficient to attract our instantaneous machine-gun fire, which meant certain death. Unfortunately, the great winter sports show had to be concluded in a most unfair manner. The German motorcycle riflemen and engineers who had started out from Natchekino on skis arrived, accompanied by several assault guns and armored reconnaissance cars, and attacked the enemy in the rear. Although the Russians, by mining the road, had attempted to protect themselves against such attacks and had in fact succeeded in driving back the vehicle in the lead, the German engineers immediately made their appearance and cleared the road. The assault guns attacked the enemy's flank and in conjunction with German ski units drove the Russians back. The four Russian ski battalions, in order to escape encirclement and complete annihilation, were forced to withdraw, crawling in the snow under fire from several directions, leaving their skis behind. It took almost three hours before the last Russians were able to reach the edge of the "Africa Forest," on which 24 guns were firing and in which they disappeared. For a long while afterward, Russian medical troops on skis were still trying to remove their numerous severely wounded comrades, and this they did without interference. The ski attack had miscarried.

e. *Russian Casualties and Captured Matériel.* We counted more than 350 dead Russian soldiers on the field of snow and captured over 200 prisoners. This amounted to almost half of the entire strength of the committed Russian ski forces. Among those killed was the commander of the ski brigade, a Russian general staff officer attached to the headquarters of the *39th Guards Army*,[18] who had been in charge of training the ski battalions and who personally had led this elite unit, which was the last available reserve.

The exhausted brigade, during its difficult withdrawal, had been compelled to leave behind in the combat area all heavy weapons and all equipment which interfered with crawling. However, most valuable of all captured *matériel* was the large

---

[18] The 6th Panzer Division was probably facing the *39th Army*, part of the Kalinin Front. There appears to have not been a *39th Guards Army* as Raus terms it. The *39th Army* consisted of at least five rifle divisions, the *183rd, 220th, 355th, 361st*, and *373th*, the last three all raised in the Ural Mountains. Robert G. Poirier and Albert Z. Conner, *Red Army Order of Battle in the Great Patiotic War* (Novato, CA: Presidio Press, 1985) p. 132. Albert Seaton states that there were six rifle divisions and two cavalry divisions in *39th Army* at this time and that it was operating with *11th Cavalry Corps. The Russo German War 1941–1945* (Novato, CA: Presidio Press, 1993) p. 233. Raus also mentions the presence of a cavalry corps in the forces facing the 6th Panzer Division. The *11th Cavalry Corps* contained the *18th, 24th*, and *82nd Cavalry Divisions*. Poirier and Conner, *Red Army Order of Battle*, p. 135.

map which was found in the possession of the Russian general staff officer who had been killed. This map showed the situation of the Russian *39th Guards Army* on the day preceding its operation. The captured map was put to very good use by the German Army, and in addition considerably facilitated the preparation of operations of a similar nature subsequently undertaken by our units.[19]

During these battles, too, it was characteristic of the enemy situation with regard to ammunition that not a single shot was fired by the Russian artillery, although at Bacharevo (eight kilometers northwest of Vasilevka) were stationed enemy batteries, including heavy guns.

IV. Evaluation

1. Significance of Supply Routes. A number of lessons may be derived from this example too. The overall situation described in the beginning already shows the result of the earlier struggle for the supply routes; in spite of all enemy efforts, these remained in our hands. In consequence, the German unit was well-supplied, whereas the supplies for the Russian unit were insufficient. The more troops the Russians moved into this region —which lacked the necessities of life and was accessible only on one single sled track—the more did their supply difficulties increase. The reciprocal effect caused by the necessity to be sufficiently strong to resist the German forces (which, although considerably weaker, were very well supplied) and the supply shortage this created, was the dilemma from which the Russians were unable to free themselves. They made an attempt to offset this handicap by disrupting our supply lines and thus gain victory; however, this was thwarted by our method of fighting, which I have described in this as well as the next example. The Russians themselves, in referring to this method, coined the expression "the mincing machine," which aptly defined the "attacks with limited objective" which were conducted with heavy weapons under firm control. Within six weeks, it was possible for a Kampfgruppe, by conducting six such surprise attacks one after another, to push one Russian guards corps consisting of three divisions back another 10–15 kilometers from the strategic railroad and Vyazma–Rzhev road on a 40-

---

[19] The operations of the 6th Panzer Division had been part of the larger offensive operation initiated by the Ninth Army's new commander, General der Panzertruppen Walter Model. After listening to his senior staff's grim forecast, "Model, a dashing commander in the field as well as a coolly calculating staff officer, nodded. 'and then the first thing to do will be to close the gap up here.' He ran his hand over the wide red arrows indicating the Russian penetration west of Rzhev between Nilolskoye and Solomino. 'We've got to turn off the supply-tap of those Russian divisions which have broken through. And from down here'—Model put his hand on Sychevka—'we shall then strike at the Russian flank and catch them in a stranglehold.' " His senior commanders and staff were stunned. One of them "summed up their astonishment in the cautious question: 'And what, Herr General, have you brought us for this operation?' Model calmly regarded his Army chief of operations and said, 'Myself.' Then he burst out laughing. With a great sense of relief they all joined in the laughter. It was the first time in many days that loud and happy laughter was heard in the map room of the Ninth Army headquarters in Sychevka. A new spirit had moved in." Paul Carell, *Hitler Moves East, 1941–1943* (Boston: Little, Brown and Company, 1963) pp. 371–2. Model's counterattacks severed the encircling Soviet forces, destroying *the 22nd Army, 11th Cavalry Corps*, and part of *39th Army*, facing the 6th Panzer Division.— Editor.

kilometer front. Thus, three reinforced German battalions, in six separate attacks, succeeded in driving back 27 Russian battalions and inflicting such heavy losses upon them that it was possible without risk for improvised German units, organized as described above, to keep the Russians in check within this new line. This victory vividly illustrates the principle of tactics mentioned in Section I of this chapter (Lessons) under item 1.

2. Commitment of Ski Units. The Russian ski brigade, in spite of its fourfold superiority, failed to achieve a victory over the attacked German forces which, one battalion strong, were occupying Vasilevka, because the Russian forces were not all committed simultaneously and had no heavy weapons at their disposal. In Vasilevka, on the other hand, were stationed one German artillery battalion with twelve howitzers and several 88mm antiaircraft and antitank guns, as well as one tank unit. In addition, one tactical reserve equipped with several assault guns and eight armored reconnaissance cars was held ready for action at Natchekino so that even in case Vasilevka was lost, they would have been in a position to recapture it in conjunction with the occupation forces, which would have been driven out. Consequently, even if the Russian ski brigade had been committed properly, it would have been defeated by the large number of powerful, heavy weapons of the German unit. This, as well as other numerous cases, witnessed by me, has proven the truth of the principle mentioned in Section I under item 2. This specifies that ski units, without the support of heavy weapons which they are usually able to take along, will not prevail against enemy troops who, even though numerically far inferior, have such weapons at their disposal. Their best chance, therefore, lies in making surprise attacks at night because in that case the enemy will be unable to use his heavy weapons and tanks with complete effectiveness. The fact that the strong Russian ski unit was unable to fulfill its mission, even in the dark, may be attributed to its piecemeal commitment, which came too late, as well as to the initiative taken by the German commanders and subordinate commanders.

From the episode described earlier (during which Russian ski troops inadvertently joined the night march of German ski forces), it becomes evident that it is necessary to mark even camouflage clothing in such a manner that would easily permit making a distinction between friend and foe. It was due to this incident that our winter clothing was marked with the German national insignia in black.

3. Dissipation of Forces. Violations against the tactical principle set down in Section I under item 3 were committed not only by the commander of the Russian ski brigade but also by the commander of the German battalion at Tatarinka, who attacked without waiting for the arrival of the heavy weapons assigned to him, and consequently had to suffer defeat. Besides, in his overzealousness, he acted against an explicit order and had to take the consequences.

4. Miscellaneous. As described previously in one incident, the Russian unit which launched the counterattack on Natchekino violated the tactical principles concerning reconnaissance, security and liaison, and paid for this with its destruction.

In addition, I wish to point out that the principle of initiative on the part of the commanders and subordinate commanders, emphasized previously in Example 1, was demonstrated in this example as well when the sergeant coming from Kishenka rushed to the rescue of his battalion, which was engaged in bitter fighting at Vasilevka, and thus helped to overcome a crisis.

Example 3: A Combined-Arms Attack
Utilized as a Training Medium[20] (22 February 1942)

I. Lessons

Example 2 has already outlined the pertinent factors with regard to the overall situation and the purpose of the attacks with limited objective, among which this operation too is included. The terrain and weather conditions equaled those encountered during the preceding operation. However, in this case the southern edge of the large forest region was considerably elevated and therefore afforded a good view into the far distance, which greatly aided the conduct of operations.

The preceding example demonstrates how quickly we succeeded in penetrating the Russian lines and driving back even considerably stronger enemy forces because they had to struggle with great supply difficulties. It is the aim of this example to illustrate that it was possible to utilize the paralyzing effect of the enemy's ammunition shortage, even for an operation of destruction. Although the reason for the enemy defeat was the same in both cases, the tactics applied were different. In the action discussed in Example 2 it was a breakthrough which led to victory, whereas in this example the operation involved was a pincer attack launched for the specific purpose of annihilating a Russian combat group which was established in typical winter positions. This operation was more dangerous than the preceding one, because in order to make the pincer attack—which was the only means of achieving the desired goa—it was necessary to divide the Kampfgruppe, which actually consisted of only three reinforced battalions. The following factors alone enabled the command to attempt this hazardous operation: it was impossible for the Russian artillery and other heavy weapons to take effect; the cooperation of strong Luftwaffe forces was assured; the German unit was imbued with good fighting spirit; and it was well-trained, and under a good command, and in addition provided with excellent equipment and supplies.

Aside from envelopment tactics, this example does not demonstrate any new rules of combat. All the more emphasis is placed, however, on the coordination of weapons under difficult conditions, and this example shows how this method of coordination as well as the principles of planning and preparation became subjects of instruction for numerous spectators. In addition, it reveals how the enemy counteraction made it possible to give them a lesson in making quick decisions, and it becomes apparent how

---

[20] This is a continuation of Example 2.

difficult it was for officers not familiar with local conditions to arrive at the proper solution for the problems presented by this unusual situation.

II. German Objectives and Measures

1. The Mission. In order to avoid jeopardizing the success attained on 18 February and to safeguard all of the supply routes to Rzhev, it was necessary for us to also gain possession of the forest region adjacent in the south as well as the enemy-occupied strongpoints in the villages grouped around Vyasovka.

The elevated terrain north of these villages offered good points of observation, from which it was possible to view the planned attack like an exercise on a drill ground. Moreover, the course of action promised to be very interesting and instructive. For this reason, I utilized this operation as a "training medium demonstrating a combined-arms attack" which, by order of the Ninth Army, I was to organize and conduct as I saw fit for the instruction of "officers who had had no combat experience in the East." It was contemplated to demonstrate for these officers of various ranks, who had been transferred to the Eastern front from other theaters of war and from the zone of the interior, the commitment and the coordination of combined arms in offensive action against a network of Russian ice bunker positions. This was a strange assignment, which was reminiscent of peacetime maneuvers but bore not the least resemblance to such exercises; for this required executing a mission which was as important as it was difficult, and which called not only for defeating a thoroughly entrenched enemy but also for withstanding the effects of a severe winter.

2. Preparations.

a. *Procurement of Attack Unit.* As a first step, it was necessary to procure battle-tried fresh troops as well as weapons and command facilities which would assure the success of this unusual operation. Due to the reverses suffered before Moscow, the entire Eastern front was in a critical situation; in particular, however, this was true as far as the depleted Army Group Center was concerned, whose front was overextended.

My own division had at its disposal merely the battalions and batteries which had been committed for the drive on Tatarinka and which were able to launch attacks, as well as the few assault guns, tanks, antiaircraft guns, telephone and radio facilities obtained from inactive front sectors. All combat units were on foot; some had skis. The delivery of supplies on local Panje sleds was handled by 800 Russian auxiliary volunteers under our control and supervision, because the German supply troops had to be used for combat. In view of the fact that, with the exception of the Luftwaffe, no additional forces were available for this new operation, it was necessary for units not capable of attacking (such as those described previously) to relieve the entire "Kampfgruppe Z" on the very day the Russians launched the ski attack; the Kampfgruppe was shifted to a rest area in the rear. This constituted a risk, which, however, the command was able to take after all Russian counterattacks had been repelled. This was all the more possible owing to the fact that all artillery, antitank, and antiaircraft forces for the time being remained as reserves in their old positions, and in the event of any emergency the Kampfgruppe could be recalled quickly.

b. *Rest and Rehabilitation.* During the period of rest, the soldiers were given very wholesome and abundant food as well as additional butter and 10,000 rations of chocolate and fat. During their ample leisure time, they had the chance to take care of their mail and to read newspapers and books. They were frequently visited by their superiors, who looked after the welfare of each individual and concerned themselves with the troubles and complaints of their soldiers. During free and unconstrained conversations, special events and experiences were discussed, as well as requests and complaints being taken up. One particularly solemn event was the presenting of decorations, and on such occasions this was always done by the division commander in person. All superiors also considered it self-understood and a duty of honor to visit their wounded troops on days of rest, and to care for their welfare.

During this period of rest, the unit, in replacement for the casualties suffered during the last operation, was assigned troops who had been restored to health; it received ample ammunition, some tanks, and numerous signal devices, all of which had been requested to assure the success of the operation. The means of signal communications were essential in order to control the large area in which the comparatively weak forces had to operate, and they included many kilometers of telephone cable and numerous telephone and radio sets, as well as the flash and sound-ranging equipment of the artillery-survey platoon.

3. Plan of Attack.

a. *Organizational Structure.* The division commander decided on conquering the system of strongpoints extending from Vyasovka to Krivakovo by means of a pincer attack to be launched from the north and east. For this purpose, Groupment North (consisting of one battalion, six assault guns and one antitank and antiaircraft battery each) was ordered to assemble for attack in the village south of Vasilevka. Groupment East (made up of two battalions, one engineer company, twelve tanks, and two antitank and antiaircraft batteries each) was instructed to move into assembly positions in the line extending from Kosmino to Chochlovka. For the advance, Groupment North had at its disposal one sled track made by the Russians and one beaten track, while Groupment East was able to use two roads which in no man's land were completely covered by snow. One ski company, which had been moved between the two groupments and was advancing from Alexandrovka to Murino, had to use the snow-covered forest path.

The artillery remained in its original positions. Instructions called for its light battalion (at Vasilevka) to support Groupment North, while Groupment East was to be supported by the heavy battalion (stationed at Sereda). It was just as possible for the artillery to quickly place the concentrated fire of all its batteries in front of one or the other groupment as it was to shift its fire to former targets.

b. *Coordination of Weapons; Liaison and Communications.* In order to ensure uniformity of cooperation with the attacking infantry, which entailed technical difficulties, the artillery command posts first of all were established close to those of the infantry commanders. Consequently, at all times, there was by the side of every tactical commander the commander of the particular artillery unit assigned to assist him. The same principle of local coordination, as practiced by the subordinate commanders or those assigned to render support, also applied to all other heavy supporting weapons. It included the commanders of the smallest tactical units, insofar as they were fighting in the front line and in strategic sectors. In such cases, one forward observer or some other communication link usually sufficed. In effect, the following elements could be found close to the division commander who was established at the advance command post:

One special-missions staff officer and several messengers equipped with skis;
One division communication officer who was in charge of telephone and radio equipment and the personnel necessary for operating it;
The artillery regimental commander with his immediate staff (similar to that mentioned above), as well as the commander of the artillery reconnaissance battalion;
One officer of the Luftwaffe, which had been ordered to render assistance; he had at his disposal radio equipment with which contact was maintained with his units.

The two groupments also functioned with the aid of a similar, but still smaller, operations staff. With the two groupments could be found the commander of the supporting artillery. Consequently, with Groupment North, there was the commander of the light artillery battalion, which, with its three 105mm field howitzer batteries, was stationed in the area south of Vasilevka; with Groupment East there was the commander of the heavy artillery battalion, which, with two 150mm howitzer batteries (eight guns with an effective range of 18 kilometers) and one 100mm flat-trajectory battery (four flat-trajectory guns with an effective range of 25 kilometers), was stationed in the Sereda–Alexandrovka area. Moreover, at the side of the commanders of the groupments and battalions, or close at hand, were the commanders or communication links of the heavy weapons assigned to render assistance. The commanders or reporting facilities of the heavy weapons assigned to support the infantry companies engaged in combat were with the commanders of those companies. In like manner, the commanders of heavy weapons were required to assign some messengers to the commander of any infantry platoon or small combat unit, respectively, if their mission called for direct cooperation. In addition, to each groupment was attached one flying officer from each wing which had been assigned to support the groupment units.

The advance command post of the division was connected by telephone cable (trunk line), which functioned via Nikite (location of the division central), with the commander of Groupment North (at Vasilevka) and the commander of Groupment East (at Chochlovka), and here the commanders of the assigned heavy weapons, too, were within immediate reach. At the two terminal points of the trunk line and at Sereda were established the telephone centrals of the two groupments, to which were linked the subordinated battalions, the motorcycle company, and the attached heavy weapons units. The terminal stations of the latter were located in the immediate vicinity of the frontmost line, and followed the advance of the groupment in leapfrog movement. The distance between the telephone stations nearest the front and the foremost line of battle, usually about four kilometers, was spanned by means of the infantry voice radio equipment or the tank radio apparatus. The latter was used wherever tanks were spearheading the advance of the infantry assault detachments.

In the event of temporary disruption of wire lines, radio transmitters were available at all times at the respective command posts of the division, the groupments, battalions, and motorcycle companies. Thus, the tactical operations network in effect extended from the division commander via the above-mentioned relay stations up to the foremost attacking spearheads.

The advance elements (forward observers) of the artillery fire control net—which functioned independently of the operations net, although it was organized along similar lines—extended as far as the infantry combat zone. The internal communication was automatically assured because of the fact that the tactical commanders were at the same time in command of the artillery fire control.

The fliers needed for artillery target reconnaissance and fire direction were also at the disposal of the artillery, and, as the fighting progressed, the artillery survey platoon which was stationed at the southern edge of the large forest area was available as well. It should also be mentioned that the heavy batteries, even prior to the first attack, had been placing their adjusted fire on all strongpoints in villages located in the Cholminka–Vasilevka–Vyasovka area by means of a photomap and guided by artillery reconnaissance fliers, and as a result had ascertained the firing data for the most important targets. In view of the settled weather conditions, these factors never changed to any marked degree. In order to be on the safe side during the attack, everything was checked once more shortly before the advance of the attacking spearheads. During the decisive battles, numerous artillery observers and the artillery survey platoon were established at the forest rims and on the roofs of buildings in captured villages, in such a manner that from their elevated posts they had a clear and direct line of vision to their targets, extending one to three kilometers. The 1st (Light) Battalion, 76th Panzer Artillery Regiment, had to fire in succession over distances of from five to eight kilometers, aiming exactly in the direction of attack of the unit it was supporting; the frontage of this unit required a gun traverse of 25 degrees. The 3rd (Heavy) Battalion, 76th Panzer Artillery Regiment, on the other hand, was firing over distances of from nine to eleven kilometers, partly slantwise to and partly almost parallel with the direction of advance, which required a gun traverse similar to that of the 1st Battalion. The shell bursts of the 3rd Battalion, in particular, were clearly visible. For that reason, and in view of the fact that the lateral dispersion was less than the range dispersion, the artillery was able to support the infantry troops until shortly before they entered the target area without endangering them in any way. Moreover, the lateral fire could be shifted more rapidly, because in most cases the firing data only had to be changed for lateral fire and not for range. Besides, the enfilading artillery fire had a much greater moral effect, which was the reason why it was employed preferably and with success, particularly in operations with Austrian troops. The drawbacks of the longer wire lines—the installation of which requires more *matériel* and time and which, owing to the distances they cover, are more frequently subject to disruptions—were more than offset by the great advantage gained by virtue of better visibility and effectiveness.

The concentrated fire from both artillery battalions first proved fully effective during the attacks on the Kolkhoz and in the Vyasovka area. This was directed by the artillery commander in person and did not require any greater than normal traverse, as described previously. In order to facilitate fire control operations, one liaison officer of the heavy battalion was attached to the light artillery battalion, and vice versa. The fire was aimed primarily at points where the roads entered the villages, at the most important strongpoints identified by means of photomaps, and at the assembly areas of enemy reserves ascertained by the Luftwaffe. Any pockets of resistance which could not be conquered by the infantry, even after being subjected to air attacks, artillery fire, and the effects of heavy weapons, were identified by the infantry through signal rockets and then again bombarded by the Luftwaffe. During the battles which took place in the large village of Vyasovka, red signal flares indicated the spots where our troops were in any way exposed to danger from friendly fire. In spite of the clouds of smoke which, caused by many fires, gradually enveloped the entire village, these signals were plainly visible. The Luftwaffe which was less hampered by the smoke furnished brief orientation reports concerning the events taking place on either side. These as well as all other measures had been arranged in advance and proved very effective.

The planning of this attack by no means implied a schematization of the attack procedure, or even any frowned-upon supervision on the part of the commanders. Its sole purpose was to ensure perfect comprehension with regard to the mission, the contemplated course of action, and the coordination of all weapons. All that remained was to provide for support of the improvised units in case the Russians were to launch an attack on the area which had been captured during the preceding operation. It was doubtful, however, whether this contingency would arise, because the Russians had used up their last reserves during their counterthrusts immediately following our attack, and there were no indications of enemy attack preparations along their entire corps front. There was all the more reason to doubt the possibility of any such danger, because in this area sufficiently large numbers of well-armed

German forces were stationed in improved positions and equipped with numerous antitank and antiaircraft guns of all calibers. To all appearances, these troops were capable of repelling any enemy attack not supported by artillery and enough heavy infantry weapons. However, the Russians, due to their critical ammunition shortage, were scarcely in a position to render such assistance. Nevertheless, we also took the necessary precautions so as to be prepared for this bare possibility, for if this contingency were to arise, it was apt to create a difficult situation for Groupment North, thus jeopardizing the contemplated new operation. These precautionary measures included providing support through additional Luftwaffe units and the available artillery. The latter had to be prepared to employ its individual batteries instantaneously, and within a very short time also the bulk of its weapons against the previous targets. It was for this reason that the communication network installed during the first attack (described in Example 2) was left intact and the observation posts remained occupied. The increased requirements for trained artillery forces were procured from among the "artillery companies on foot" stationed at that point and taken from the same artillery regiment. In order to facilitate the shifting of artillery fire by 90 degrees in the new direction of fire, the batteries were echeloned in such a manner and the individual guns of the batteries so grouped around the control gun—which remained in one position—that they had a free field of fire before them even after changing their direction of fire. In order to make it possible for these shifts to be executed rapidly, the snow was removed from the roads leading to the alternate firing positions, and, whenever needed, the guns were moved there on skis. The shifting to the alternate emplacements was practiced and the correct firing data ascertained at that time; checkups were made to determine the efficiency of the old lines as well as of the observation posts.

As can be seen from the description of the actual course of action, the Russians, as we had estimated, did not attack the western front, which eliminated the necessity for shifting the artillery fire.

The support aviation and bomber wings of the "Richthofen" Air Corps,[21] whose assistance had been promised and which could be committed continuously from their nearby airfields, constituted a very valuable and powerful aid.

c. *Issuing of Commands.* The plan of attack was, in all its essential points, outlined and all issues clarified by the division commander in the presence of the commanding officers and the commanders of all supporting weapons. This was followed by discussions between the battalion commanders and the chiefs of the attached heavy weapons units, which were attended by the division commander and during which all details with regard to coordination were set forth. These personal discussions

---

[21] Generaloberst Wolfram Freiherr von Richthofen (1895–1945) commanded the Luftwaffe's 8th Air Corps. He was a cousin of the "Red Baron", Captain Manfred Freiherr von Richthofen of World War I fame. The 8th Air Corps was the only mobile support available to Army Group Center in the grim days of January–February 1942. Seaton, *The Russo-German War*, p. 233.

were an absolute necessity prior to attacks launched according to plan. They were the only means of guaranty that frictions and misunderstands would be kept at a minimum.

The written attack order was issued a short while later. It served merely as a reminder and historical document. Upon conclusion of discussions, the men who were participating in the training course were separated from the others, apprised of the contemplated operation, and then assigned to various units in accordance with their respective branch of service, in order to become acquainted with the details of the preparatory measures.

III. The Course Of Action On 22 February 1942
1. Events at Groupment East.

a. *Final Preparations.* The three days spent in preparation and recreation had passed very quickly. As the next step, it was necessary to carry the plans into effect the best way possible. The weather continued to be steady and beautiful; the temperature had even fallen a few degrees lower than −12°F, so that individual troops were able to move across the snow without skis. The sled tracks and the wider beaten paths were frozen solid and could be used even by tanks. All in all, the weather was ideal for the contemplated "training attack."

One obstacle still remained to be eliminated. This was the deep snow which covered the roads on which the attack was to be launched in the area between the German and Russian outposts (in the sector of Groupment East). This snow would have considerably handicapped the movement of tanks, antiaircraft and antitank guns. It was therefore necessary during the night of 22 February to remove the snow from these roads and to clear them beyond the German outpost area. Since both sides were engaged every night in removing snow from their last piece of respective road, the Russians were familiar with these sounds, which therefore did not arouse their suspicions. Moreover, during the moonlit nights, which were bright with stars, skirmishes were always taking place between the reconnaissance patrols who advanced beyond the outpost area, and on these occasions the forward security detachments of the one side were pushed back by their respective opponents as far as the main line of resistance. Consequently, the Russians attached no special significance to these incidents either.

Such were the events which, during the night of 22 February, were taking place on the roads leading from Kosmino and Chochlovka in the direction of enemy lines. Small units composed of elements who had previously occupied the position had attacked the Russian security detachments, as they had frequently in the past, and had pushed them back as far as the most advanced Russian bunker position at Krivakovo. They were followed close behind by engineers who carried on their snow removal operations as far as the vicinity of the Russian lines. The rest of the road to the German lines had to be cleared of snow by armed construction battalions. Now and then a Russian searchlight swept the outpost area but could not detect anything suspicious because the hill sloping toward the brook valley, where the constructions were taking place, could not be observed. The beam of light therefore passed over the engineers and construction battalions without disturbing their activities in any way.

b. *Preparations for Action.* In the meantime all attack units also moved into the above-mentioned assembly areas. Every unit commander had been briefed concerning his mission, and every soldier knew what was at stake. There was no uncertainty whatsoever with regard to the cooperation with the artillery, the tanks, and all other heavy weapons. Forward observers and liaison officers were assigned to the unit commanders, with whom they had made friends long since. The commanders who had been detached from the Luftwaffe, antitank, antiaircraft, and other units had already earlier established close contact with the division, and were vying with each other to do their best in serving the division. The feeling of comradeship which united everyone created a bond of confidence between these men, who were dependent on each other for better or for worse, and this offered the best guaranty for victory. All commanders and subordinate commanders were well-trained and experienced, and in unforeseen situations acted on their own initiative, but always in keeping with the overall mission. They had complete confidence in their respective units. Only under such conditions was it possible to achieve the maximum in performance which was the very thing absolutely essential in unusual situations.

c. *Attack on Krivakovo.* The construction troops were withdrawn while it was still dark. On the roads which they had cleared, the attack columns stood ready to advance. Groupment North, too, was ready to strike, and waiting for the right time so that the assault would be launched simultaneously by the two groupments poised for attack 16 kilometers apart. They were to meet each other mid-course, and were to join forces at Vyasovka; as far as could be calculated, this was expected to happen around noon.

Suddenly the night, which was coming to a close, was illuminated by fire flashes, which with great intensity blazed up in the north. These were followed by thunderlike rumbling, and then the droning and roaring of heavy and light shells, which, fired in unbroken succession from all guns, were striking the eastern outskirts of Krivakovo and battering the ice bunker positions to pieces. After ten minutes of intense bombardment, the bursts of fire gradually shifted toward the western part of the village. At that moment—it was 0640—all columns started out simultaneously. Shortly thereafter, the silhouettes of the German infantry troops who were penetrating the village from three sides could be seen in the glow of the burning huts. However, the shapes of other men could be seen taking the opposite direction, and these were followed by numerous others. This made us wonder whether there had been a setback, but we did not have to remain long in doubt, for green signal rockets which were beginning to appear at the western outskirts of the village indicated that the village had been captured by the infantry battalion. And soon afterward we also received the first situation report by telephone, informing us that 80 Russians had been captured. Those were the men who earlier had taken the wrong direction and had caused us to doubt the outcome of the attack.

By the time the sun rose, the remaining piece of road up to Krivakovo had been cleared of snow to such an extent that it was possible for the tanks to push forward and take their place at the head of the attacking column. Every tank in the lead was followed by one engineer assault detachment. The latter were charged with the mission to penetrate the village of Chmelevka, which was already subjected to our heavy artillery fire, and to clear the Russians out of the still intact ice bunkers by means of hand grenades and flamethrowers. During that time, the tanks had the task of keeping the enemy troops in the adjacent bunkers and machine-gun nests in check.

d. *Events at the Division Observation Post.* From this observation post, which was located at the southern rim of the forest, it was possible to observe the skillfully coordinated action of the tanks and engineer assault detachments. Just a short while ago, this division observation post had been snatched from the enemy by some elements of the ski company. The officers "participating in the course" and acting as spectators had also arrived at this observation post, covered by the ski unit and antitank guns. After a brief disturbance caused by a Russian reconnaissance tank which had burst forth from the forest but was very quickly put out of action by the antitank guns, we were able to continue the "course of instruction" through observation and training. The lesson proved very instructive inasmuch as the short distance made it possible, even without field glasses, to observe all particulars with regard to our attack procedure and the Russian defensive measures. At this observation post were also received all reports sent by the unit in combat, and from here the fighting troops, as the need arose, received additional orders and the observers were able to listen in on their transmission.

e. *Assault Detachment Battle for Chmelevka.* The tactics of joint assault detachment and tank operations had proved successful because the Russian antitank forces, blinded by smoke and pinned down by the heavy artillery, were unable to function. When they attempted to change positions, they were recognized and shot down by tank fire. On the other hand, in every ice bunker which had remained intact, the Russians were offering desperate resistance and hampered the advance of the attacking infantrymen. However, other German infantry troops, who had by then forced their way through the nearby gaps, had become aware of the plight of their comrades. Some of these elements turned and attacked such tenaciously fighting Russian strongpoints in the rear and mopped them up. In this way, the southern part of Chmelevka had already been captured by the infantry battalion. At the northern outskirts of the village, the Russians were still vehemently resisting the 4th Infantry Battalion, whose arrival had been delayed by snowdrifts. Only through the commitment of infantry reserve forces who, supported by tanks, attacked from the southern part of the village, was it possible to break this resistance. Chmelevka was in German hands.

f. *Drive on Vyasovka.* The two German infantry battalions, advancing in wedge formation and on both sides of the road, continued their attack. The armored spearheads, advancing by bounds, had soon reached a point halfway to Vyasovka, when suddenly their flank was attacked by antitank fire. This came from fortified positions which the Russians had established in depressions and hollows on a rise in the ground which followed the southern side of the road; these positions were expertly camouflaged. The Russians commanded a perfect view of the terrain, which gradually sloped toward the forest. The German infantry companies, advancing at that point in loose formation, were bombarded intermittently by Russian artillery fire from the west, which, however, was not heavy enough to pin them down. Only when they began to be subjected to the fire of heavy mortars and machine guns from Vyasovka were they compelled to halt their brisk drive, and the advance was continued by very small groups in short jumps. The battalion adjacent to the south for a time was pinned down by the fire coming from the bunkers and ditches in the rise in the ground, which were occupied by large numbers of enemy troops.

The armored points, too, in order to avoid the fire of the antitank guns, were forced to withdraw to nearby farmsteads. Not until ground attack airplanes forced the Russians to take cover was it possible for the tank spearheads to move up to the troublesome targets and put them out of action. Fortunately, the ice bunker positions established by the Russians on the rise in the ground were open to view from the sector of the division command post. One 88mm flak battery which was emplaced in that area took these positions under direct fire and silenced the weapons which had been harassing our troops. The entire Russian position became untenable only when it was hit by the enfilading destructive fire from all heavy batteries. The Russians in the demolished ice bunkers suffered heavy losses and rushed back to the west. However, these shaken troops instantaneously were confronted by commissars with pistol in hand and—as we were able to observe closely through our field glasses—were driven back. At this critical point, several German tanks veered in that direction and covered the Russian lines surging back and forth in the open terrain with artillery and machine-gun fire. The effect was devastating. Under cover of this fire, the German infantry battalion renewed its assault and seized the entire fortified intermediate terrain in front of Vyasovka, which by then the battalion of the 4th Motorized Infantry Regiment had also penetrated.

2. Events at Groupment North.

a. *Penetration by Assault as Far as Pribitki.* Groupment North started its advance at the same time as Groupment East, but without preliminary bombardment. In two columns, spearheaded by its assault guns and assault detachments, Groupment North advanced southward. At first, the Russians, as was to be expected, offered very feeble resistance. At the approach of our assault guns, the Russian security detachments immediately withdrew to the forests on both sides in order to harass with their flanking fire from there the German infantry companies following on foot. The Russians were greatly taken by surprise, however, when they were attacked and scattered by the German ski units which had been detached along the forest rims in order to serve as flank protection.

For the first four kilometers, the advance continued without difficulties. Not until they had reached the *Kolkhoz*[22] and the edge of the patch of woods east thereof did the advance guards come across well-fortified ice bunker positions, which were supplied with numerous heavy weapons. It was considered inadvisable to attack these positions. Consequently, the groupment came to a halt and requested artillery and Luftwaffe support for its attack on the *Kolkhoz*. While the fire of the close support airplanes, which quickly appeared in waves, pinned down the Russians in the bunker positions and the immediately available light batteries were pounding the *Kolkhoz*, the battalion of the 114th Motorized Infantry Regiment was grouping for attack. No sooner had this been accomplished when the artillery fire, in which the heavy batteries too were now participating, sharply increased in intensity. The 88mm flak battery of Groupment North was by then also bombarding the Russian bunkers which had been identified previously, and demolished them with its well-aimed fire. The bomber squadrons which had been held in readiness, subject to call, now arrived exactly on time. Their salvo bombing attack on the positions at the *Kolkhoz* was coordinated with the fire of all batteries and heavy weapons, which had been increased to maximum intensity. This was the signal for starting the assault on this fortified strongpoint.

The last bombs and heavy shells had scarcely struck when the assault guns and forward assault detachments were already breaching the bunker position. They were quickly followed by the infantrymen, who mopped up the crushed strongpoint. Nothing but a handful of completely worn-out soldiers remained of the two Russian guards companies which had been charged with the task of holding this key position at all costs so as to prevent the Germans from striking at the rear of Vyasovka. Although the spectators were as yet unable to see anything of this attack, they could hear the tremendous noise of battle in the Russian rear area and the roaring of the bomb hits. They were steadily kept informed, however, about the course of events.

Rolling across the ruins which was all that had been left of the *Kolkhoz*, the German assault guns immediately continued pushing southward; their goal was Pribbitki. Again the German close support airplanes, which the Russians dreaded, made their appearance: they circled and roared over the fortified group of farms and in approved fashion pinned down the Russians occupying this position, which was

---

[22] *Kolkhoz* is the Russian acronym for "collective farm," often a village or collection of farm buildings supporting the farm. Collective farms were created during the great and bloody wave of collectivization in 1930–32, when the State confiscated the peasant farmsteads, effectively reintroducing serfdom but of a sort so brutal that no tsar would have dreamed of it.—Editor.

already under fire of the assault guns. Bypassed on both sides and under concentric attack, this Russian strongpoint, which was occupied by merely one company, also succumbed to the superior strength of our weapons.

b. *Measures Taken by the German Ski Company.* The ski company, which had been placed between and connected the two groupments, by then finally had succeeded in fighting its way out of the forest region. This company was repeatedly held up in the forest, and, since it was unassisted, succeeded only after bitter fighting in taking by assault an enemy strongpoint located in a clearing. This battle took place just two kilometers from the point where the immediate division headquarters and the spectators were established. On that occasion, they were all alerted to stand by for action in the defense of this important observation post. However, the victory of the ski company in this battle made their commitment unnecessary.

After detouring the fortified strongpoint in the village of Murino, the ski company launched an attack in the rear of the previously mentioned forest bunker position, in front of which one company of the 114th Motorized Infantry Regiment was still tied down. Through the coordinated action of both units, supported by the heavy weapons assigned to them, this tenaciously defended position, too, was taken by assault. Thus, all outlying strongpoints of the defense system of the Russian regimental combat group at Vyasovka had been captured, with the exception of that at Murino. As the next step, it was necessary to encircle and, by means of an all-out attack, conquer the main stronghold of Vyasovka, which now resembled an octopus deprived of its tentacles.

3. Changed Situation, Lesson in Tactics on the Battlefield.

a. *Arrival of Fresh Enemy Troops.* All German forces were already in the process of making their concentric advance on Vyasovka when suddenly German planes reported that fresh Russian troops were approaching from the south. Observers estimated their strength at one regiment, consisting of two to three battalions. It was expected that this regiment would reach the Vyasovka area within two hours and attempt to eliminate the danger of encirclement which threatened Vyasovka, either by reinforcing the sorely pressed Russian units or by attacking one of the two German groupments.

Thus a changed situation had suddenly arisen which made it necessary for the division commander to make a new decision. This he did without delay, and he put his plan into effect by issuing the necessary orders in the adjacent building which housed the spectators and where his assistants and command facilities had been established.

b. *A Lesson Formulating Decisions.* Afterward the members of the training course were apprised of this interesting turn of events, and everyone was requested to state what his decision would be if he were to face the same situation as that which confronted the division commander. In addition, each man was asked to write down in keywords the orders necessary for the execution of his respective plan. This meant that they were required to solve a real problem in tactics while under fire. "Hic Rhodus hic salta!"[23] They obviously had difficulties in arriving at the proper decision in this unusual situation. They were not as yet sufficiently familiar with the mentality of the enemy, the peculiarities of the theater of war, or the effects of the exceptional situation. Consequently, their judgment was based on their theoretical knowledge or their experiences gained in other theaters of war, and the following three alternatives for solving the problem were proposed by them: (1) to annihilate these fresh Russian forces by means of the Luftwaffe and to continue the attack; (2) to contain the Russians at Vyasovka with some forces and to attack the new Russian troops with the bulk of the German forces; and (3) to withdraw the German unit to the line extending from the farm buildings across the edge of the forest to Chmelevka and there assume defensive positions.

They were thunderstruck when later they were informed about the decision the division commander had actually made and the few brief orders he had issued, which were worded as follows: "The attack will be halted; they enemy regiment will be allowed to continue its march and is to be annihilated at the same time as the Russian forces occupying Vyasovka." The unit, as well as the Luftwaffe, was apprised of the new situation and instructed to act in accordance with the above-mentioned order. The execution of the all-out attack, which had been scheduled for noon, was postponed until 1500.

c. *New Orders.* In keeping with the above plan, the two groupment commanders and the Luftwaffe were given the order "Stop the attack!" by telephone, and the operations officer and the artillery commander, as well as the liaison officers present, were briefed about the new situation and objective. Following that, the two groupment commanders were summoned to the telephone, and, after being informed about the changed situation, they were given the following order:

> The line reached so far will be held and the enemy troops who are advancing toward Vyasovka from the south will not be hindered in any way. You will strike only if they attack your positions or attempt to bypass them. If, as expected, they march into Vyasovka, you will close the gap behind them at the sector boundary between the two groupments and prevent all enemy troops from breaking out of the encirclement. It is contemplated to annihilate the new Russian troops, together with the Russian forces occupying Vyasovka, by means of the concentric attack planned originally. The artillery and the Luftwaffe have been given instructions along the same lines. The attack will probably start at 1500; you will wait for instructions to this effect.

Under constant observation by the Luftwaffe, the Russian regiment, just as had been assumed, marched to Vyasovka, rejoicing that it had been possible to arrive there on time to be able to assist their hard-beset comrades. The three hours during which the attack was delayed were utilized to study the excellent aerial photographs

---

[23] This probably refers to an incident in one of Aesop's Fables dealing with a man boasting about his exploits on the iIsland of Rhodes, and in the course of the story, he is told: "Hic Rhodus his salta"—Here's Rhodes, go ahead and jump (literally translated), and meaning "Show what you can do."

which had just been received and to check and supplement them by means of ground reconnaissance reports. Then these findings were evaluated with reference to the plan of attack, which was prepared in all particulars.

The plan outlined the sector boundary between the two groupments. This boundary followed a north-to-south direction along a road in the western part of the village, and this road was explicitly marked on the basis of aerial photographs. The plan also outlined the action to be taken against Murino by the motorcycle company in conjunction with portions of Groupment North, and these forces were moreover charged with the task of preventing the Russians from escaping to the large forest area north of Vyasovka. All details of the execution of the plan were discussed in a conference between the two groupment commanders and the necessary orders transmitted to the subordinate units.

4. *The Final Battle.* No sooner had the last Russian companies arrived at Vyasovka when the German support aviation and bomber wings appeared on the scene in majestic flight and attacked the Russian units which had not yet been committed and in groups were pressed against the buildings. At the same time, all artillery, tanks, assault guns, antiaircraft and antitank guns, and heavy infantry weapons, bombarded those enemy strongpoints and trenches which most seriously hampered our penetration of the village. The furies of war were raging as if all hell had broken loose. Soon the large village was enveloped by smoke and flames. The German attack columns, advancing from all sides, were drawing ever closer. In the south, the two groupments had joined forces. The Russian regiments were encircled, no longer able to escape. The frontmost bunkers had already been demolished by tanks and captured by the accompanying assault detachments. German engineer detachments were engaged in blowing up the antitank obstacles at the main road and in clearing minefields. The way was open. Assault detachments and tanks in ever-increasing numbers dropped out of sight behind the thick smoke of burning buildings. The concentrated fire of the artillery and the heavy bombing raids were now aimed at the fortifications in the center of the village and later shifted more and more to the north. It was possible to closely trace their path through the violent explosions and the huge lumps of earth which were thrown high into the air. The crackling and rattling of machine-gun and submachine-gun fire repeatedly rent the air, indicating that additional enemy strongpoints were being taken by assault.

Gradually the noise of battle in which the unit was engaged also shifted northward, until it ceased when night was beginning to fall. It flared up only once more, far off in the north, when the strongpoint at Murino, the last place of refuge for the remaining enemy forces, was attacked and captured. At that point one or two battered enemy companies in the darkness still succeeded in escaping to the adjacent woods. Several hundred Russians were captured and marched off eastward. These were the only forces who had managed to escape the "holocaust," as the prisoners called it. It had cost the Russians two regiments, whose destruction had been witnessed by numerous observers. Never before had these spectators attended a class in tactics as convincing as that. This was a lesson which was taken from life and initiated these officers in the tactics of winter combat in the East, of which the pincer attack on Vyasovka was always regarded as a classical example.

IV. Tactical Lessons

1. Even during severe winter weather, it will be possible for a unit equipped with warm clothing to conduct decisive operations. These troops are, however, as they are during every season, dependent on the cooperation of heavy weapons (tanks, assault guns, artillery, antitank and antiaircraft guns, etc.) as well as the support of the air forces.

2. Nevertheless, winter campaigns are difficult operations and consequently require particularly thorough preparations and a firm conduct of operations. In this connection, the coordination of all weapons and tactical commanders is of decisive importance. Therefore, the secure functioning of communication facilities of every description between the tactical commanders and the fire controllers of the heavy weapons and the air forces is just as essential as is the reliable liaison between these fire controllers and the attacking spearheads.

3. In view of the fact that the heavy weapons are indispensable and necessarily confined to the roads, the choice of the direction of the assault and points of main effort is determined by these roads.

4. It is important to make a roadway through the mined no man's land, which is covered with snow as soon as it has been crossed by the attacking infantry, otherwise the infantry troops, being separated from their supporting weapons too long, run the risk of being stranded.

5. Enemy troops who are handicapped by shortages of ammunition can be conquered even by numerically weak forces who are equipped with heavy weapons and sufficient ammunition.

6. Commanders and troops who are to be committed for operations under difficult conditions in a theater of war with which they are not familiar should be retrained there promptly in order to prevent failures and heavy losses.

Chapter 3

"To Liberate Stalingrad!"

Preface

This study was written especially for the Historical Division, USAREUR, by a distinguished commander of German armored forces. The author, whose experience on the Eastern front ranged from command of an armored division to that of an army group, desires to remain anonymous.

As the author points out, the "unusual situations" described here were direct products of a German command decision to relieve the German forces in Stalingrad at all costs. The examples cited in this study concern the 6th Panzer Division, an excellent, experienced unit which was rushed all the way from France to spearhead the relief thrust. This whole undertaking may be described as an attempt to regain the initiative against a numerically superior enemy by the commitment of better-trained and -equipped troops. That problem probably has confronted every opponent of Russia throughout her history, so the strategic background for these tactically "unusual" situations is normal.

W. S. Nye
Colonel Artillery
Chief, Historical Division

Introduction

Whereas, in previous parts of this study, it has been shown that the peculiar behavior of the enemy resulted in unusual situations, in the present cases it was primarily a great and almost insoluble task, forcing the German command to take hazardous and, at times, prohibited measures, which was conducive to such situations.

"Liberate Stalingrad!" was the momentous mission, upon the execution of which the fate of 300,000 troops depended. A task of historic magnitude was to be attempted, and the further conduct of the campaign hinged on its successful completion. Officers and men down to the lowest-ranking private were fully aware of this. Conscious of the great task and of their responsibility to their own people, whose eyes were anxiously turned toward Stalingrad, officers and men did their utmost to master the difficult assignment. It is this attitude and this readiness to sacrifice their lives, in addition to their extraordinary ability and the experience gained in combat in the East, which led to exploits bordering on miraculous.

Example 1: Defense Against Partisan Raids

In the middle of November 1942, after being adequately rehabilitated, provided with a complete reissue of weapons, and thoroughly trained in the West, the 6th Panzer Division, with its units again above T/O[1] strength, rolled eastward in 78 trains. During the 4,000-kilometer journey from France, there were unpleasant incidents, since the large-scale troop movement, which crossed the whole of Europe in scarcely two weeks, did not remain hidden from the enemy. In the extensive marshy forests in the Pripyat region, the German troops were the targets of numerous partisan raids directed especially against the trains carrying tanks and artillery, since these seemed to offer prospects of greater rewards and were less dangerous. The tarpaulins camouflaging them did not prevent the trained eyes of the partisans lurking in ambush from identifying the big weapons.

The trains would have been defenseless if the division had adhered to the entraining regulations governing troop movements. These regulations, which were designed to economize in the use of freight cars, provided that troops, weapons, combat equipment, and ammunition were to be loaded as compactly as possible. In the process, units were split up and the preparedness of the troops for action was not considered. (In addition to the *matériel* referred to above, the trains carrying the tanks had to include compressed forage to facilitate the difficult winter provisioning of horse-drawn units in the East.)

Although fully acknowledging the reasons for this measure, the division, experienced as it was with conditions in the East, was primarily concerned about its preparations for immediate action. It gave priority to these preparations over all other considerations. Allowance for other factors was made only to the extent that they did not interfere with the troops' readiness for action during the movement. Hence, in spite of the fact that it was prohibited by regulations, and in spite of the protests voiced by the rail transportation authorities, the men were entrained in "combat trains."

This involved a different way of loading men and equipment, as well as a different order and distribution of the various combat elements. Allowance was made for the necessity of fighting off partisan raids and of leaving the train to fight. Care had also been taken to insure that, in the latter case, the men in each train, together with the men in the trains immediately following, would form a combined-arms force able to fight alone until further reinforcements arrived.

The course of the movement and the arrival at the destination proved the value of these measures. The partisans everywhere encountered a well-prepared, abruptly initiated defensive operation, no matter whether they blasted tracks, attacked the train from one or both sides or placed obstacles in its path. Defensive measures had been

---

[1] T/O = Table of Organization, the equipment authorized for a particular unit.—Editor.

envisaged against all these possibilities. In dangerous sections, trained sentries, with their weapons ready to fire and with hand grenades, were placed along both sides and at either end of each car. The men in each car had their weapons and other items of combat equipment handy. Machine guns had been placed in the brakeman's boxes; at night searchlights went into action whenever necessary. Their cones of light, which shone out from both sides of the train as soon as the first shot was fired, dazzled the enemy and made it possible to see every movement he made and to discern his intentions. Thereupon, rapid fire and hand grenades subdued him.

The brakes were applied and the train came to a sudden halt. At the same moment, active defensive operations set in. It had been drilled into the men, and hence they functioned automatically. While the machine guns, which fired from the brakeman's boxes, were providing protection, the Germans rapidly mopped up the forest edges, and presently the train was on its way again.

More time was necessary when tracks had been destroyed, but this predominantly happened at points where it was possible to repair the tracks quickly, since all stations, bridges, and other important objectives were protected by permanent sentries. In order to prevent derailments and to protect locomotives from being damaged, they were driven through partisan-infested areas at a slow pace and with two or three empty cars in front of the engine.

In most cases, technical damage could be quickly eliminated by the engineer teams riding in the leading sections of each train. These engineers had been provided with appropriate tools and equipment. During such halts, too, the train was secured from all sides and the immediate vicinity was searched by patrols. At night, the tarpaulins were removed from the turrets of the tanks, and they were made ready to fire. They were a very effective means of defense. A large number of emergency ramps, which were included in the trains, made it possible to unload tanks whenever necessary and to commit them against strong enemy elements. In order to increase the protection of the artillery transports, which the enemy liked to attack, 20mm antiaircraft guns were frequently assigned to them, since the partisans particularly feared the tracer ammunition of these guns.

The above precautions yielded good results. It was due to them that, in spite of numerous partisan raids, most of the trains suffered only few losses and arrived at their destinations in time. Only one artillery train suffered the loss of a battalion commander and several men, who were killed in a surprise raid undertaken by a strong partisan force in conjunction with a demolition of the tracks. Even this train, however, arrived at its detraining point without any delay to speak of. The partisans, on the other hand, sustained severe losses as a result of the powerful defensive operations which were immediately undertaken. They were particularly taken aback by the sudden and vigorous counterattacks which forced them either to engage in bloody close combat if their forces were strong or to flee at once.

The damage of inadequately protected trains had far more unpleasant effects. It necessitated time-consuming halts or detours of the trains, which particularly affected armored units. In one of the following examples, the consequences of these delays will be described. The value of forming combat trains in spite of protests and of taking precautions which the regulations did not provide for will likewise be shown.

Example 2: Raid on a Troop Train in Kotelnikovo, 27 November 1942

The scenes which the soldiers had observed on their way across the European continent were still passing through their minds. The coasts of Brittany, washed by the booming waves of the Atlantic, lay far behind. Far behind also lay the peaceful towns, villages, and hamlets of the West and of their homeland which they had passed through quickly. The verdure of meadows and fields brightly reflected the autumn sun, and the spires and gables of churches and castles were radiant. Paris and Berlin, the two great cultural centers of Europe, and the ruins of Warsaw left a great impression on everyone who had seen them. All that was now a distant dream.

For days and nights the troops had been rolling through striking country, through its extensive forests and marshes, its infinite plains and steppes, its sluggish streams and rivers. By the time the transports had reached Rostov on the Don River, the gateway to Caucasus, after passing through Kharkov and Stalino, traversing the Donets river basin, and passing the Sea of Azov, the men had already forgotten their adventures with the partisans.

Instead of moving on in the direction of the Caucasus, however, the trains veered northward. Their destination was now uncertain. No one was able to say where the trains were headed. The situation was still obscure when, on the evening of 26 November, the first train passed Tsimovniki, where the headquarters of the Fourth Panzer Army was situated, on its way northward. Trains were jammed in all stations. The side tracks were clogged with huge Russian locomotives captured during the German offensive.

A cold wind blew through the monotonous brown steppe, driving before it innumerable balls of tumbleweed. They resembled greyhounds chasing game at top speed, moving forward in great leaps. A few camel riders moved alongside the train on steppe trails, trying to reach their solitary huts before darkness fell. At every halt, the personnel of the numerous evacuation trains running southward were asked which was the last station which it was possible to reach. "This morning it is still Kotelnikovo," was the answer. This was the information the army commander had given the division commander at a briefing at headquarters, for which the division commander had been summoned from the leading train.[2]

The situation was even worse than the first conference with the commander of Army Group "Don,"[3] held on the way to Rostov, had led the division commander to expect.

---

[2] Raus's 6th Panzer Division and the 23rd Panzer Division were subordinated to General F. Kirchner's LVII Panzer Corps, which in turn was part of Generaloberst Hermann Hoth's Fourth Panzer Army. Although part of the panzer corps, the 17th Panzer Division had been diverted by Hitler and only rejoined in the middle of December.—Editor.

[3] Generalfeldmarshal Erich von Manstein had only received orders to assume immediate command of Army Group Don on 20 November 1942. Only a few days before, von Manstein had been traveling to the front

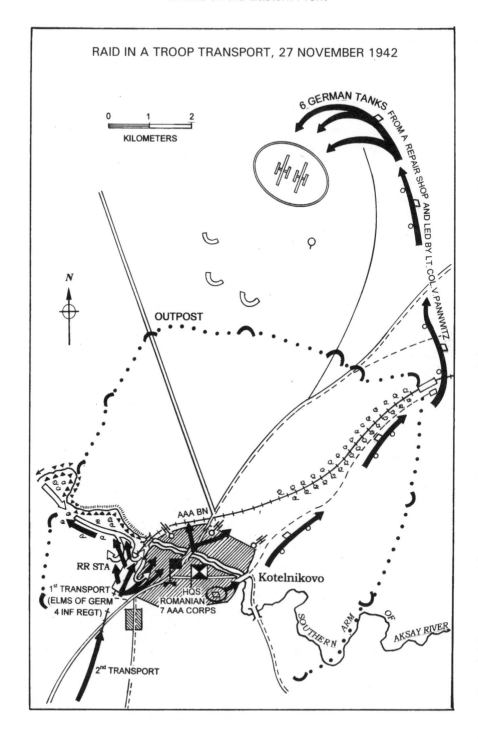

RAID IN A TROOP TRANSPORT, 27 NOVEMBER 1942

An enemy cavalry corps,[4] reinforced by tank units, was advancing along the southern bank of the Don River, and its points had already crossed the southern branch of the Aksay River. A hostile infantry corps was slowly advancing on both sides of the railroad in the direction of Kotelnikovo.[5] The Russian *3rd Tank Army*[6] was being assembled behind the northern branch of the Aksay River; two corps of this army had already been identified there.

These enemy forces, of considerable strength, were faced, south of the Don River, by a few German antiaircraft guns which had just been moved up from the Caucasus, and a Rumanian corps headquarters staff with its headquarters guard totaling 30 men. Far off in the steppe, the remnants of two Rumanian cavalry divisions with a total combat strength of 1,200 cavalrymen were retreating. Thus, there was no longer a German front; in fact, there was not even a single German unit which would have been able to offer temporary resistance to the advancing enemy. This was in part due to the fact that the German and some of the Rumanian units composing the Fourth Panzer Army were encircled in Stalingrad and that the Rumanian divisions employed on a very broad front south of this city, along the edge of the Kalmuck Steppe, had been equipped with inadequate antitank weapons. As a result, their front had been pierced and the units had been scattered by strong Russian armored units. The weak remnants were disintegrating. Even the army headquarters staff barely escaped disaster. It was learned that a battle-weary panzer division was about to be moved up, but this was small comfort since this division only had the combat strength of two weak battalions and, having artillery but no tanks, would first have to undergo emergency rehabilitation behind the Sal River.

The approaching troops as yet knew nothing of this highly unpleasant situation; but they felt that they would enter combat soon, and relied on their strength and ability. Their trains went ahead at full speed. Comprising 50 cars each, they slowly, in broadly sweeping curves, climbed the hills between the river valleys and then quickly descended into the

---

and had been delayed by a mine explosion under his train. Manstein, *Lost Victories* (Novato, CA: Presidio Press, 1982) p. 272.

[4] The author is referring to the Soviet *4th Cavalry Corps (51st Army)* commanded by General T. T. Shapkin. G. Zhukov, *Reminiscences and Reflections* (Moscow: Progress Publishers, 1985), p. 115; Robert G. Poirier and Albert Z. Conner, *The Red Army Order of Battle in the Great Patriotic War* (Novato, CA: Presidio Press, 1985) pp.63–4, 95–6, 123.

[5] The Soviet force facing LVII Panzer Corps was the *51st Army* commanded by General N. N. Trufanov The army had taken part in the Stalingrad counteroffensive in November. According to Zhukov, the mission of "the *51st Army* of Stalingrad, which had been reinforced with armoured formations [was] to hurl the smashed enemy units further back from the encircled Stalingrad groupings and build up a firm exterior perimeter so necessary for annihilation of the trapped enemy. Zhukov, *op. cit.*, p. 127. In December, when LVII Panzer Corps began its offensive, the *51st Army*'s order of battle included the *4th Cavalry Corps*, the *13th Tank Corps*, and the *91st, 96th, 126th*, and *302nd Rifle Divisions*. Poirier and Conner, *op.cit.*, pp. 63–4. On 14 December the *51st Army* was further reinforced with the *87th* and *300th Rifle Divisions* from STAVKA reserve. *Battle for Stalingrad*, p. 121.

[6] The *3rd Tank Army* was being held as a reserve of the High Command (RVGK) near Tula at the time Raus's division was fighting outside Stalingrad. Von Manstein refers to this situation as well but identifies the formation correctly in his memoirs as the *3rd Guards Army* and locates it north of Stalingrad, possibly presenting a threat to Rostov. Manstein, *op. cit.*, p. 331; Poirier and Conner, *op. cit.*, pp. 19, 20, 27.

next valley. Climbing and descending the grades in a pitch-dark night, the trains neared their destination. The guards and sentries did their duty in the usual manner, just as they had done in the partisan-infested regions. All the men in the first train rested on benches, in baggage racks, and on the floor; they were fully clothed and had their weapons handy.

It was dawn by the time the train had climbed the last hill between the Sal and the Aksay river valleys. The aroma of morning coffee was drifting over from the field kitchen when the train entered Semichnaya. This was the last station before Kotelnikovo, the destination of the movement. The long voyage, the endless rolling and grinding of wheels, the rattling and bumping of the cars, would soon be over—so the gradually awakening soldiers thought as they searchingly looked over the dim outlines of the area in which the small town was likely to be situated, where comfortable quarters should be awaiting them after several weeks of rail travel.

Just then, a long evacuation train from Kotelnikovo entered the station. Two engines had strained to push it up an ascending stretch of 20 kilometers. With intense curiosity, the men asked the personnel in the evacuation train how things were progressing in the town:

> There is complete calm and order. Two more evacuation trains are waiting for your arrival and they will be the last to leave the town. Aside from a few planes, we saw no Russians. Except for a few old men constituting the railroad station guard, there are no German soldiers in the town. A few groups of unarmed Rumanians drove herds of sheep past us. That is all we were able to see.

On the previous evening, the German soldiers had seen signs of breaking-up of camps from their trains. "The Russian farmers are surprised at the evacuation of the town," the narrators continued, "and they regret it very much. They were always polite and ready to help, and they will be very glad to see you."

A few short shrill whistles sounded by the train commander called the soldiers back into their cars and put a sudden stop to the question-and-answer game. A few minutes later, the train started again with the same jerk and the grinding of buffers. Quickly it neared its destination. The soldiers packed their "stuff" and felt happy at finally being able to leave the train in which they had been tormented for weeks. A nice little town in the valley of the northern arm of the Aksay River was already coming into sight. At the edge of town stood a triumphal arch adorned by withered wreaths of flowers. This arch, which was visible from afar, had been inscribed in large Rumanian letters: "It is good that you have come!" This welcome had been meant for the Rumanian troops which had marched in several months ago and were now encircled in Stalingrad waiting, along with their German comrades, to be rescued.

No sooner had the men tried to guess the meaning of this strange welcome than the train pulled into the large station. Suddenly the train was shaken by a hail of shells. The ground quivered, black earth was thrown up on all sides, the windows were shattered, the brakes screamed, the wheels screeched, and, with a sudden jolt which threw men and equipment into a heap, the train came to a halt. All the men leaped from the cars, just as they had done on the occasion of the partisan raids which they had so frequently gone through. The Russians, coming from the station building, were already storming the train with cries of "Hurrah!" At this instant, the German machine guns and submachine guns began to fire from the car roofs on the earth-brown figures advancing on the train from both sides.[7]

In the next minute, however, the infernal din caused by detonating shells and yelling Russians was drowned out by ear-splitting cheers from the German infantrymen who, led by their regimental commander, rushed forward with bayonets and hand grenades to fall upon the Russians and, in ferocious hand-to-hand fighting, to wrest the station from them. In bitter fighting among the freight cars, buildings, and railroad installations, they managed to mop up the entire railroad area in the course of an hour.

The hostile artillery which, during this action, had aimed its fire at the end of the station where the train had entered and at the western exit of town, now redirected it toward the center of the station, ostensibly with the intention of incapacitating this part of the installation for any further detrainment of troops and destroying the full transport train waiting in it. It was not difficult to see that the enemy would soon achieve this objective, since he was certain to employ local observers wearing civilian clothes who, with incredible accuracy, always adjusted the fire on those points where it did the greatest damage. Abruptly, however, the fire, which two to three batteries had directed on the center of the station and which had been very effective, ceased. The guns were expected any moment to resume their work of destruction once a new target had been selected; but nothing of the kind happened—they remained silent. This was fortunate. The fire had already done a good deal of damage, which was now rapidly being repaired by the engineer platoon of the 4th Panzergrenadier Regiment with the assistance of railroad personnel, who had by now fairly recovered from their initial confusion.

The intention of the railroad administration—to quickly move to the rear all rolling stock still present in the station and to stop directing troop trains to Kotelnikovo—was not approved and, on the contrary, a demand was made that all movements to the rear be halted and that the trains following be driven into this station with the utmost speed. Thus, the second train arrived soon after the raid, and it was possible to unload it, as happened with all the subsequent trains, without the slightest interference, since the hostile cavalry unit which had dismounted and crept up through the floodplains of the river without being noticed and which had carried out the raid had meanwhile been vigorously pursued and scattered, and since the artillery still remained silent.

It was only in the late morning that it was possible to find out the reason for the silence of the enemy batteries. In the emergency, a genius had been found to remedy the

---

[7] These were troops of the *81st Cavalry Division, 4th Cavalry Corps.* Louis C. Rotundo, ed., *Battle for Stalingrad: The 1943 Soviet General Staff Study* (Washington, DC: Pergamon-Brassey's, 1989), p. 115. The *4th Cavalry Corps* consisted of the *61sth, 81st,* and *115th Cavalry Divisions.* Poirier and Conner, *op.cit.,* p. 123.

situation. This was Lieutenant-Colonel von Panwitz, who, during the surprise fire in the morning, happened to be in a tank repair shop situated at the eastern edge of the town. Realizing the great danger threatening the station and the town, he quickly rallied all tanks that were at all battleworthy, appointed the maintenance team as tank drivers and gunners and, with six tanks, immediately conducted a raid against the enemy batteries. Since he came from the cavalry, a daring enterprise of this sort was natural to him.

Making a quick decision, he had his improvised force advance by bounds behind the hedges of the railroad embankment and through defiles in the terrain in so skillful a manner that he suddenly appeared in the rear of the firing guns. Seeing his chance, he attacked the batteries without an instant's hesitation. The surprise of the enemy batteries was even greater than that of the Germans in the arriving transport train. Every round was fired at extremely close range and was a direct hit. The machine-gun fire of the tanks cut down the Russian crews before they could turn a single gun on the Germans. As a result, the German tank men were able to complete their work of destruction in a few minutes. Piles of wrecked guns, ammunition and wrecked limbers, which the Russians had tried to rush to the scene, surrounded the large numbers of dead, who had thus paid a high price for their successful surprise fire.

After giving them an honorary salute, which is every brave enemy's due, the small armored force, which had suffered no losses, returned to its repair shop. This day—on which they had proved that they not only knew how to hammer, weld, bore and drive, but also how to fight—remained unforgettable to them. The gallant leader and his group of fighters received decorations which they had fully deserved. Of course, they at once became the friends of the infantrymen whom, in the spirit of true brotherhood in arms, they had helped save.

The day, which had begun so adversely, had finally brought complete success. The enemy had been dealt a crushing defeat, and Kotelnikovo, which was highly important as a detraining point for the action planned by the Germans, was firmly in German hands.[8] The troops which had arrived by that time comprised the division headquarters, the headquarters of the 4th Panzergrenadier Regiment, its 2nd Battalion, and one engineer company, all together constituting a Kampfgruppe that, in conjunction with the antiaircraft batteries and the brave "damaged-tanks unit" which had been there from the outset, was able to defend the town even against heavy enemy attacks.

The previously described measures for counterattacking enemy surprise raids accordingly yielded good results, as did the "combat transports" set up for troop movements in spite of the regulations and the transportation authorities. These trains made it possible to advance the concentration area of the troops up to the Aksay River, thereby making the distance to be covered in an attack on Stalingrad as short as possible.

---

[8] The Soviets admitted that a second formation, the *61st Cavalry Division*, was also roughly handled that day. *Battle for Stalingrad.*

Example 3: The Cannae[9] of Pokhlebin, 6 December 1942

During the following days, the detraining of the troops proceeded without incident. On 28 November, the advance elements of the 114th Panzergrenadier Regiment, including some artillery, arrived. These elements had been detrained the day before in the Tatsinskaya area on the rail line north of the Don River leading to Stalingrad, and had reached the Kotelnikovo area overland by way of the bridge across the Don River at Tsymlyanskaya. They were followed by the combat echelons, which alternately used the southern and the northern routes and established themselves in the assembly area around Kotelnikovo. It is hard to understand why the Russians discontinued their advances when the first German troops appeared, although they had certainly been assigned the minimum objective of reaching the southern arm of the Aksay River and of occupying Kotelnikovo.[10] Instead of attacking the German forces with their superior numbers, they idly watched for ten days while the Germans constantly increased in strength. It was impossible to solve this enigma just as it was impossible to explain the fact that neither the German troops which were being detrained nor the endless truck convoys moving along in broad daylight were attacked even once from the air, although no German fighter planes were aloft.

Had the Russians been active, they could have compelled the German command to locate its troop assembly areas at a point behind the Sal River, that is to say 50 kilometers further back. This would have substantially reduced the probability of success of the German action. As it was, however, it was possible to assemble the division in peacetime fashion in spite of the proximity of superior enemy forces. Still, the German command ran a great risk in virtually sending the troops it was assembling into the lion's mouth.

To forestall a "fatal bite," the division grouped its units in an unusual defense pattern which displeased the panzer corps (LVII) headquarters and worried Army headquarters, but which fortunately was not changed since the division commander had sound arguments in its favor and stood by them energetically. He rejected the proposed establishment of a defense line along the Aksay River with the left flank anchored on the Don River because the area was too wide to be held, even if all available forces were assembled, and it would also have been impossible to protect the open right flank. Instead, a network of local strongpoints occupied by combined-arms forces was set up.

This network, which was in the form of a perimeter defense position covering an area ten by twenty kilometers, had Kotelnikovo for a focal point and offensive bridgehead. Behind it, at Semichnaya, a strong mechanized general reserve was assembled, which could easily be shifted in all directions on the rolling terrain which makes a broad sweep south of the Aksay River. Consequently, every enemy force infiltrating into the defense

---

[9] The battle at Cannae, near Rome, in 216 BC, in which Hannibal inflicted a crushing defeat on the Romans, was the first historic battle of encirclement.

[10] Raus does have a good point, especially when the Soviet General Staff Study on Stalingrad stated, "For the further development of the offensive, was as necessary to capture Kotelnikivo, since it was the most important road center in the given operational direction." *Battle for Stalingrad.*

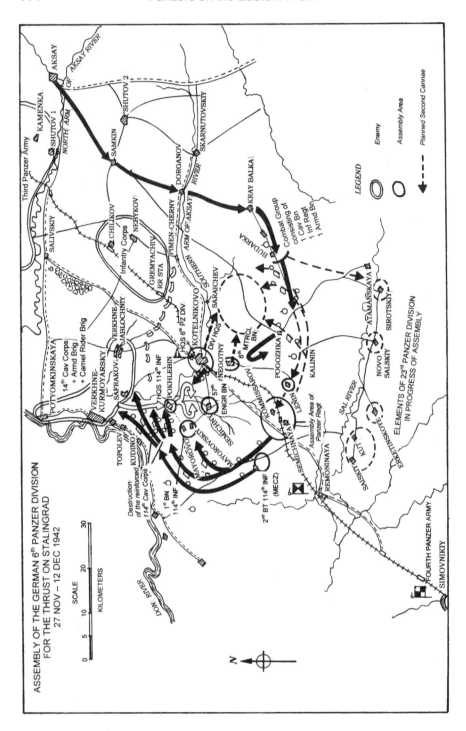

ASSEMBLY OF THE GERMAN 6th PANZER DIVISION
FOR THE THRUST ON STALINGRAD
27 NOV – 12 DEC 1942

network was threatened with destruction by crossfire and concentric attacks from several strongpoints. By employing the mechanized general reserve, it was possible to prevent any attempt on the part of the enemy to force his way through the gap to the Don River or to unhinge the division by bypassing it on the east.

This unusual form of organization also had the advantage of permitting the Germans to unexpectedly start their planned offensive from it at any time by assembling the mechanized general reserves in the bridgehead at night and forming them into a spearhead. Only weak covering parties were stationed at the flanks. The twenty modern armored reconnaissance cars of the motorcycle battalion were employed to watch the gap and undertake reconnaissance on the flanks and in the rear.

These tactical measures and the planned manner of operation had been thoroughly discussed in the field with all commanders, in order to insure the cooperation of all elements in any situation in the interests of the whole. The immediately subsequent events were to show whether the conduct of operations as planned—which was dictated by the situation, the terrain, and the mission and was, as it were, made to order for a mobile force—was the proper one. In contrast to this, the regulations made in peacetime state that armored units constitute a well-defined means of attack and hence are not suited for defense. They also state that tanks must not be moved at night, since their crews cannot observe in the dark and the tanks are thus exposed to serious damage.[11]

It seemed appropriate to preface the following example with these considerations, although they actually transcend the scope of small-unit tactics, in order to facilitate a proper appraisal of the actions of the officers and the men, and to demonstrate how the specific necessities of warfare often made it mandatory to discard the dogmatic rules contained in peacetime manuals and to replace them by action which met the requirements of reality.

This was the case when the enemy made his first attempt to destroy the German units assembled in the area around Kotelnikovo by a flanking attack from the northwest. On previous days German personnel in armored reconnaissance cars had already observed hostile scout patrols mounted on steppe horses at various points along the fifteen-kilometer gap to the Don River. These patrols would disappear with the speed of lightning as soon as they saw a German armored vehicle. Their chief interest, however, was centered in a defile at Pokhlebin and the hilly ranges north of Mayorovo. Dismounted scouts crept up the defile through the high steppe grass and the rush in the Aksay Valley, but vanished as soon as they were accordingly unable to penetrate. They were visibly amazed, on the other hand, to discover no Germans on the hilly ranges situated west of the defile; they were sometimes seen by artillery observers on those

---

[11] Here Raus is admitting to an error. The combat diary of the 11th Panzer Regiment stated, "Gen. Raus intended to commit tanks at night to reach the Aksai crossing, but Colonel von Hünersdorff refused, because it was very difficult to orient at night, and the chance of tanks slipping into icy ravines was high." Combat diary quoted in Werner Haupt, *Army Group South: The Wehrmacht in Russia 1941–1945* (Atglen, PA: Schiffer Military History, 1998), p. 215.

ranges. The same observation had been made by enemy scouts on the morning of 5 December, the day of the enemy attacks.

Russian combined-arms forces, comprising dismounted cavalry and tanks, which poured out of Verkhne-Kurmoyarskiy at dawn, attacked the motorcycle company stationed in Topolev on the Don River to provide protection, and pushed the company back as far as Kudino. This was the prelude to interesting and instructive events.

The enemy advance did not come as a surprise; it had been expected in this area for the past few days. It had been presaged by the situation and by the active reconnaissance which the enemy had been conducting there. Soon after the introductory engagement at Topolev, it was clearly discernible that the Russians, after pushing through the gap, would either lunge westward and attack the rear or move directly southward and attack the German force in the flank.

The enemy force attacking along the Don River remained in front of Kudino, which the motorcycle company that had withdrawn to this locality managed to hold. At the same time, the main body of the cavalry division, preceded by the tank brigade attached to it, veered southward and pushed toward Pokhlebin. Presently it was caught in the fire of the heavy batteries situated at Semichniy, and soon afterward was hit by fire from the entire artillery. The sixty-four Russian tanks, however, moved on unconcernedly, in spite of the hail of shells pounding down near them. The dismounted cavalry at once disappeared into the floodplains of the Aksay River, from which they later reappeared north of Pokhlebin to undertake an attack after the artillery fire had followed them there, too, and had inflicted severe losses on them.

The long column of tanks came to an abrupt halt in front of Pokhlebin when the leading tanks received fire from antitank guns and were destroyed. Shortly before, the cavalry units, attacking on foot, had been forced to take cover against machine-gun fire from a reinforced company of the 4th Panzergrenadier Regiment, which had the mission of blocking the town and the defile of Pokhlebin. More and more forces came up to reinforce the attackers, who hoped to capture the town by encircling it. Advance elements of these forces, strong armored units, broke into the town, after several previous armored attacks had been repulsed by the antitank platoon, which was fighting against overwhelming numerical superiority. But the strength of this platoon decreased as the individual guns were, one by one, identified and finally overrun by the enemy.

The enemy believed that he had won out when his two leading tanks had reached the center of the town, but the last gunner of the last German antitank gun destroyed these tanks too. Six tall black columns of smoke indicated the total losses the enemy had suffered at the hands of the three antitank gun crews, who had perished to the last man in an unequal fight. A sublime drama had thus drawn to a close.

This exemplary heroism on the part of a small group of staunch and courageous soldiers had made it possible for the enemy's tank brigade to be held up in the defile for almost two hours. The time thus gained was sufficient for the main body of the 1st Battalion of the 114th Panzergrenadiers, coming from the Mayorovo strongpoint, to attack the enemy's infantry forces on the flank and to detain them in the Pokhlebin defile until the afternoon.

Only the enemy tanks, utilizing a passage through the swampy valley of the Siberachnaya Stream, managed to make headway in the direction of Kotelnikovo. Without regard for the battle for Pokhlebin raging in their rear, or the loss of tanks inflicted by the antitank guns of the attacking German infantry battalion, they presently crossed the Semichnaya Stream, which was difficult to ford as a result of the partial melting of the snow which had fallen a short time previously.

The next intention of the Russian tanks was to seize the village of Sakharov, situated three kilometers to the east, on a bend of the Aksay River. This village was being stubbornly defended by the 6th Company, 4th Panzergrenadiers, which had been pushed back from Pokhlebin, plus one artillery battery. The Russians forced their way into the village, but the Germans destroyed several enemy tanks by armor-piercing, hollow-charge shells and knocked out the leading enemy tanks by magnetic antitank hollow charges. The majority of the enemy tanks then withdrew to the west in a broad sweep, in order to still try to reach their objective, Kolelnikovo.

While they did so, they came under crossfire from six batteries, whose heavy and light shells hit them on both flanks from a range of two to four kilometers. The hail of fire was so formidable t hat several tanks were damaged, while others fell into marshy holes. They were driven here and there in an effort to free them, but they only sank deeper and deeper into the morass. It so happened that the main body of the Turkestan cavalry managed to push back the 1st Battalion of the 114th Panzergrenadiers so far from Pokhlebin that it was able to penetrate into the area between the two streams already mentioned.

Before they were able to aid the tanks, however, an unexpected turn of events occurred in the early hours of the afternoon. This had been brought about by the first two companies of the 11th Panzer Regiment, which, in view of the critical situation in the Kotelnikovo area, moved forward as far as this town and were at once committed in a counterattack. Although outnumbered by the enemy, they managed during bitter fighting, which caused losses on both sides, to drive the hostile tanks back across the Semichnaya Stream. The attempts on the part of the ever-increasing masses of enemy cavalry to cross this stream in an easterly direction were balked by the combined German artillery fire, which hit the Russians simultaneously from the strongpoints in the south, east and west, thus breaking their aggressive spirit.

When darkness fell, the din of battle gradually subsided. The day was drawing to a close, and the outcome of the fighting was as yet undecided. Although the enemy had managed to achieve a local penetration into the German defensive system, his intention of seizing Kotelnikovo had been frustrated. The situation of his forces, which, driven through a defile and squeezed in between marshes and the Aksay River, were caught in the crossfire of the surrounding German local strongpoints, was highly unfavorable. On the next day, however, the enemy was able to commit the *2nd Turkestan Cavalry Division* and to have the infantry corps, which so far had been looking on idly, attack from the east. If both corps had given each other the proper tactical support, their large numerical superiority would have placed the German forces in a very serious predicament. The only asset of the Germans consisted of the possibility of timely commitment of the main body of the 11th Panzer Regiment and of the mechanized 2nd Battalion, 114th Panzergrenadiers, which had not yet arrived. To solve the problem of having them available in time was the sole concern at the end of this day of battle. This concern was not unjustified, since it was not only victory or defeat on 6 December , but also the liberation of Stalingrad, which depended on the solution of this problem.[12]

As had already been mentioned, the partisans were especially interested in tank trains. The continual raiding caused such delays that the panzer units, which had been placed at the head of the movement, were finally at the rear of the combat troops. Although these trains had priority, it would normally have been impossible for them to arrive and be unloaded before 6 or 7 December. This would have been too late. Only unusual measures could still make their timely commitment feasible. The first of these measures was to halt all rail movements in the area concerned and, contrary to the safety provisions of the railroad regulations, to let the trains move within sight of one another. Since the few stations near enough to permit the tanks to arrive in time would be insufficient for the unloading of the trains, it was necessary for the tanks to be unloaded in complete darkness with the aid of the ramps available on the trains. Furthermore, contrary to regulations, night marches of several hours' duration had to be undertaken in completely unfamiliar terrain.

In spite of these unusual measures, it was not until 2000 hours that the first tank trains arrived at the Semichnaya station and were unloaded there. The tanks which had been unloaded in the two preceding stations were already moving toward the hilly ranges surrounding the above-mentioned station. They were followed by the tanks and mechanized infantry units which had been detrained in the open. Since, on the basis of experience gathered previously at Moscow, such measures, as well as the movement and commitment of armored units in the dark, had been drilled into the troops in France, everything went smoothly. By 0100 hours on 6 December, the last units had arrived in the assembly area. An hour before, the commander[13] of the panzer regiment had set out with the first elements of his combat troops to carry out the mission which had been indicated on a map and explained to him by the division commander after the latter had briefed him concerning the situation. Led by armored reconnaissance cars whose crews

---

[12] The Soviet General Staff Study placed their first attack as taking place on 3 December instead of 5 December. It stated that the *51st Army* "met heavy counterattacks of enemy infantry and tanks," and that the *61st Cavalry Division* "was engaged in battle in the jump-off position for the attack and did not set out." The *81st Cavalry Division*, "after suffering heavy losses, withdrew to the line Verkne-Kurmoiarskaia, Verkne-Iablochnyi, and the *832nd Infantry Regiment* of the *302nd Rifle Division* was thrown back in the direction of Chilekov." *Battle for Stalingrad.*

[13] Oberst Walter von Hünersdorff, who was later to command the 6th Panzer Division at the Battle of Kursk, where he died of wounds (Appendix 1).

were familiar with the area, the mechanized combat forces arrived at 0400 hours and, despite the darkness, were already for a counterattack an hour later in the area of Mayorovo, the site of the command post of the 114th Panzergrenadier Regiment, and north thereof.

As soon as there was enough light to permit firing, the noise of battle was again heard on the previous day's battlefield. This area was situated in the valley. German tanks and infantry again attacked the enemy, who offered stubborn resistance and threw new reserves into the fighting. The Soviet commander meant at all costs to keep open the defile at Pokhlebin, his route of approach of Kotelnikovo, especially as he knew that the second division of his corps would move up and bring about a decision. In long columns, the tank, cavalry, and motorized infantry units of this division were advancing toward Pokhlebin, along the same road which the *1st Cavalry Division* had used on the previous day.

Substantial elements had already vanished into the town and into ravines, when, all of a sudden, German tanks, organized in several wedge-shaped formations, appeared on the snow-covered hills. Plodding through the snow, they slowly advanced toward their victims, who as yet were unaware of their imminent disaster. This was in part due to the fact that the Russian cavalry corps had only recently been transferred here on foot from the Afghan border, and had previously performed border patrol duty without ever seeing combat. Inexperienced as they were, the commanders failed to observe the most elementary rules of precaution. Not a single cavalryman, infantryman, or tank climbed to the concealed parts of the rugged terrain to reconnoiter or provide protection. If this had been done, the movements of the numerous German armored units would never have escaped attention. The inexperienced commanders were not even aware of the fact that the possession of this hill range was of decisive importance for their attack on Kotelnikovo, or else they would have occupied it. As it was, the catastrophe overtook them.

Crippled by paralyzing terror, the enemy suddenly saw more than 200 tanks and armored vehicles descend from the hills and fall upon his columns. Two hundred guns fired from close range at the enemy's tanks, artillery, and vehicles. Flames went up; columns of black smoke from tanks which had been hit rose to the sky; trucks were overturned and burned. Three hundred machine guns took a terrible toll among the riders and horses. Those who escaped from this inferno tried to get across the river, but the thin ice broke. Men, tanks, vehicles, and equipment were lost in the cold waters. The men at the end of the column thought they would be able to escape a similar fate by running in the opposite direction, but their attempt to do so was in vain, because they were immediately taken under fire by twenty armored reconnaissance cars and by the machine guns of the panzergrenadiers who, in compliance with their orders, blocked the withdrawal route of the column. As a result, the enemy was forced into a pocket which was rapidly tightened by a concentric attack on Pokhlebin.

By 1000 hours, the fate of the cavalry corps had been sealed. There was no longer any escape. However, the enemy, although encircled in the area around Pokhlebin,

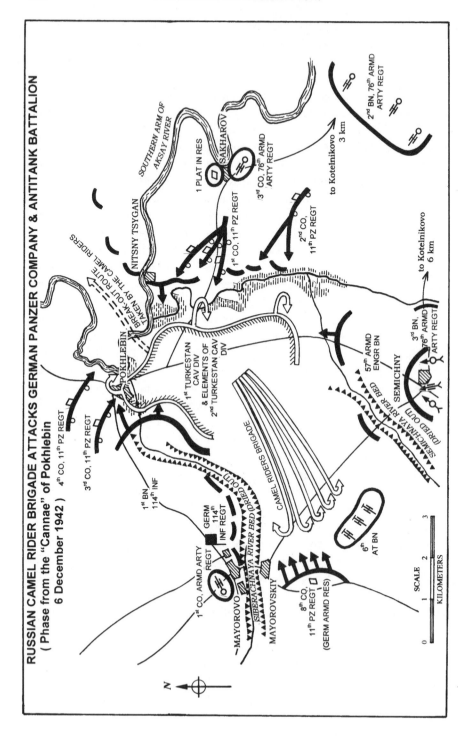

RUSSIAN CAMEL RIDER BRIGADE ATTACKS GERMAN PANZER COMPANY & ANTITANK BATTALION
(Phase from the "Cannae" of Pokhlebin
6 December 1942)

continued to offer very stubborn resistance for hours. The Russian tanks and numerous antitank guns engaged the German tanks coming down from the hills in a fire duel for life or death. The tracer stream of the armor-piercing shells traveled up and down in rapid succession. More and more shells came from the hills, fewer and fewer were the responses which flashed from below. One volley after another from the heavy batteries boomed into the town and threw up columns of black earth; the town began to burn. A sea of smoke and fire veiled the horrible end of the brave garrison. Fire still flashed up occasionally from isolated antitank guns when the German armored points entered Pokhlebin. The panzergrenadiers who followed were obliged to use hand grenades in order to break the resistance of the enemy's motorized infantrymen, who stubbornly fought on for every house and every hole. They lay around their wrecked antitank guns by the dozens. The few survivors clung to the marshes and the brush. It was not until noon that Pokhlebin was clear of the enemy.

In the area between the town and the previous day's front, a few hostile tanks still fought in order to support the attempts of the Russian elements encircled there to break out. They tried to escape across the river, but only a few managed to do so. Others attempted to break through between the local strongpoints, but had to give up after being caught in crossfire and having suffered heavy losses. Finally, a larger force thought it had found a gap between two dry river beds and tried to escape westward at this point. The covering parties had not seen it at first owing to the smoke. They then reported the approach of something that was neither men, horses nor tanks. It was only when it had surged over the crest of the range and was preparing to storm forward in the direction of Mayorovski that it was identified as a camel brigade. It ran up against fully prepared German armored and antitank units. whose mission it was to prevent the encircled tanks from breaking out at this point. The enemy was received with such a burst of fire that his leading elements broke down at once and those following behind ran back wildly. The attempt on the part of the tanks to overtake the camel riders and destroy them failed, since some sections of the area were marshy and, as a result, the tanks were unable to follow quickly enough. The camels proved quicker and better able to move across the country and consequently won the race. As a result, they also regained their freedom since they alone were able to ford the Aksay River.

Early in the afternoon, the pocket had been mopped up and the two-day battle had ended. During the next few days, however, stragglers and isolated cavalry troops continued to be discovered in the dried river beds where they had hidden themselves. The men and the puny steppe horses were captured in a half-starved condition and were provided for. The battlefield clearly showed the traces of the deadly struggle. One division had been smashed in the Pokhlebin area, the other one on its way there. On the highway and in the town, there were 56 wrecked enemy tanks, which, burned out and blackened by smoke, topped the debris around them. Just a few hours ago, they had been the proud backbone of the cavalry corps. Guns, vehicles, ammunition and military equipment of all kinds had been turned over, smashed and burned. In between, there were piles of dead men and horses. Cart roads and meadows had been trampled and plowed up by tank tracks. Smoldering planks and demolished blockhouses choked up the lanes of Pokhlebin and added to the chaos. A smell of burning vitiated the atmosphere. Innumerable prisoners of war and more than 2,000 horses fell into German hands. The two Russian division commanders had been killed. The corps commander had fled across the Aksay River and had escaped the shots which German outguards posted on the other side of the river had fired at him. His escorts were taken prisoner.

The hotly contested Pokhlebin defile had witnessed immortal deeds of heroism. The German antitank platoon which, on 5 December, had stopped the first onrush of Russian tanks, had sacrificed itself. The guns, smashed by enemy shells, lay on the ground, and at their side lay the bodies of the company commander (First Lieutenant Count Plettenberg) and the crew. The counterpart to this "battery of the dead" in the "Cannae" of Pokhlebin was to be found in the Russian antitank guns and the tanks in the town itself. A brave though inexperienced enemy had found his grave there.

It will be difficult to find an example which shows more clearly than that above that it is not always possible to adhere strictly to regulations when unusual conditions arise. There is no set formula for dealing with such conditions. Only experience and a proper grasp of the situation will show the measures which must be taken in such cases. The example also demonstrates, however, that a battle-tried and skillfully commanded force can cope with an unusual situation, even under the most difficult circumstances.

Example 4: "The Golden Bridge"

In good spirits, the troops now awaited the order to advance on Stalingrad. As yet, however, it was still necessary to wait for the arrival of the most important supplies. Above all, it was necessary to wait until the remnants of the 23rd Panzer Division, regrouping behind the Sal River, had been rehabilitated.

In the meantime, the men of the infantry regiments which had originally come from the cavalry had fun riding the small steppe horses which had fallen into their hands by the hundreds. With fur caps on their heads and sabers dangling from their sides, they galloped all over the area. Their long legs almost grazed the ground. The riders actually made the streets look different, since the streets were now full of horses instead of tanks. It was almost as if the Turkestan riders, rather than the German tanks, had been the victors.

After a few days, signs appeared that the enemy was about to try to throw the 6th Panzer Division off balance by attacking from the opposite side. On 9 December, air observers and armored reconnaissance cars had identified a combined-arms column which seemed about to bypass the Kotelnikovo area in a broad eastward sweep. A cavalry battalion comprising two to three troops was up in front, and was followed at a great distance by two infantry battalions and some tanks. Obviously this was a strong hostile reconnaissance force, whose mission it was to find out what the situation was and also the strength of the German forces now concentrating. The assumption was justified that this reconnaissance force might be followed by a strong armored force from the Russian *3rd Tank Army*, assembled behind the northern arm of the Aksay River, or even by the main body of this army, with the intention of throwing back the German forces while they were still preparing to relieve Stalingrad.

The operations staff of the division, however, had anticipated such intentions on the part of the enemy from the beginning and had taken appropriate countermeasures. By 7 December, the 11th Panzer Regiment and all other panzer units had been assembled again in the vicinity of the Semichnaya station. Out of the sixteen German tanks that had been disabled in the battle of Pokhlebin, it had been possible to quickly repair a few which had sustained only light damage, while the others were replaced by tanks which had recently arrived.

Accordingly, the German panzer force stood ready twenty kilometers behind the front on the same dominating rolling terrain from which it had advanced on the night of 5 December to deal the Russians a decisive blow. The enemy force about to attack Kotelnikovo from the southeast was to be defeated in the same manner as the cavalry corps had been defeated the day before.

Possibilities for shifting troops on the rolling terrain were excellent in this new direction, too, no matter whether the movements had to be carried out by day or by night. The gently rising ground was covered by a thin layer of snow, from which the brown steppe grass protruded. Neither the snow nor the dry grass were able to impede movement in any way.

An enemy force, on the other hand, advancing from the above-mentioned rolling terrain into the valley of Kotelnikovo, would have been caught between two very deep dried-out river beds which were several kilometers long. These river beds constituted an absolute antitank obstacle. Men and horses could not cross without bridge-building equipment. With these river beds on his flanks and the Aksay River in front of him, the enemy would have no way of escaping once the mechanized general reserve came out of its assembly area and attacked his forces in the rear. A second Cannae would surely have been in store for him.

For this reason, and also to permit the Germans to defeat the greatest possible number of hostile forces before the beginning of the relief of Stalingrad, it was desirable that strong armored forces should follow the enemy reconnaissance force. Hence it was necessary to build a "golden bridge" for the enemy in order to lure him into the trap. To this end, the Germans pretended to be careless and placed no obstacle in the path of the Russians in order to induce them to "pick the seemingly ripe fruit" of Kotelnikovo. The reconnaissance force actually did choose the route leading into the lion's den.

By 9 December, the enemy was already advancing through Budarka; his cavalry points had already reached Pogozhka, but not a single German soldier was to be seen far and wide. All the German armored reconnaissance cars and other forces which had been employed there had withdrawn in accordance with their orders and had watched the enemy's movements from well-camouflaged hideouts. The enemy was visibly ill at ease when his forward scout patrols reached the first farms of Kalinin and Lenin and found them clear of Germans. They had not discovered the well-camouflaged mechanical general reserve in the Semichnaya–Kommissarov area. On the other hand, German railroad trains rolled past them barely three kilometers away. There was considerable truck traffic on the road west of the railroad tracks.

The same movements were observed by hostile cavalrymen feeling their way forward to the edge of Negotny, in which the 6th Motorcycle Battalion was situated. The place was filled to capacity with soldiers and camouflaged vehicles. Holding their weapons in their hands and ready to leap up in case the enemy attacked, motorcycle riflemen crouched on the floors of the farm huts. Men with machine guns were lurking in hidden corners waiting for the appropriate signal to fire at the unsuspecting enemy, whose movements were being closely watched by scouts from dormer windows. But nothing happened. Only fowl moved about in the village, which otherwise seemed quite dead. The barking of dogs indicated the approach of hostile cavalrymen and the stealthy advance of scouts, who at some points had already crept up to within 100 meters of the outermost houses.

The two infantry battalions which had previously been entrenched in the rolling terrain west of Budarka now also followed, reaching Pogozhka in the course of the afternoon. They dug in again north of the latter town. The few tanks accompanying them protected the risky disposition of the troops on both flanks and in the rear. But for two days now German air observers had been looking in vain for the strong Russian tank forces which had been virtually invited by the actions of the Germans to follow their reconnaissance force, since the latter had so far not suffered the slightest interference. The Germans even allowed the Russian reconnaissance force to go to the extreme limit permitted by the situation. The Russians accepted the offer.

Their infantry advanced an additional eight kilometers in the direction of Negotny. The cavalry in Kalinin was reinforced, and its scouts went forward almost as far as the Semichnaya station without being disturbed in their activity. Now, however, the extreme limit of what was possible in the way of concessions had been attained. The railroad and the garrison of Negotny were already seriously threatened as a result of these concessions. The command decided to set off the alarm in order to catch the small fish already in the net. At that very moment, however, enemy movements to the rear were observed. Apparently his courage failed him and he was withdrawing before nightfall. No raid was forthcoming. An unusually tense but completely peaceful day drew to its close. It extended an invitation to the main body of the enemy armored force to follow on the route which had been found to be safe. But, when there was no sign of an advance of strong hostile forces on the following day either, it was evident that the enemy refused to use the "golden bridge" built for him.

What may have been the reason for this refusal? There was only one, and this one was significant enough. It was the "Cannae of Pokhlebin" which paralyzed his initiative. This defeat had hurt him too deeply to make him feel any desire to undertake a similar venture after so short a period. Not even the "golden bridge" was able to change his attitude. It remained unused.

Example 5: Flank Protection by Means of a Sideways Thrust

On the evening of 10 December, the order for the relief attack on Stalingrad arrived. This order provided that the 6th Panzer Division was to effect a breakthrough at the railroad line on 12 December and reach the northern arm of the Aksay River as quickly as possible. The 23rd Panzer Division was to accompany the attackers echeloned right and protect the eastern flank of the 6th Panzer Division. The latter division had to provide protection itself for its vulnerable western flank. This provision in the plan of the attack confronted the division with a problem which was not easy to solve.[14]

On the one hand, a quick breakthrough through the Russian infantry corps entrenched between Pimen-Cherni and the road leading northward from Kotelnikovo would require the concentration of all forces. On the other hand, it was impossible to ignore the remnants of the hostile cavalry corps defeated at Pokhlebin, since these remnants had been assembled in the Verkhne-Yablochny and Verkhne-Kurmoyarskiy areas and new forces had been moved in to strengthen them. At present, these reinforced remnants comprised several troops and dismounted camel units supported by fourteen tanks.

Although this motley force was no match for the German division, its presence was a serious threat to the supply which depended upon the railroad line and the road running parallel to it. A disruption of this vital artery might have had a fatal effect on the whole operation. Precautions had to be taken to meet this danger.

The customary way for a unit to protect its flanks had been to detach a flank security patrol to accompany the main body. In the present case, such a patrol would have had to be in at least battalion strength, with supporting artillery and an armored detachment. It was impossible, however, to permanently detach a force of this size from the division, either during the initial breakthrough or in the course of the attack, without decreasing

---

[14] Von Manstein describes the onslaught of the 6th Panzer Division: "The versatility of our armour and the superiority of our tank crews were brilliantly demonstrated in this period, as were the bravery of the panzergrenadiers and the skill or our anti-tank units. At the same time it was seen what an experienced old armoured division like 6 Panzer could achieve under its admirable commander, General Rauss and the tank specialist Colonel v. Hünersdorff (who, I am sorry to say, was later to be killed at the head of this same division) when it went into action with its full complement of armoured vehicles and assault guns. How hard, in contrast, was the loss of 23 Panzer Division (commanded by General v. Vormann, a former colleague of mine in the O.K.H. Operations Branch who had been five times wounded in World War I), which had a bare twenty tanks to work with!" *Lost Victories*, p. 330. The relief expedition was just not an armored spearhead: "The column was spearheaded by the 57th Panzer Corps, with part of two Luftwaffe field divisions, and its flanks protected by the re-formed remnants of the 4th Rumanian Army. At the rear a mass of vehicles of every kind, trucks of French, Czech, and Russian manufacture, English Bedfords and American GMCs captured during the summer, agricultural tractors towing carts and limbers—pressed into service by the resourceful Colonel Finkh—waited with three thousand tons of supplies which were to be run through the corridor to revictual the 6th Army." Alan Clark, *Barbarossa: The Russian-German Conflict 1941–1945* (New York: Macmillian, 1985), pp. 266–7.

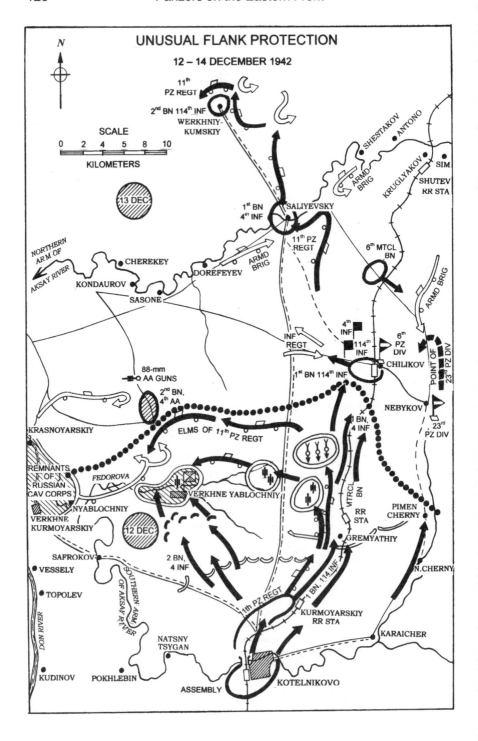

UNUSUAL FLANK PROTECTION

12 – 14 DECEMBER 1942

the division's striking power to such an extent that the planned breakthrough would be jeopardized. Detachment of a "stationary" flank security patrol had the same disadvantages.

As a result, it was necessary to immediately deal the enemy a single blow which would eliminate him completely. For this purpose, the division commander decided to concentrate the division within a very small area behind the covering parties of the bridgehead, which were in contact with the enemy, and then push forward along the hilly range on both sides of the rail line and to penetrate through the entire depth of the enemy corps. Thereafter, the 11th Panzer Regiment, together with the 2nd Battalion, 4th Panzergrenadiers, which had been covering the bridgehead and would then be available, was to liquidate the enemy forces situated on the western flank in the Verkhne-Yablochny area by a powerful blow so as to render any further detachment of troops for the protection of the flank superfluous. In order to employ a maximum number of troops for both these missions, it was necessary to carry out the missions successively. The large-scale breakthrough had to be followed as soon as possible by a lunge to the side to crush the remnants of the cavalry corps situated on the flank. The following narration of the course of events shows how this unusual plan was realized.

Before dawn on 12 December, the 6th Panzer Division and, on its right, echeloned in depth, the 23rd Panzer Division were ready for the attack. The combat troops of the 6th Panzer Division had assembled without incident in the bridgehead north of Kotelnikovo. It was still dark. The occupied old sectors looked the same as ever. A sunny winter day dawned. The officers looked at their watches. They and their men were fully conscious of the significance of the approaching hour.

Suddenly the silence was disrupted by the sounds of explosions. All the guns of the division fired, and it almost seemed as if the shells were going to hit the assembling German troops. Involuntarily, everyone flinched and stooped, but the first salvo had already screamed over the heads of the men and was coming down on the Gremyachi station. The earth quivered from the explosion of the heavy shells. Stones, planks, and rails were hurled into the air. The salvo had hit the center of the enemy's chief strongpoint. This was the signal for the Witches' Sabbath which followed. Both corps were assigned to the *51st Army* during the Stalingrad operation.[15]

---

[15] When the offensive began on 12 December, Colonel-General Vasilevsky (General Staff coordinator for Stalingrad operations) was visiting HQ, *51st Army*, with Nikita Khrushchev. "He immediately perceived the danger" and attempted immediately to shift the *2nd Guards Corps* from Rokossovsky's *Don Front*. Rokossovkiy persuaded Stalin not to authorize the immediate move. The next day, Stalin conferred with Vasilevsky and agreed to allow the transfer on 15 December. By 19 December the *2nd Guards Corps* was in action. Zhukov, *Marshal Zhukov's Greatest Battles*, New York: Harper and Row, 1969), p. 184, note by by Harrison E. Salisbury, citing Vasilevsky and Rokossovky, *Stalingradskaya Epopeya* (Moscow: 1968), pp. 103–7, 172–3. The commander of the Stalingrad Front, Colonel-General Yeremenko, was also on the phone to Stalin. "There is a danger that Hoth may strike at the rear of our *Fifty-Seventh Army*, which is sealing off the south-western edge of the Stalingrad pocket. If, at the same time, Paulus attacks from inside the pocket, toward the south-west, it will be difficult to prevent him from breaking out." "Stalin was angry. 'You will hold out—we are getting reserves down to you,' he commanded menacingly. 'I'm sending you the *Second Guards Army*—the best unit I've left.'" Paul Carrell, *Hitler Moves East*, pp. 604–5.

While the artillery maintained a rapid rate of fire, the motors of the tanks were started. The majority of the tanks began to move. Like a spring tide, they overran the enemy position and advanced through the steppe in deep wedge formations. Their guns sent death and ruin into the fleeing enemy forces.[16]

So abrupt and forceful was the impact of the catastrophe on the surprised enemy that he was unable to rescue his heavy combat equipment. His light and heavy batteries stood intact in their firing positions. They had been enveloped and caught in the rear by German tanks before they had been able to fire an accurate round. The limbers which the Russians had moved up quickly had not reached the guns. The horse teams drawing them had fallen under the machine-gun fire. Horse-drawn limbers and ammunition carriers, which had overturned, continued to lie about for hours afterward. Horses which had survived were nibbling at the frozen steppe grass while standing in teams together with the bodies of those which had bled to death in the fire. Here and there, horse teams dragged a dead horse along. Blood on the snow marked their paths. The remnants of the Russian infantry had been scattered and had disappeared in the tall steppe grass as if they had been whisked away by a gust of wind.

By early morning, the command post of the Russian division had been reached and soon afterward that of the Russian corps. The enemy had been obliged to evacuate both these posts in great haste. As a result, he had been paralyzed in the conduct of his operations. The German motorcycle battalion, which had advanced east of the railroad, maintained contact with the 23rd Panzer Division, which had set out for its attack at the same time as the 6th Panzer Division and had advanced eighteen kilometers through the hilly region on both sides of the Kremoyarski Aksay River as far as Pimen-Cherni. In the beginning, it met with stubborn resistance from a Russian infantry division. After the 6th Panzer Division had severely defeated the main body of the Russian corps, however, the resistance offered by the Russian infantry division very soon decreased noticeably.[17]

The principal action had thus led to a complete success within a few hours. Now the moment had come for the German division to eliminate the threat to its flanks. For this purpose, the main bodies of the German panzer units, comprising approximately 100 tanks, turned westward as planned and attacked retreating enemy elements which had not been directly affected by the breakthrough. Everywhere there were rewarding objectives which held no danger for the tanks and could, therefore, be liquidated quickly. The numbers of captured Russian guns and other heavy weapons, as well as of horses and vehicles of all kinds, including field kitchens, increased by the hour.

A few hours before, the 2nd Battalion, 4th Panzergrenadier Regiment, had prepared the drama of Verkhne-Yablochny. The plan here provided for a feint attack from a

---

[16] "Show it to them; give it to them!" shouted Colonel Hünersdorff, as his 11th Panzer Regiment led off the attack at 0515 that morning. Quoted in William Craig, *Enemy at the Gates: The Battle for Stalingrad* (New York: Bantam Books, 1982), p. 210.

[17] Raus ruptured the enemy front at its weakest point—the point where the flanks of the already weakened *81st Cavalry Division* and *302nd Rifle Division* joined. See map 19, *Battle for Stalingrad*, p. 118.

Red Army BT-26 tanks destroyed in a Lithuanian town in the path of XVII Panzer Corps, late June 1941. (Courtesy Army Art Collection, US Army Center of Military History)

Red Army surprise: the superheavy KV-1 (right) and KV-2 (left). The appearance of these unknown model tanks came as a complete surprise to the Wehrmacht, which had no tank remotely as powerful or well-armored. It took all the tactical and leadership skills of the Panzertruppen and its flexible all-arms approach to combat to overcome these giants. For the 6th Panzer Division, the surprise came a few days after the German invasion of the Soviet Union, near the Lithuanian town of Rossienie. (Editor's Collection)

In the face of Soviet superheavy tanks, the Germans found that no antitank weapon on their inventory was of any use, except medium and heavy artillery in the direct-fire mode, and especially the magnificent 88mm dual-purpose gun, shown here advancing to the front. (Courtesy Army Art Collection, US Army Center of Military History)

Raus was everywhere at the right time and the right place as commander of Kampfgruppe Raus in the 6th Panzer Division's drive to seize the twin bridges over the Luga River in early July 1941: "Throughout the march I stayed with the advance guard battalion and at times also with the advance party." (Editor's Collection)

In defense of the twin bridges over the Luga River, Raus employed his dismounted motorized infantry superbly in the surrounding forests. (Courtesy Army Art Collection, US Army Center of Military History)

The days from September through November 1941 were heady with victories for Raus and the 6th Panzer Division as they broke down one barrier after another on the roads to Leningrad and Moscow, only to have each prize snatched from them by the decisions of the Supreme Warlord—Hitler. (Editor's Collection)

Freezing temperatures and Soviet reinforcements from the Far East stopped the 6th Panzer Division and the rest of the German Army as the Red Army turned on its heel and launched the great Moscow counter-offensive on 5 December 1941. Soviet cavalry were particularly adept at the rough winter going that confounded mechanization.

While detraining at the railroad hub of Kotelnikovo outside Stalingrad in late November 1942, the 4th Panzergrenadier Regiment was attacked by elements of the Soviet *4th Cavalry Corps.* The swift counterattack of the Panzergrenadiers in the railyard of the town crushed the Soviet cavalrymen. (Editor's Collection)

Raus's 6th Panzer Division smashed the Red Army's *4th Cavalry Corps*'s two Central Asian cavalry divisions in swift actions around the railroad hub of Kotelnikovo on the road to Stalingrad in late November, and on 6 December 1942 in the action he dubbed the "Cannae of Pokhlebin" (Courtesy Army Art Collection, US Army Center of Military History)

"The attempts on the part of the ever-increasing masses of enemy cavalry to cross this stream in an easterly direction were balked by the combined German artillery fire, which hit the Russians simultaneously from the strongpoints in the south, east and west, thus breaking their aggressive spirit."— Raus. (Courtesy Army Art Collection, US Army Center of Military History)

A knocked-out Soviet BT-26 tank and its frozen crew from the *51st Army*, part of the trail of wreckage left by the 6th Panzer Division in its drive 'to liberate Stalingrad' in December 1942. (Courtesy Army Art Collection, US Army Center of Military History)

The Panzergrenadiers of the 4th and 114th Panzergrenadier Regiments demonstrated prodigious valor against overwhelming numbers in the fighting to relieve Stalingrad. (Editor's Collection)

The center of the "revolving battle" in the drive to Stalingrad was the village of Verkhniy-Kumskiy, which was reached first by the Germans and was held by them until the end of the operation. The Panzergrenadiers of the 2nd Battalion, 114th Panzergrenadier Regiment, held the village against repeated attacks until the end of the operation, while the 11th Panzer Regiment maneuvered around it, taking a great toll on Soviet tank and mechanized forces. (Courtesy Army Art Collection, US Army Center of Military History)

Under leaders like Erhard Raus, the German motorized infantry were a vital part of the panzer army. (Courtesy Army Art Collection, US Army Center of Military History)

The tank brigades of the *2nd Guards Army* were Stalin's prize reserve and were thrown into the 6th Panzer Division's path to stop its attack to relieve the garrison of Stalingrad, only to be ground up by the 6th Panzer, well-supported by the Luftwaffe. It was a brilliant example of the lethality of the German combined attack, wielded by one of the finest generals of World War II. (Courtesy Army Art Collection, US Army Center of Military History)

The defense of Kharkov after the Battle of Kursk in the late summer of 1943 by Raus's XI Corps ignited desperate fighting along the line of the Donets River north of the city as the Germans drove back one attempt after another by several Soviet armies to breach their defenses. (Editor's Collection)

Raus's skilled use of panzer and antitank forces in the defense of Kharkov in August 1943 took an enormous toll of the *5th Guards Tank Army*, fresh from its victory at Kursk the month before. (Courtesy Army Art Collection, US Army Center of Military History)

Raus employed the 6th Panzer Division, now back under his command in the defense of Kharkov, to wipe out a Soviet unit that had penetrated the city and seized part of the huge factory that produced spare parts for the German Army. (Editor's Collection)

SS Infantry attacks. In early February 1945, on Hitler's orders, the weak and outnumbered 11th SS Panzer Army attacked far superior Soviet forces. Though not in command of the operation, Raus vehemently advised against it to Himmler, but to no avail. (Courtesy Army Art Collection, US Army Center of Military History)

A destroyed German Panther Mark V. Referring to the ill-advised attack of the 11th SS Panzer Army, Raus wrote: "After achieving insignificant initial success, it came to a standstill on the second day with the loss of many of our tanks," just as he had predicted. (Editor's Collection)

southerly direction against the long, stretched-out village. This attack was to simulate the presence of strong forces and induce the enemy to commit the remnants of his cavalry corps situated between the Don River and Yablochny in the defense of the endangered village. In addition, this maneuver was to divert the enemy's attention from the German armored forces which, situated to the north of the enemy, were threatening to annihilate him.

In accordance with these tactics, the 2nd Battalion, 4th Panzergrenadier Regiment, undertook a surprise attack on the hostile covering parties situated opposite it. The enemy were at once overrun and scattered in various directions. Stragglers entering the village spread grossly exaggerated news of the advance of heavy German forces toward Verkhne-Yablochny, as a result of which the Russian garrisons in this village and in the villages situated along the lower Aksay and Don Rivers were alerted. The German Air Force, which was very active that day, soon afterward reported considerable activity in all villages occupied by the enemy and a heavy reinforcement of the enemy positions on the southern edge of Verkhne-Yablochny.

The attack of the German infantry made rapid headway. The plan to feign the presence of strong forces and the necessity of advancing in open terrain covered by a thin layer of snow called for broad and deep echelonment of the troops. Occasional weak fire from a light Russian battery in no way impeded the progress of the movement. The machine-gun fire setting in as the Germans came closer to the village was much more unpleasant, since it forced the German infantrymen to the ground and made it necessary for them to use their heavy weapons.

The manner of advancing, too, had to be changed. In order to avoid excessive losses, the alternate rushing forward of whole groups was discontinued. Instead, the men were ordered to work their way forward individually from cover to cover. This practice of creeping up, which had been adopted from the enemy, was familiar to the German infantrymen, who were well versed in Eastern combat methods. Favored by the steppe grass protruding from the snow, scouts and a few patrols were able, during the morning hours, to advance almost as far as the edge of the village which the enemy was stubbornly defending and in which he was constantly reinforcing his troops. According to reports from German air and ground reconnaissance, there was a continuous movement of numerous small groups of enemy forces from the Don and Aksay Rivers along the Fedorova Stream to Verkhne-Yablochny. By noon, the whole German battalion had worked its way to within a few hundred meters of the village. Its chief concern was its left flank, which the enemy was able to threaten and attack from the west with infantry as well as with tanks. Hence, the flank was protected by a deeply echeloned reserve and a tank platoon.

But the remnants of the Russian cavalry corps had still not quite recovered from the blow which had been dealt them scarcely a week before. They were not ready to think of offensive action. They were content with hastening to the aid of their comrades in threatened Verkhne-Yablochny. Thus, they did precisely what the Germans desired them to do: they fell into the trap. However, the Germans still feared that the enemy would draw the only correct conclusion from the defeat of the adjacent corps, which had already occurred by that time, namely to withdraw hurriedly northward or westward. Had they withdrawn northward, the German tanks would have pushed into a void and would have had the enemy in their flank again the next day. The result would have been a regrettable loss of time. If the enemy withdrew in the direction of the Don River, the infantry battalion would have had to follow him there and the armored force would have been obliged to double the speed of its thrust in order to be able to destroy this enemy force on the Don River in time.

As yet, there was still time for the enemy force to elude the German blow. But it had neither realized the threat to its rear nor received orders to withdraw. Accordingly, it continued in its staunch defense of the village against all penetration attempts on the part of the German infantry. Here and there, German combat patrols captured a house which the enemy was defending or a section of trench which the enemy recaptured with the aid of tanks. The German infantry had to feign eager attempts to capture the town until German armored forces appeared in the rear of the enemy.

Every hour seemed endless. It took the tanks a long time to bypass a swamp east of the town and to assemble for the decisive stroke, which they did with their front toward the south behind a range of hills. They were able to do this barely one hour before nightfall. With their flanks echeloned forward, they stormed ahead in a wild chase. Innumerable tank turrets appeared in the steppe grass. Immediately thereafter, the tanks rattled down the slope. Muzzle flashes and thundering bursts from numerous guns gave an indication of the enemy's ruin. His efforts to throw his few tanks and defense weapons against the new adversary in order to keep the way to the west open for his men were in vain. It was too late.

After a short, unequal struggle, ten of his fourteen tanks went up in flames. The columns of their fires and the blazes of Russian strongpoints situated in burning houses colored the evening sky a deep crimson. A field of debris formed from demolished huts, weapons and equipment buried the Russian garrison. The tanks had done a perfect job. But they disappeared again as quickly as they had come, in order to continue their main thrust toward the north.

The German infantry battalion, which had witnessed the tragedy from dugouts, encountered scarcely any resistance when mopping up the town. Afterward, it was reassembled and was available for a new assignment. The few surviving Turkestan riders were taken prisoner. Only four tanks and a few stragglers managed to fight their way westward.

On the following morning, the last enemy tanks were disabled by a German antiaircraft battery which had awaited them in ambush on a hill situated north of the captured town, as they were about to reconnoiter the situation of the defeated adjacent corps. Now every threat had been eliminated. The thrust sideways had been a complete success. It had cleared the flank.

Example 6: The Armored "Revolving Battle"[18] at Verkhniy-Kumskiy, 13 December 1942

The 11th Panzer Regiment had a right to be proud of its achievements on 12 December. In a single day, it had won two battles and fought its way forward for a distance of 70 kilometers without sustaining losses. This was a favorable prelude to the Stalingrad operation; but it was still far from a triumph. The objective was still far off, and the hard battles were yet to come. The task of defeating the hostile armored forces, who were numerically greatly superior and blocked the way north, seemed almost insoluble to the German command.

Behind the northern arm of the Aksay River, the "Popov" Russian *3rd Tank Army*,[19] which was very ably led, stood ready to attack and destroy the German relieving forces as they crossed the river. It had neither used the "golden bridge" of Kotelnikovo nor entered the fighting of 12 December, in order to avoid dissipating its forces. But its positions were spread over a large area, thus offering the German attackers a chance to gain local superiority each time they attacked and defeated its various elements successively.

These thoughts gave rise to the decision to push forward during the night of 12 December across the northern branch of the Aksay River and into the hilly region surrounding Verkhniy-Kumskiy, using all the armored elements of the division in order to defeat the hostile armored forces wherever they were found. This plan greatly exceeded the mission assigned by the army, which provided that on this day the troops were to pursue the enemy as far as the Aksay River and that they were to form a bridgehead. The fact that the intended operation was dangerous and might lead to an unusual situation was no reason for shrinking from its execution. Its objective was not the capture of a village or the defense of an area; on the contrary, the objective was to weaken the enemy while keeping the German losses as small as possible and to continue to do this until the German tanks outnumbered those of the enemy and were thus able to defeat them. Accordingly, the German tactics consisted of defeating the various enemy elements separately, eluding a defeat, and maintaining the initiative.

In view of the heavy demands made on the German troops on the previous day, a brief rest was ordered, during which the armored units refueled their tanks and received supplies. Soon afterward, they resumed their advance. It was still dark. Only the pale light of the stars made it possible to identify, from a very close range, the dim outlines of the tanks and their dark trail in the thin layer of snow. The rattle of their tracks was suddenly heard in the previously silent steppe. It aroused the enemy, who was just trying to close

---

[18] The German term is *Drehschlacht.*

[19] General-Lieutenant M. M. Popov commanded the *5th Shock Army*, which was coming into the line north of the Aksay River on the right flank of the *2nd Guards Army* and *51st Army*. Had the 6th Panzer Division penetrated any further, it undoubtedly would have met this strong force. The author's continued mistaken references to the *3rd Tank Army* indicate that the Red Army's deception efforts were successful, or that German military intelligence was doing a poor job of analysis, or that the author's memory had gone astray (an understandable failing).—Editor.

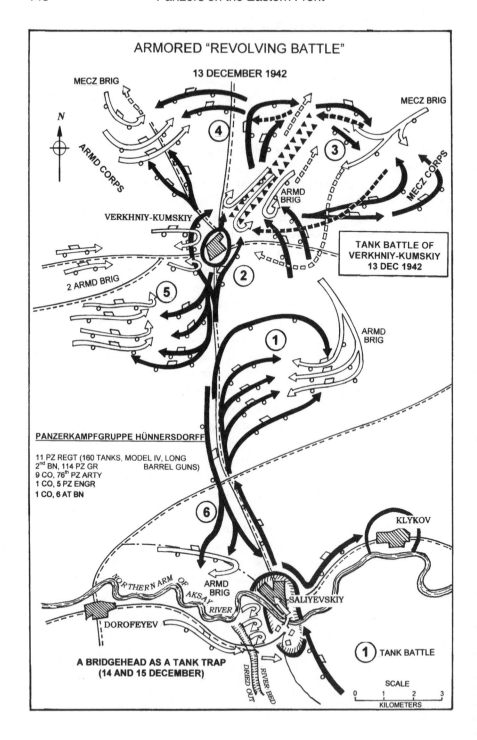

ARMORED "REVOLVING BATTLE"

13 DECEMBER 1942

MECZ BRIG

MECZ BRIG

N

ARMD CORPS

MECZ CORPS

ARMD BRIG

VERKHNIY-KUMSKIY

TANK BATTLE OF VERKHNIY-KUMSKIY 13 DEC 1942

2 ARMD BRIG

ARMD BRIG

PANZERKAMPFGRUPPE HÜNNERSDORFF

11 PZ REGT (160 TANKS, MODEL IV, LONG
2nd BN, 114 PZ GR   BARREL GUNS)
9 CO, 76th PZ ARTY
1 CO, 5 PZ ENGR
1 CO, 6 AT BN

KLYKOV

NORTHERN ARM OF AKSAY RIVER

ARMD BRIG

SALIYEVSKIY

DOROFEYEV

A BRIDGEHEAD AS A TANK TRAP
(14 AND 15 DECEMBER)

RIVER BED DRIED OUT

① TANK BATTLE

SCALE
0   1   2   3
KILOMETERS

the gap caused by the German breakthrough north of Chilikovo. Since the enemy had lost his antitank weapons on the previous day, it was possible for the German tanks to overrun Russian forces without any loss of time. It would be the task of the German infantry units following behind to come to grips with them. By the first light of dawn, the armored points had reached the northern arm of the Aksay River and were looking for a crossing point. After they had been searching for some time, they discovered a ford at Saliyevskiy and crossed the river. The 1st Battalion, 4th Panzergrenadier Regiment, followed up immediately and formed a bridgehead. Soon afterward, the engineers began to build a bridge. The 6th Motorcycle Battalion threw the enemy back north of Chilikovo and across the railroad. It protected the right flank, since movements of Russian tanks and trucks had been observed on the southern bank of the Aksay River. The 1st Battalion, 114th Panzergrenadier Regiment, had driven the enemy from the rolling terrain west of Chilikovo and was now occupying this region and protecting it from attack from the west.

As though they had been "fired from a rocket," the German tanks now pushed northward. The thrust "hit the enemy in the heart" and upset his plans. This was the starting point of the dramatic struggle for Stalingrad. Only by defeating the enemy, who was twice as strong as the Germans, would the way to Stalingrad be open. The commanders of the armored forces on both sides knew this. Accordingly, they brought to bear all their strength, courage, and ability in an effort to be victorious. The result of this awareness of the significance of their actions was the armored "revolving battle" around Verkhniy-Kumskiy, in which 500 tanks were engaged for ten hours in a bitter struggle.

The center of this "revolving battle" was the village of Verkhniy-Kumskiy, which was reached first by the Germans and was held by them until the end. Supported by the mechanized units employed there (2nd Battalion, 114th Panzergrenadier Regiment; 1st Company, 6th Reconnaissance Battalion; 1st Company, 57th Engineer Battalion; 9th Heavy Battery, 76th Artillery Regiment), the whole of the 11th Panzer Regiment had full freedom of action and was to exploit its advantage of being able to fight on interior lines. As a result, at all times and in all places, it arrived ahead of the enemy, to whom all passages leading through Verkhniy-Kumskiy remained blocked. The German regiment enjoyed the further advantage of having a more flexible command than the Russians, which was due to the fact that the radio equipment in the German tanks was more modern. On the other hand, the enemy had at his disposal twice as many tanks, and these were fully a match for the German tanks. Moreover, the Russian tanks were followed by numerically superior infantry forces, which, however, arrived on the battlefield relatively late.

First Phase

The course of this tank battle was just as unusual as the situation from which it took its start. The immediate objective of the reinforced German panzer regiment was Verkhniy-

Kumskiy. The valley of the Aksay River was still veiled by ground fog, which even the first light of dawn was not able to penetrate. Tank after tank forded the river and rolled northward. A column apparently without end moved toward its target. The country and the cart roads between the Aksay River and Verkhniy-Kumskiy were passable for track-laying vehicles and wheeled vehicles of all kinds.

When the beginning of the column had reached the hilly range south of Verkhniy-Kumskiy, the first rays of the sun were breaking through the haze. The steppe spread peacefully before the eyes of the Germans. The large village of Verkhniy-Kumskiy, whose outlines it was now possible to make out clearly, lay in the valley. German reconnaissance tanks had already reached it and had reported it to be clear of the enemy. At a rise in the ground identified as Point 140,[20] which was situated west of the route of advance, German covering parties had already been posted. They were not in contact with the enemy. Suddenly, the following message was received from armored reconnaissance elements situated at Hill 147 west of the advance route: "There is a heavy concentration of hostile tanks in a broad depression south of here. More tanks are following."

The situation was clear: the enemy had been roused by the appearance of the strong column of German tanks and was throwing his nearest available force against it. This was a Russian tank brigade which intended to push into the flank of the German column and tie it down. The Russians planned to have another of their tank brigades, which was approaching Verkhniy-Kumskiy, attack the flanks and the rear of the German tanks as the latter turned eastward, and to defeat them.

The Russians, however, underestimated the striking power and the flexibility of the German tanks. Even before the enemy had completed his assembly south of Hill 147, he attacked the German flank with concentrated force. But no sooner had his troops reached the edge of the depression than the guns of 60 tanks, which had moved into position behind a low range of hills in the vicinity, suddenly began to fire at them. The enemy stopped his advance immediately. More than a dozen hostile tanks which had come in full view of the German gunners were set ablaze. The other tanks withdrew into the depression in order to escape a similar fate.

The German tanks pushed after them and formed a wide ring around the depression. A concentric attack began; it ended with the complete encirclement of the Russian brigade by German forces which, after lunging north and south, now had met again. The enemy tanks, which were caught in an extremely tight pocket, formed an all-round defense system and offered fierce resistance. Their attempts to break out toward the east remained fruitless. Shells from German tanks hit them from all sides and prevented their escape.

The unequal battle was soon over. The enemy tank brigade had perished heroically at the precise spot where, an hour before, it had triumphantly assembled for its attack.

---

[20] Apparently not of sufficient height to be designated a hill.—Reviewer.

More than 70 Russian tanks remained on the field. The guns were still turned menacingly toward all sides against the Germans. The enemy attack ended in a "tank graveyard" which continued to impress both friend and foe for a long time to come. It was often mistaken by Russian and German aircraft for a tank assembly area and bombed by both. Many a soldier was terrified when he suddenly came on this mass of enemy tanks and, then, deeply moved when he realized his error, raised his hand to the salute.

Second Phase

The battles south of Hill 147 were still raging when German armored elements at the end of the column began to enter Verkhniy-Kumskiy, which they occupied before the enemy arrived. Soon afterward, however, they were engaged in combat with the hostile tanks hurrying to the scene to help the encircled tank brigade, whose calls for support they had received. As a result of the advance of the Russian tanks, the German elements were compelled to withdraw to the northern edge of the village, which, since here they were supported by a constant flow of reinforcements, they were able to hold. Under their protection, the mechanized units now also moved up and took over the defense of the village.

As a result, the German armored forces again became available for a flexible conduct of operations. This was desirable since the Russians had already tried to drive their tanks past Verkhniy-Kumskiy on both sides in order to be able to take part in the battle on Hill 147 in time. By means of skillful maneuvering and rapid redistribution of forces, the German tanks, although outnumbered, managed again and again to prevent the enemy from enveloping them.

However, the situation became critical when the two Russian armored units were joined by a third which pushed forward on the eastern flank, thereby threatening to cut off the German panzer force which had advanced as far as Verkhniy-Kumskiy from the main body of the German tanks. Suddenly, the din of the tank battle on the hilly range located south of the village ceased. Apparently the fighting had been decided there. But nowhere were enemy tanks seen to withdraw. Was it possible that the enemy had succeeded?

Just then the commander of the German panzer regiment radioed for the German tanks to try and hold out, and that his forces were coming to the rescue. The hearts of all the men leaped. To them it meant victory. Indeed, the familiar outlines of German tanks were already appearing on both sides of Hill 147. Their number constantly increased. At top speed, four wedge formations of tanks raced down the slopes; more and more appeared on the horizon.

The enemy became visibly uneasy. For quite some time, no radio messages had come in from his advance brigade on Hill 147. Now the German tanks suddenly poured down into the valley in large numbers. The enemy knew that this meant a first defeat which threatened to be followed by a second one. The situation called for immediate action; no time was to be lost. Both the German and the Russian commanders understood this, and, as a result, all radio messages were sent in clear. The Russians in front of Verkhniy-Kumskiy sent out repeated calls for help. Finally there was an answer: "Mechanized brigade on way; hold out, hold out!"

Meanwhile, the points of the German armored wedges had already reached the valley. From Hill 147, it was possible to observe that they were carrying out their orders accurately. The officers were aware of the necessity of acting quickly if a decision at Verkhniy was to be brought about before the arrival of the hostile mechanized brigade. The plan behind the German attack, which consisted in a double envelopment of the enemy while holding on to Verkhniy-Kumskiy, began to materialize on the battlefield. The enemy, too, recognized the plan of the German tanks. He tried in vain to increase the length of his front in order to escape envelopment by the Germans. Again and again he was prevented from doing so by heavy fire and by the tanks pushing forward from Verkhniy-Kumskiy. The German tanks had already reached his flanks and were tightly compressing his armored forces. Still the enemy kept trying to eliminate the threat to his flanks by bending them back. The German pressure, however, constantly increased, and at the same time the Russian flanks drew out more and more and their protection became weaker and weaker. What was the use of the promised aid unless it came in time?

By now, the German tanks had already appeared in the enemy's rear to block his last route of retreat, a deep sunken road. But their number was small and a breakthrough to the rear was still possible. Soon it would be too late. The enemy's losses were already very high. Further resistance might spell his ruin. These considerations apparently induced the enemy to withdraw. He took advantage of the last chance he had of escaping utter destruction and broke contact with the Germans. Sacrificing the covering parties of their flanks and their rearguard, the latter being overtaken and crushed by the German left wing, the defeated remnants made good their escape through the sunken road leading northeastward.

This brigade, too, had now been beaten. It had lost 35 to 40 tanks and could no longer be considered a dangerous adversary. The remaining tanks, however, might still regain a certain importance if they reinforced the mechanized brigade which was on its way. Hence the victory was not a total one, although it did constitute another severe blow for the enemy.

Third Phase

The radio messages coming from east and west in rapid succession, and intercepted with increasing frequency, seemed to presage a simultaneous concentric attack by numerically superior forces. These forces consisted of armored units and motorized infantry to which Verkhniy-Kumskiy had again and again been assigned as an objective which was to be reached as soon as possible. The reason was that the German Panzer Kampfgruppe Hünersdorff, which had penetrated 20 kilometers deep into the assembly area of the Russian corps and had done great damage there, had to be eliminated as soon as possible. The Russian forces were still adequate for this task.

The German armored unit commander (Colonel von Hünersdorff), however, who was accustomed to think calmly even in the heat of battle, had already been informed of the enemy situation by air reconnaissance, and realized that the strong adversary coming from the west would not be able to arrive at the scene for the next hour or two. Making a quick decision, he had his forces attack the mechanized brigade which approached from the northeast around noon. First he attacked the armored elements of this brigade on the west flank, and, when they had turned to meet the attack, he pushed through a depression which shielded him from sight and had the main body of his force attack the Russians in the rear. In the resulting confusion, the motorized Russian infantry following behind the armored elements withdrew across country in a northwesterly direction and escaped the German attempt to "strangle" them. The enemy tanks, on the other hand, suffered heavy losses in the crossfire of the numerically superior German units and retired after offering heroic resistance. Even the Russian forces which were approaching from the northwest to give help and which had already come into contact with German armored reconnaissance elements arrived too late. They were no longer able to avert the defeat of the mechanized brigade.

Fourth Phase

Soon afterward, the newly arrived Russian force, which also was a mechanized brigade, veered northeastward in order to attack the German Kampfgruppe in the rear. But it unexpectedly ran up against a defensive front made up of well-protected German tanks. These had been detached from the German forces pursuing the first mechanized brigade, had pivoted at an angle of 180 degrees, and were now blocking any further advance by the Russians. A bitter tank duel took place in which the Russian tanks, which had advanced without cover, suffered considerable losses. Although, soon afterward, the German tanks were attacked in the rear by motorized enemy infantry and were taken under fire by antitank guns, they bravely held their ground. They had been told by the commander of the Kampfgruppe to hold out until he could come to their aid with the majority of the tanks. The situation, however, was becoming very critical owing to the hostile armored forces which were coming closer and closer from the west.

The main body of the German force, which now likewise pivoted around through an angle of 180 degrees, selected the route through Verkhniy-Kumskiy. Here enemy armored points were already engaged in combat with the German garrison. Hostile artillery, firing from the west, also entered the fighting for the village. The German 150mm howitzer battery committed in the defense of the village returned the fire and soon silenced the enemy guns. Individual enemy tanks which had come too close to the village had already been liquidated by German antitank guns, even before the main body of the German armored force arrived.

A few tanks from the main body drove back the enemy's armored advance guard in a quick thrust, while the majority of the tanks pushed on through the village and continued straight into the flank of the second Russian mechanized brigade so quickly that the latter scarcely had time to form a new defensive front. Attacked on both sides of the road by two strong German panzer wedges, and under heavy attack also by the northern German force, the enemy was compelled to retreat. More than 30 enemy tanks were left on the battlefield.

Fifth Phase

In the meantime, strong motorized enemy forces, which their infantry had dismounted, had approached the village and took it under fire with mortars and machine guns. Infantry guns, too, were active. Under the protection of their heavy weapons, the infantrymen filtered closer and closer to the village, which they soon hemmed in from the north and the east. In addition, Russian tanks had resumed their attacks and were making rapid headway on the road from the west. A few hostile combat patrols had actually entered the village, but they had either been liquidated in bitter fighting or been driven out of the village.

The situation became critical when some T-34 tanks broke into the village and destroyed a number of heavy artillery and antitank guns before close-in antitank teams of the German engineer company were able to liquidate them. To make the predicament worse, radio messages were arriving from the reconnaissance tanks to the effect that strong hostile armored forces were advancing on Point 140, which was situated southwest of the village. It was the enemy's intention to occupy Verkhniy-Kumskiy and the hills south of the village, in order to cut off the Kampfgruppe from its route of retreat and to destroy it. This was the enemy's final desperate attempt to offset, before the day drew to a close, the severe defeats which he had suffered previously by a decisive victory.

Kampfgruppe Hünersdorff, however, after its successful operation against the second Russian mechanized brigade, had quickly turned around and now its massed tanks broke through the enemy's encirclement. Without delay, they attacked the hostile armored forces, which reached Point 140 at the same time they did. Here the heaviest clash of the day occurred. More and more Russian armored forces ran up against the strong front of the German units, but each time they were stopped by the fire of the German tanks.

The enemy, however, did not give up his attacks. Finally, he staked everything on one card. Heavily concentrated and echeloned in depth, all his tanks rolled forward like a huge wave about to swallow up the German forces. This mass attack, too, was stopped in the hail of fire of more than 100 German tank guns. The German armored unit commander had waited for this favorable moment to play his trump.

After having held back his panzer reserve all this time, he now used it to counterattack. He undertook a surprise thrust into the enemy's flank and caused his lines to waver. Now the German defensive front also attacked. After engaging in bitter close fighting, the enemy's main force finally flooded back. Countless wrecks of tanks covered the scene of this heavy struggle, and were eloquent testimony of the proportions of the enemy's defeat.

Meanwhile, the defenders of Verkhniy-Kumskiy, who had again been encircled in the village, were in a very distressing situation. Enemy forces attacked the village from all sides. More weapons were disabled and ammunition became scarce. So far, brave German infantrymen had still managed to finish off the penetrating Russian tanks by means of magnetic antitank hollow charges, but new tanks used from ambush always took their place. Nevertheless, the German troops did not yield a single inch of ground to the enemy's motorized infantry. The calls for help from Verkhniy-Kumskiy did not escape the attention of the commander of the German panzer regiment, although his forces were engaged in heavy battle. No sooner had they achieved victory than they pushed northward again to help their comrades.[21] For the second time, the German panzer regiment broke through the encirclement and freed the garrison in the village.

Afterward, the garrison was escorted on both sides by the weapons and vehicles of the armored forces while they moved together toward the bridgehead at Saliyevskiy. On the hills situated south of the village, the enemy once again tried to block the progress of the Kampfgruppe, but the panzer regiment quickly opened up an exit toward the south and formed a rearguard to prevent the enemy from harassing the movement any further.

The unexpected thrust across the Aksay River by the German tanks had induced both friend and foe to dispatch strong air forces to the scene. First, Russian bomber wings and fighter planes had hastened to the aid of their distressed armored units. They circled over the battlefield at lower and lower altitudes in order to identify their targets clearly. But their efforts to distinguish the enemy's troops from their own in the rapidly changing picture of the battle were futile. The same thing happened to the German planes.[22] Both Germans and Russians finally were obliged to attack less rewarding targets, of which many were to be found on supply roads and on the open steppe. There the bombs went down in large numbers, causing the officers great concern for their vehicles. Actually, however, things were not half as bad as they seemed. The trucks maintained large distances between each other, and as a result, the effect of the attacks was very limited.

---

[21] Apparently the situation was a little more tense than Raus indicates. "Colonel Hünersdorff appeared in the midst of his weary troops. Leaning out of his tank, he screamed: 'You want to be my regiment? Is that what you call an attack? I am ashamed of this day!' He kept it up, hurling invective on all sides, and his soldiers reacted with cold rage. Some openly questioned his right to tell them how to fight. But Hünersdorff's motive was to galvanize his tankers. This he did. His tirade was followed by another desperate call from Verkhne-Kumski. Hünersdorff gave the order to burst into the village 'at maximum speed whatever the losses,' and five companies formed a column with the few tanks carrying armor-piercing shells leading the way. Still furious at Hünersdorff, the panzer crews roared ahead, spraying the fields on both sides with indiscriminate machine-gun fire. The unorthodox approach terrified the Russians, who jumped up and ran wildly across the plains. Inside their Mark IVs, the Germans assumed that the Russians thought they were insane." Craig, *Enemy at the Gates*, pp. 218–19.

[22] An account of the fighting presents a more positive impression of the Luftwaffe's contribution. "The effect of the Stuka bombing was devastating. The tanks wildly drove into each other and tried to seek cover in the Yablochnaya Ravine. The Stukas renewed their attacks in the afternoon and continued until darkness fell." From *Fire Point (6th Panzer Divison)* (Krefeld, 1977), quoted in Haupt, *op.cit.*, p. 216.

The raging armored battle tempted the air forces into an effort to join in it directly, but since the respective strengths of the air forces kept increasing, their attacks on each other became more and more vehement. Around noon, the fighting developed into a three-dimensional "revolving battle" involving the air and ground forces. The Russian bomber wings outnumbered the German, but the German fighter planes inflicted severe losses on them time and again and eventually repulsed them. On the ground and in the air, the same strength ratio prevailed and the same tactics were employed. The "revolving battle" in progress on the ground found its true reflection in the battle being fought in the skies. Above and below, the result was the same: the Germans were victorious.

It was already getting dark by the time the last planes disappeared and the point of the German armored column was sighted by the men in the German bridgehead. The latter had repulsed two hostile attacks in the course of the day, thus frustrating the enemy's intention of seizing the bridgehead and stopping the movement of supplies for the panzer Kampfgruppe.

The third attack was just in progress when a multitude of tanks descended from the hills south of Verkhniy-Kumskiy. The bridgehead would have been lost if these tanks, as was first feared, had been a hostile force. But they were German, and they arrived just in time to attack the rear of a hostile armored brigade which was hammering violently at the gates of the bridgehead. In the prevailing semidarkness, the German force managed to incapacitate several fleeing Russian tanks and to thwart the enemy's plan.

The unique armored "revolving battle" was over. Its end was as unusual as its beginning. To the enemy's great surprise, the German armored forces again withdrew to the Aksay River, in spite of the successes they had achieved. The enemy did not dare to pursue them or to launch a counterattack of his own during the following days. He was content to have his motorized infantry occupy the hills south of Verkhniy-Kumskiy. Later on, it was discovered that the enemy had lost more than half his tanks in this heavy struggle. That was the main reason for his reluctance to attack again. Moreover, he was unable to find a plausible explanation for the voluntary withdrawal of the German tanks, and regarded it as a feint designed to lure him into a trap. In reality, the shortage of fuel and ammunition and the situation of the main body of the German division made it impossible for the German armored forces to advance across the Aksay River. Furthermore, the purpose of the unusual thrust had been achieved. The armored "revolving battle" had broken the enemy's backbone and had achieved a numerical superiority for the German tanks.

Example 7: A Bridgehead as a Tank Trap, 13–15 December 1942

In order to shield the rear of the German armored forces which had advanced across the Aksay River, and to protect their long supply routes, the 1st Battalion, 4th Panzergrenadiers, which had been attached to these forces, had formed a bridgehead covering both banks of the Aksay River. At the same time, two engineer companies had begun to build a bridge. Within a few hours, a military bridge which was passable even for tanks had been erected. Upon completion of the bridge, the two above-mentioned companies, which belonged to the 57th Engineer Battalion, and the tank destruction training battalion,[23] which was also attached to the 57th Engineer Battalion, assumed the task of securing the northern bridgehead. The 1st Battalion, 4th Panzergrenadier Regiment, reinforced by an antitank platoon, was now able to concentrate its entire forces in the southern bridgehead and thus strengthen the latter substantially.

As a result of the unusual situation of the division, the southern bridgehead was the more vulnerable sector. North of the Aksay River, the enemy forces were tied down by the armored "revolving battle" at Verkhniy-Kumskiy. South of the river, on the other hand, it was temporarily necessary to detach a battalion for the support of the adjacent division and to employ the remaining battalions in various sectors. There they became involved in combat with elements of the Russian infantry corps which had been defeated on the previous day. These elements still controlled the region up to the Aksay River.

On the morning of 13 December, enemy infantry, escorted by a few tanks, appeared at the west flank of the southern bridgehead. It assembled along the lower course of a deep, dried-out river bed which, lined by tall shrubbery, stretched for several kilometers alongside the supply route of the German division and which German troops had not yet been able to mop up. Since the Russian tanks were unable to cross the river bed, which was three to four meters deep and five to ten meters wide, they fired through gaps in the shrubbery at the German truck convoys moving toward Saliyevskiy. As a result, it was necessary for the supply traffic to use a detour avoiding the point under enemy fire and to reach the bridgehead from the east.

After the Russians had failed to stop the movement of supplies in this manner as they had intended, they attacked the bridgehead around noon with two battalions which, supported by the fire of their armor from the bank, advanced across the dried-out river bed. Their attack, however, was stopped by lively fire from the German infantry. A German counterattack presently threw them back across the river bed. In the afternoon, the enemy repeated his attack and reached the eastern bank of the river bed. Eight to ten tanks thereupon advanced from the bed of the river. To the surprise of the German defenders, the enemy had managed to move his tanks across the river bed through the use of field expedients. Although they were met with heavy fire from all weapons and immediately sustained losses, they overran the German infantry and pushed over the Aksay bridge into the village. However, the hostile infantry which tried to follow the tanks was soon forced to take cover as a result of intense fire and finally became separated from the tanks. Soon afterward, there were heavy detonations in the village. The tanks were silent; six columns of smoke and fire gave clues as to their end. Not a single tank managed to escape from the scene. The German tank destruction training elements had done a good job.

---

[23] Used for demonstrations and the like.

A third attempt on the part of the enemy to advance on Saliyevskiy, this time by means of an enemy armored movement during twilight, also failed. This unit had the misfortune to clash with the strong Panzer Kampfgruppe Hünersdorff, which was just returning from the "revolving battle" at Verkhniy-Kumskiy. The previous example has described how the Russian unit lost several tanks in this clash and was able to escape destruction only by a hasty retreat.

Nevertheless, the enemy attacked the southern bridgehead on three more occasions with newly arrived armored and infantry forces, twice on 14 December and once on 15 December. Each time, the German infantrymen in their narrow trenches and deep dugouts were run over by the tanks without suffering the slightest injury. As experienced fighters in the East, they also had long since been immune to the shock effect of hostile tanks. As soon as the black monsters were past, the heads of the German infantrymen appeared, and devastating machine-gun fire swept across the open battlefield, forcing the Russian infantry following the tanks to return to its line of departure or remain motionless in shallow depressions in the sand until the fall of darkness. Both courses of action involved heavy losses. Hostile detachments which, by following close behind the tanks, reached the German positions or crossed them were liquidated in close-in fighting or taken prisoner.

Out of the eight to twelve tanks reaching the village during each attack, not a single one returned to its line of departure. They were not able to use the village street, which was blocked by the burned-out wrecks of their predecessors. Hence, they tried to force a way to the center of the village from the side, through the gaps between groups of houses. Wherever such a possibility existed, however, German tank destruction elements had been systematically distributed. Hidden in houses or camouflaged in holes which the Russian tank crews drove over unsuspectingly, they awaited the approach of their victims and, at the proper moment, attacked them with magnetic antitank hollow charges. A thunderous blast, usually followed by a jet of flame, signaled the abrupt end of each tank and its crew. Even if one or the other of the tanks did manage to escape a German destruction team and continue its advance, it was all the more certain to fall into the hands of the next team. Moreover, the Germans, who had emplaced a few well-camouflaged antitank and antiaircraft guns in readiness and had also laid mines, were able to give a good reception to any tank which might try to approach the village from the north, and to give a proper send-off to any tank trying to escape in this direction.

In this manner, the Saliyevsky bridgehead was turned into an organized tank trap which twenty hostile tanks entered but none was able to leave. The mysterious tank destruction teams became the terror of all enemy tank crews who had the habit of driving their tanks singly or in small groups through villages, forests, or shrubbery in order to avoid German antitank guns, antiaircraft guns, and airplanes. How good the achievements of these well-trained, courageous men were appears alone from the fact that 15 percent of all the Russian tanks incapacitated in the thrust for the liberation of Stalingrad were credited to the tank destruction teams. Their most brilliant achievement, however, was the destruction of all the hostile tanks which entered the tank trap of Saliyevsky during the three days of fighting to keep open the supply route.

Example 8: Lunge into the Void
by Two Panzer Regiments, 16 December 1942

During the fighting of the last few days, the Panzer Kampfgruppe of the German division had been deliberately spared. After the heavy armored battle of 13 December, the tanks of the Kampfgruppe needed a brief reconditioning, which they underwent in the Klykov area on the northern bank of the Aksay River. It was there that the division had also moved its command post.

By 16 December, all minor damage to the tanks had been repaired, and 22 out of the 30 tanks which had been incapacitated at Verkhniy-Kumskiy were fit for reemployment. Forty-two assault guns which had recently arrived increased the strength of the Kampfgruppe for the impending decisive battles.

On that day, the 6th Panzer Division planned to make a concentrated attack with all its forces against the Russian *3rd Tank Army*, [24] which had established itself in the rolling terrain south of Verkhniy-Kumskiy. This attack was forbidden by higher headquarters. Instead, army headquarters issued orders for an armored thrust to be undertaken by the combined panzer regiments of both divisions. By means of a flank attack starting at the southern enemy flank, they were to roll up the enemy forces on a range of hills twelve kilometers in length. Again, endless columns of tanks pouring out from Klykov climbed the gentle slopes of the Aksay valley. Their objective was the line of hills situated south of Verkhniy-Kumskiy, the area which had already been the scene of heavy tank battles on 13 December (Example 6). The mission of the present panzer force, however, was quite different from the mission of the forces employed on that day.

This force had the mission of sweeping away the hostile motorized infantry forces which had established themselves on the hills after the armored "revolving battle" and which had so far remained completely inactive. It seemed an easy task to overrun the Russian infantrymen, who had dug in like fieldmice, and to drive them off the hills. The second part of the mission, which consisted of seizing and holding the extended range of hills, seemed somewhat more difficult to the armored commanders. The infantry of the accompanying mechanized 2nd Battalion, 114th Panzergrenadier Regiment, was far from sufficient for this task: it could at most occupy a few strongpoints. The broad gaps between the strongpoints, however, had to be secured by flexible conduct of operations on the part of the armored force.

For this purpose, it would have been necessary for the panzer force to divide itself into several groups and keep these ready behind the gaps in such a manner that they would be able to stop any breakthrough by a counterattacking force. This would be a

---

[24] The author continues to identify his main opponent as the *3rd Tank Army*; however, he was actually fighting Trufanov's badly beaten-up *51st Army*, reinforced by the *4th* and *13th Mechanized Corps* and two more tank brigades from General A. I. Yeremenko's *Stalingrad Front*. Seaton, *The Russo-German War*, p. 327.

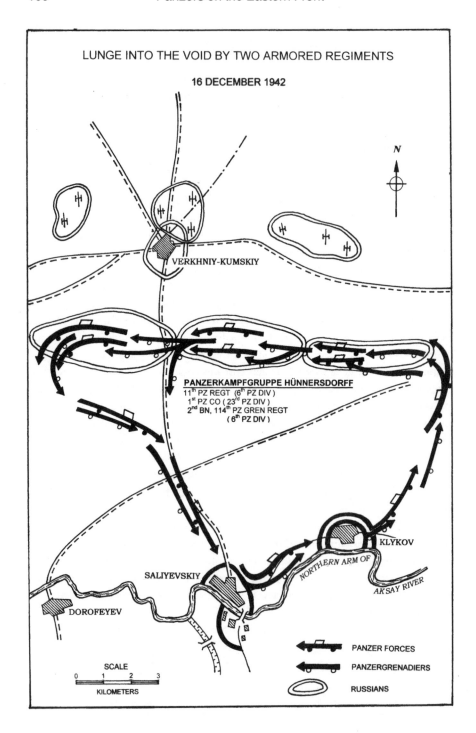

LUNGE INTO THE VOID BY TWO ARMORED REGIMENTS

16 DECEMBER 1942

N

VERKHNIY-KUMSKIY

PANZERKAMPFGRUPPE HÜNNERSDORFF
11th PZ REGT (6th PZ DIV)
1st PZ CO (23rd PZ DIV)
2nd BN, 114th PZ GREN REGT
(6th PZ DIV)

KLYKOV

NORTHERN ARM OF

AKSAY RIVER

SALIYEVSKIY

DOROFEYEV

SCALE
0   1   2   3
KILOMETERS

PANZER FORCES

PANZERGRENADIERS

RUSSIANS

difficult assignment if the enemy once succeeded in infiltrating without being observed in the tall steppe grass, and if it were then impossible to find him. Hence, it is understandable that the tank crews were uneasy. They hoped, however, that their appearance would induce the enemy's armored forces to engage in battle again. The Germans would then definitely have achieved a great victory.

In reality, the course of events was quite different from what the army headquarters and those of the German panzer force had expected. The well-camouflaged enemy motorized infantry, which was situated in groups of two to four men in a system of deep foxholes and narrow trenches, allowed itself to be overrun by the German panzer regiments. Then, using its innumerable antitank rifles, each of which was operated by one man, it opened fire at close range against the lightly armored vehicles of the panzergrenadiers following in the rear of the armored forces, and inflicted losses on them. Over and over again, it was necessary for the tanks to wait or give active help while the German panzergrenadiers were deployed to engage the invisible enemy in combat on foot. The various nests, however, were so well hidden in the steppe grass, which was brown like the Russian uniforms, that the only way to find them was actually to stumble over them. Usually, however, the Germans were killed by a bullet before they had been able to find a nest. Even the German air forces were unable to eliminate "this invisible ghost." Never before had the German tank crews felt so powerless, although they would have been able to stand their ground against the strongest hostile armored force. The enemy's armored forces, however, were too cautious to run the risk of another defeat.

In the first hours of the afternoon, the German armored force reported that it had reached its objective but was unable to eliminate "the invisible enemy." The lunge into the void brought losses but no success. The strong combined panzer force returned to its line of departure without having achieved anything. The result of the action was a lost day.

Example 9: Two Infantry Battalions Do What Two Panzer Regiments are Unable to Do, 17 December 1942

On the following day, the enemy was attacked by the 6th Panzer Division, which applied the methods which it had intended to use on the previous day. It was not the tanks but the motorcycle riflemen and the dismounted panzergrenadiers which had to bring about the decision this time. They were assembled for the attack in extended order in the bridgehead of Saliyevskiy. The whole artillery was assembled behind them. In the rear and somewhat to the right, in a village and in a depression, the armored force had assembled and remained there as a reserve at the disposal of the division commander. All movements were carried out at night.

By dawn, seasoned combat patrols of the 6th Motorcycle Battalion advancing through a gully covered by tall grass had worked their way close to their immediate objective, an observation post of the enemy artillery on Hill 140 which alone afforded a full view of the outpost area. All troops had been camouflaged to such an extent as to be almost indiscernible.

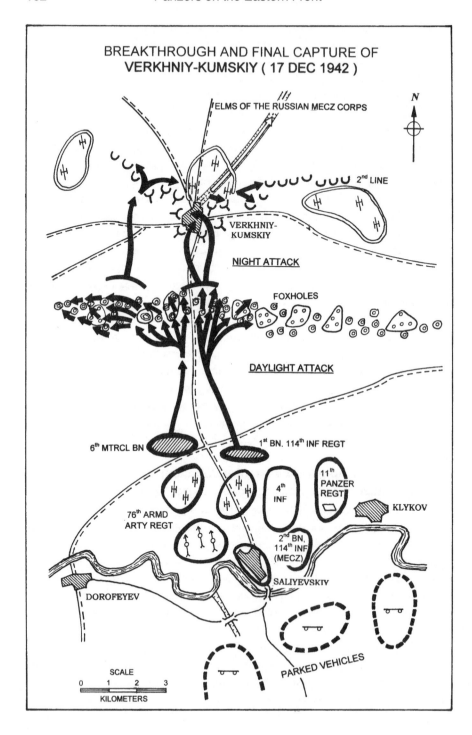

BREAKTHROUGH AND FINAL CAPTURE OF
VERKHNIY-KUMSKIY (17 DEC 1942)

N

ELMS OF THE RUSSIAN MECZ CORPS

2nd LINE

VERKHNIY-
KUMSKIY

NIGHT ATTACK

FOXHOLES

DAYLIGHT ATTACK

6th MTRCL BN   1st BN. 114th INF REGT

11th
PANZER
REGT

4th
INF

76th ARMD
ARTY REGT

2nd BN,
114th INF
(MECZ)

KLYKOV

SALIYEVSKIY

DOROFEYEV

PARKED VEHICLES

SCALE
0   1   2   3
KILOMETERS

The division planned first to paralyze the main observation post of the enemy, which was situated on a "projecting point" in the terrain, to penetrate the enemy's defenses, and to extend this penetration on both sides. Then the German forces were to advance toward Verkhniy-Kumskiy and capture this bastion. The artillery was given the mission of supporting the infantry in its attempt to infiltrate by concentrating the fire of all its guns on the penetration point, of supporting the infantry in rolling up the enemy's position, and of preventing hostile counterattacks. In addition, the heavy batteries, together with dive-bomber squadrons, were to smash the enemy artillery and his potential armored concentrations. Engineer assault detachments and flamethrower and mine-clearing teams had been attached to the infantry battalions. The armored forces were intended only to pursue the defeated enemy. They were to be also ready, however, to attack and destroy any hostile armored force appearing during the attack. In addition, the whole 4th Panzergrenadier Regiment stood in reserve, ready to help if needed.

Aerial reconnaissance was active on both sides; nothing stirred on the ground. The enemy's position seemed unoccupied. No shot was fired. Owing to their good camouflage, even on the side of the assembling German troops, there were no indications of an impending attack.

At 0800 hours, like a thunderstorm from a clear sky, all the German guns suddenly started firing as fast as they could. A hail of shells hit the hostile observation post and smashed it to pieces. Smoke from the burning steppe grass and reddish clouds of dust deprived the enemy of all visibility. The first German assault detachments were already advancing toward the hill under the protection of the clouds of dust. A few minutes later, light signals sent by the German detachments showed that they had captured the hostile observation post and had penetrated into the enemy's position. The artillery shifted its fire. The difficult job of the assault detachments began. The first German dive bombers appeared on the horizon and approached their targets with majestic calmness. The leading plane turned its nose toward the ground and swooped down on a hostile battery which it had identified; the remaining planes of the squadron followed. It almost seemed as though the planes were about to crash into the ground when, at the last moment, the bombs were released and the planes shot up again. Tremendous detonations caused the surroundings to quiver; huge mushrooms of smoke shot up into the air. Where enemy guns had been situated a minute ago, ten-meter-deep craters now gaped. The German dive bombers assembled, assumed a wedge formation, and flew off again. They had not yet disappeared from sight when the next squadron appeared and continued the work of destruction. Other squadrons followed. The hostile artillery was silent.

Balls of smoke immediately followed by the booming of antiaircraft guns announced the approach of a hostile bombardment wing. Before it arrived, there was an air battle between the hostile fighter plane escort and German Messerschmidts, during which three blazing Russian Ratas were downed so quickly that the column of smoke from the first still hung in the air when the second and third met their fate. Then the six German fighters pounced upon the hostile bombers and downed several of them, which exploded in tall columns of flame immediately after hitting the ground. The others turned around and disappeared. For some time the air was clear. Then the same scenes recurred over and over again.

Unconcerned about the events taking place in the air, the German assault detachments advanced step by step at both sides of the original penetration. Machine-gun crews and sharpshooters kept their eyes on the enemy. Every enemy soldier who showed himself was hit by a well-aimed shot; every enemy patrol which was seen crawling forward was hit by a rapid burst from a machine gun or submachine gun. If any rounds were fired from a nearby foxhole, a volley of hand grenades was the answer. The enemy's weapons were silent.

The flamethrowing teams of the engineers smoked out a number of bunkers. Flames and smoke visible from afar were an indication of the activity of these teams. Even the most stubborn pockets of resistance were unable to endure these "infernal fireworks." At some places, the effect of the fire was heightened by the burning steppe grass, which drove the enemy out of his hideouts. The snow, however, prevented the steppe fires from attaining large proportions. Fire for direction from signal pistols pointed out particularly annoying targets to the artillery and the mortars. The forward observers of these weapons immediately directed the fire of their batteries to the spot. The artillery fired with great accuracy and aided the advance of the infantry.

It was not the fascinating spectacle of a tank battle which presented itself to the eyes of the spectators, but the laborious and arduous small-scale operations of assault detachments and individual infantrymen. More and more small groups appeared along the crest of the hill, and the din of battle continually moved forward along both sides of it. By noon, the motorcycle battalion had cleared all enemy forces from the assigned sector, and an hour later the 1st Battalion, 114th Panzergrenadier Regiment, had done the same in its sector. A three-kilometer wide breach had been opened for further advances.

The reserves followed up and assembled for an attack on Verkhniy-Kumskiy. Scouts sent there reported that the village and the hills fronting it on the north were occupied by strong enemy forces. Upon approaching the village, hostile fire had been directed at the patrols from all directions. Reconnaissance aircraft identified numerous antitank guns and entrenched tanks on the edge of the village and in the positions on the hills. Movements of enemy tanks from the west toward the village were also observed.

The division, however, had no intention of sending its tanks to certain doom. The infantrymen, too, descending completely exposed hill slopes devoid of any cover, would have come into destructive enemy fire. Heavy losses would have been the result. These might have jeopardized the attack on Stalingrad. For this reason, the attack was stopped in spite of objections voiced by higher headquarters, and was continued only after the nightfall. The infantrymen, who had been well-trained for night combat, had to go it alone.

During the afternoon, the heavy weapons of the enemy, which had been identified at the village outskirts and in the hill terrain, were shelled by the German artillery operating with ground and air observation. The dive-bomber units which had been requested arrived again and attacked the tank concentrations, the entrenched tanks and the antitank positions until evening. Misled by the "tank graveyards" left by the previous battles for Verkhniy-Kumskiy, the first German squadrons had dropped their heavy bombs on these instead of on the well-camouflaged tanks of the enemy. The following squadrons, however, attacked the real enemy. The flames of burning tanks confirmed the good results achieved during these air attacks.

After nightfall, the German Panzergrenadiers and the motorcycle riflemen attacked as planned. Preceded by assault detachments, they noiselessly advanced along guiding lines which had been determined by observers during the daylight hours. The smoldering ruins of burned houses facilitated orientation. The movements and the calls of the enemy showed that he did not expect a night attack. Like specters, the assault detachments crept up to the edge of the village and observed the distribution of rations and the unconcerned activity there. The moment was appropriate for a surprise attack. From three sides, the German panzergrenadiers and motorcycle riflemen stormed forward, cheering, and entered the village. The surprised enemy was gripped by panic and tried to escape from the village. The panzergrenadiers and motorcycle riflemen made numerous prisoners and hurled the remainder of the enemy forces back to the hills. The tanks which had stood in the village turned northward in order to escape the German tank destruction teams which were advancing on them. Several, however, remained stuck in the confusion of fleeing vehicles and were blasted. All the antitank guns and damaged tanks, as well as a great deal of heavy equipment, fell into the hands of the German battalions.

The Germans had captured the enemy's key position almost without sustaining any losses. The intensive training of the troops in night combat and in the destruction of tanks had yielded good results. Two panzergrenadier battalions had gained the victory which had been denied the panzer regiments on the previous day.

Example 10: A Panzer Attack with an Inverted Front Decides a Battle on the Mushkova River, 21 December 1942

The last phase of the struggle for the liberation of Stalingrad also brought unusual situations which only an iron will, coupled with bravery and a skillful conduct of operations, was able to master.

After the capture of Verkhniy-Kumskiy, the main body of the 6th Panzer Division, with the 11th Panzer Regiment leading, was assigned the mission of pursuing the defeated Russian tank army, pushing through it, and, in a speedy advance, reaching Stalingrad. No sooner had the tanks passed through Verkhniy-Kumskiy on their way northward, however, than they were ordered back and told to turn eastward in the valley. They were followed by the main body of the division. The task was now to help the adjacent 23rd Panzer Division, which was being attacked by a newly arrived hostile infantry corps and some armored units, and was being pressed back across the Aksay River.

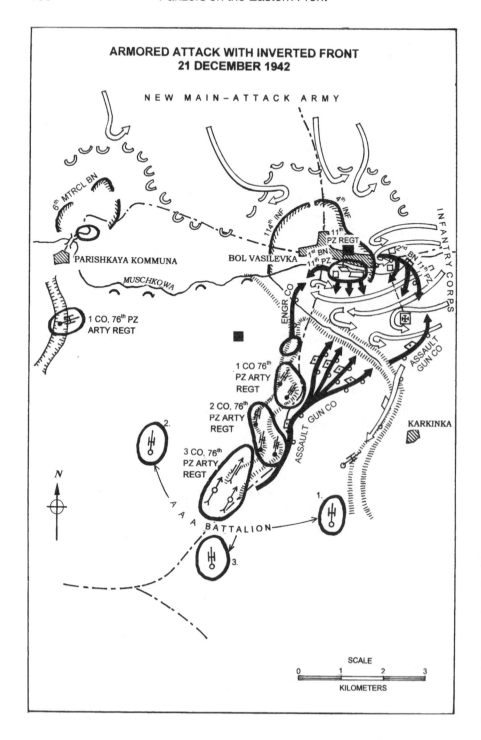

**ARMORED ATTACK WITH INVERTED FRONT
21 DECEMBER 1942**

One after another, the German units quickly moved in this direction on a good road. The mission of pursuing the enemy forces defeated at Verkhniy-Kumskiy was taken over by the 17th Panzer Division, which had arrived on the battlefield in weak combat strength only the previous evening after completing an overland march of 1,000 kilometers from the Orel area.[25]

Early in the afternoon, twelve kilometers east of Verkhniy-Kumskiy, the tanks encountered a hostile antitank front consisting of approximately twenty antitank guns, which the enemy infantry corps had set up on both sides of the approach route for the protection of its west flank. Making a quick decision, the commander of the German panzer force had his tanks envelop the enemy guns from three sides, and pour such a hail of shells on them that the entire antitank unit was smashed in a few minutes. Not a single man, horse, gun or vehicle survived this hail of steel. The German forces moved on. When the seemingly endless column of tanks appeared, the Russian corps instantly discontinued its attack at the Aksay River and withdrew east. Supply columns, seized with panic, fled to the rear. Uncoded distress calls telling all units to rally east of the railroad as quickly as possible were sent on all the radios of the Russian corps. The corps commander himself hurried there and kept urging his men on.

Freed from its distress, the 23rd Panzer Division at once advanced across the Aksay River again. It was tempting to undertake a joint attack on the confused enemy corps and to inflict a crushing defeat on it, but the overall situation made it mandatory to desist from this project in order to save Stalingrad before it was too late. Immediately the tanks stopped pursuing the enemy and veered northward again. Without having sustained any losses, the entire tank force, followed by the main body of the division, moved toward the Mushkova sector, the meeting point with the garrison of Stalingrad, during the night of the 18th. On its way there, the panzer regiment encountered only weak resistance, which it was able to break quickly. Much greater difficulties were caused by the problem of finding the correct way in the pitch-dark, monotonous steppe. The few existing tracks had been snowed under. Only with the aid of compasses and maps was it possible to advance toward the objective. At a few points, dried-out river beds and isolated marshy sections caused extensive delays, since it was first necessary to reconnoiter detours. It was a difficult night march.

It was not until dawn of 19 December that the point of the advancing force reached the Mushkova River, which was protected by strong enemy forces. An advance by surprise on the part of the tanks brought the only bridge across the river and the center

---

[25] The 17th Panzer Division was commanded by Generalmajor Fridolin von Senger und Etterlin, who assumed command only a short time before its hurried deployment to LVII Panzer Corps. Unlike the 6th Panzer Division, and very much like 23rd Panzer Division already fighting, it had not been rebuilt and reequipped. In mid-December it had only 30 tanks, no armored cars, and only one or two reconnaissance vehicles; 30–40 percent of its motor vehicles were under repair, forcing one company from each [anzer grenadier battalion to march on foot, following after the division. Senger und Etterlin, *Neither Hope Nor Fear: The Wartime Memoirs of the German Defender of Monte Cassino* (Novato, CA: Presidio Press, 1989), p. 63.

of the village of Bolshaya-Vasilevka into German hands. All efforts which the enemy undertook to eliminate this small bridgehead were futile.[26]

About noon, the whole artillery had moved into position and the 4th and 114th Panzergrenadier Regiments, supported by the artillery and the tanks, attacked in order to extend the bridgehead, the attack of the first regiment being directed toward the east, and that of the second regiment toward the north and the west. In the course of these attacks, after bitter house-to-house combat, the whole village, which was two kilometers long, was captured by the Germans.

The enemy realized the danger threatening the ring around Stalingrad from the south, and hurriedly moved all available units to the scene in order to destroy the German spearhead. His armored corps were no longer able to do this. They had suffered so heavily in the recent battles that they had ceased to constitute a serious threat. Hence, the Russian command resorted to the time-honored practice of trying to smash the Bolshaya-Vasilevka bridgehead by means of concentrated fire from the artillery and rocket launchers and then to "wash it away" by massed infantry attacks.

The new main-attack army, which had been detached from the troops besieging Stalingrad and had been reinforced by reserves from the eastern bank of the Volga River, assembled in the northern hills and in the valley east of Bolshaya-Vasilevka for an all-out attack against the 6th Panzer Division.[27] Thousands of Russians filled the snowfields, slopes, and depressions of the endless steppe. No soldier had ever seen such multitudes advance on him. Their leading waves were thrown to the ground by a hail of high-explosive shells, but more and more waves followed. Any attempt on the part of the Russian masses to reach the German lines was thwarted by the fire of machine guns and guns. The frontal attack was blocked.

A few hours later, however, the Russians poured into the village from the east like a stream of lava, pushing the flank of the 4th Panzergrenadier Regiment back some 100 meters. A short time later, they pushed through the gap to the 23rd Panzer Division and

---

[26] The Soviet General Staff Study denies that the Germans ever got across the Mushkova River; yet the document is full of artful omissions. It goes to great length to discuss the strengthening of the *2nd Guards Army* and *51st Army* for the express purpose of a major counterattack on 19 December, but then it says nothing of that operation. It does admit, though, that the Germans drove the Soviet armies back to the river at that point. *Battle for Stalingrad*, pp. 121–3. This would not be the first time that Soviet military history attempted to cover up severe defeats. In July 1991, the deputy commander of the Russian Military History Institute told the editor of this book that his military historians needed to cite Western analyses of operations in the Great Patriotic War to write the truth of what happened, so often had Communist Party censors forbidden it.

[27] These strong forces included Malinovskiy's newly committed *2nd Guards Army* and Trufanov's strengthed *51st Army*. Zhukov, *op. cit.*, pp. 133–4. The *2nd Guards Army* consisted of the *1st* and *13th Guards Rifle Corps* and the *2nd Guards Mechanized Corps* when it was committed from STAVKA reserve; it was further strengthened with the *7th Tank*, the *4th Mechanized*, *4th Cavalry Corps*, and the *300th Rifle Division*. The *2nd Guards Mechanized Corps* consisted of the *4th*, *5th*, and *6th Mechanized Regiments* and the *21st*, *22nd*, *23rd*, *24th*, and *25th Tank Regiments*. At the same time, the *51st Army* was reinforced with the *38th Rifle Division* taken from the *64th Army* holding the ring around Stalingrad to the rear of the fighting. In addition, the *5th Shock Army*, west of the Don River, was to cooperate with the offensive of the *2nd Guards Army*. *Battle for Stalingrad*, pp. 121–2; Poirier and Conner, *op. cit.*, p. 93.

rolled forward toward the rear of the troops in the bridgehead. The eastern part of the village and the vicinity of the cemetery were lost. But the division stood unshaken, like a rock in the surging sea. It was only when the encirclement of the division seemed on the point of becoming complete that the Russian masses were mowed down by a sudden thunderous concentration of the German artillery and were at the same time caught in the flank by 150 tanks coming from the village, and in the rear by 42 assault guns. As a result, they were overwhelmed. Even the strongest nerves of the enemy were unequal to this eruption of fire and steel. The Russians threw their weapons away and tried like madmen to escape the infernal crossfire and the deadly armored envelopment. This was a thing which rarely happened in World War II. In mobs of several hundreds, shelled even by their own artillery and their own rocket launchers, they ran west toward the only open spot, and surrendered to the German covering parties stationed there.[28]

The battle raged on, but it had passed its climax. The crisis had been weathered. The threatening masses on the flank and in the rear had either been smashed or were prisoners. Even the enemy's combat method—the mass attack, which so often yielded good results—had failed this time. The defensive battle on the Mushkova River had been crowned by a German victory.[29]

Example 11: A Panzer Kampfgruppe
Prepares for a Final Thrust, 23 December 1942

On 23 December, the 4th Panzergrenadier Regiment, with the support of artillery and tanks, undertook a counterattack, recaptured the eastern section of the village, and occupied the cemetery located south thereof which had previously been seized by the Russians. This last operation completely restored the situation of 20 December. Much more important, however, was the fact that both the enemy tanks and the masses of infantry had been overcome, so that there was no longer any insuperable obstacle between the liberators and Stalingrad. The initiative had again passed to the German command. The troops now awaited the breakout attempt by the Sixth Army which had long been hoped for. Now such an attempt would be easier for the German Army, since substantial elements of the encircling forces had been beaten on the Mushkova River. The continued delay was incomprehensible.

An order issued in the morning of 23 December, however, seemed to remove all doubt. This order provided for a thrust over a distance of 33 kilometers, to be undertaken by all armored elements on the morning of the 24th. They were to approach close to the encircled city in order to link up with the garrison, which, it was said, was no longer in a position to fight, and, under armored escort, to take it behind the Mushkova sector,

---

[28] This section describes the attack of the *2nd Guards Army* with its infantry corps, its armored elements having been chewed up in the preceding fighting.—Editor.

[29] The view of the situation lower on the chain of command was not so positive. The war diary of the 11th Panzer Regiment recorded, at 0600, 20 December: "The gradually increasing resistance is becoming stronger every hour. . . . Our weak troops—twenty-one tanks without gasoline and two weak assault gun companies—are insufficient to widen the bridgehead." Craig, *Enemy at the Gates*, p. 235.

which remained occupied by the main body of the 6th Panzer Division and by the two adjacent divisions. This was an unusual mission, but, in view of the enemy's defeat on the Mushkova River, its success seemed possible. Since the railroad line had long since been extended up to the Aksay River, and since, in addition, several thousand trucks were available to the liberators, the problem of supplying and evacuating the German troops would not be insoluble. It was likewise to be assumed that German troops, who had been encircled for only a month, would muster the strength necessary for a march behind the Mushkova River if their freedom and lives were at stake.

All preparations for the final thrust which was to decide the fate of Stalingrad were quickly made. The combat force, which consisted of 120 tanks, 40 assault guns, 24 armored reconnaissance cars, one panzergrenadier battalion, one mechanized motorcycle company, one mechanized engineer company, and one armored artillery battalion, was ready for the final lunge on the afternoon of 23 December, when a counterorder called for the 6th Panzer Division to be pulled out immediately. It was to cross the Don River bridge at Potemkinskaya during the night of 23 December and reach Morosovskaya in a forced march.[30] At dawn on 24 December, the 6th Panzer Division, in a column 130 kilometers long, rolled over the blood-drenched steppes on which it had fought so successfully toward an uncertain future. (Von Manstein describes in detail the reasoning behind his redeployment of the 6th Panzer Division in his memoir; the prospect of the division's success was as apparent and tantalizing to him as it was to Raus: "In the days following its arrival at the Miskova on 19th December, the relieving army had become embroiled in heavy fighting against the never-ending waves of forces thrown in by the enemy from Stalingrad to halt its advance. Despite this, 57 Panzer Corps had succeeded in gaining a foothold on the north bank of the river and, after a series of ding-dong engagements, in forming a bridgehead there. Mass attacks by the enemy brought him nothing but bloody losses. Already, on the distant horizon, the leading troops of the corps could see the reflection of the gunfire around Stalingrad! Success seemed to be within striking distance if only Sixth Amy would create a diversion by going over to the attack and at least prevent the enemy from constantly throwing fresh forces in the path of Fourth Panzer Army. . . . However, Sixth Army's attack never materialized.[31] On the afternoon of 23rd December the Army Group was regretfully compelled to take account of the situation on the left wing, which was more than critical at this time, by shifting forces to that area. Third Rumanian Army on the Lower Chir was directed to release H.Q. 48 Panzer Corps and 11 Panzer Division to restore the position on the Army

---

[30] Raus stated: "This move definitely sealed the doom of the German forces at Stalingrad. The remaining two panzer divisions, the 17th and 23rd, were not even sufficient to make a stand against the Russian forces, let alone repulse them. But also the enemy was so weakened by his losses, which included more than 400 tanks, that he was unable to make a quick thrust against Rostov, an action which would have cut off the entire Caucasus front." Rauss, *Fighting in Hell*, p. 87.

[31] This attack never materialized because its commander lacked the initiative and independence to defy Hitler's orders which required him to do the impossible—not give up any of the Stalingrad pocket in order to assist the relieving forces.—Editor.

Group's western wing, and to make good this loss Fourth Panzer Army had to give up one armoured division, without which the Lower Chir could not possibly be held."[32] Zhukov offers a description of the same events but from a different perspective. "A fierce battle unfolded in the Verkkne-Kumsky sector taking a heavy toll on both sides. But despite heavy losses, the enemy continued to drive forward to Stalingrad. Battle-seasoned Soviet forces doggedly contested their defence lines. Only when the 17th Panzer Division returned and aerial bombardment was intensified did units of the 51st Army and General Shapkin's Cavalry Corps retreat across the River Myskova The enemy was only 40 kilometers from Stalingrad and apparently believed victory was within reach. But these hopes were premature. In conformity with orders from the Supreme Command, Vasilevsky moved into action the 2nd Guards Army under General R. Ya. Malinovsky, well-reinforced with tanks and artillery; it reversed the tide of the battle in favour of the Soviet forces."[33] Von Senger und Etterlin's viewpoint is closer to the fighting. "During the next two days the 6th Panzer Division was pulled back. It had barely maintained its position against heavy attacks in a small bridgehead north of the river sector. The corps was forced on the defensive and took up positions further back. This alone could ensure keeping contact with surviving units. This was really a complete defeat. The enemy had evidently brought up strong forces. What I had feared at the start of the relief operation had now come to pass. The Russians had no intention of allowing one weak corps to rob them of their great vitory at Stalingrad, especially after our attack had brought us within 30 kilometers near to the great city. The attempt to relieve 6th Army had to be abandoned. My division had suffered heavily."[34])

Conclusion

The preceding series of examples corroborates the thesis that unusual situations lead to peculiar decisions, and the latter, in turn, to odd forms of combat which place an enormous strain on both officers and men.

---

[32] Manstein, *op. cit.*, p. 345.
[33] Zhukov, *op. cit.*, pp. 133–4.
[34] Senger und Etterlin, *Neither Hope Nor Fear*, pp. 74–5.

Chapter 4

Struggle Along the Donets, August 1943

Preface

This section contains four examples of Russian tactical expedients taken from the defensive operations of the German XI Corps along the upper Donets River front in August 1943, preceded by an introduction which addresses the development of the Corps' situation as background; and German defensive tactics to prevent Russians crossing the river.[1]

Example 1. Description of the Russian "Swamp Battalion," whose personnel gain a foothold on the western bank by remaining all day in a swamp submerged to their chests; rifles are hung in tree branches and floated on boards.

Example 2. During the heavy fighting, a unit appears in the German positions wearing German uniforms, carrying German equipment, and speaking German; they open fire on the Germans at close range, thus revealing themselves.

Example 3. The Russians succeed in crossing the river with tanks and without a bridge, much to the surprise of the Germans; a counterattack reveals an underwater bridge which has been made by pushing tanks into the river and tying planks to their tops.

Example 4. Another unusual tactical measure of creating a "defensive bridgehead within an offensive bridgehead, which saves the Russians a foothold on the western bank when a German counterattack almost succeeds in eliminating the salient.

Introduction

The following examples were taken from a different situation facing XI Corps (Hanover) during the defensive operations along the upper Donets River in the early days of August 1943. In this situation, not only the commanders of large units, but also those of small and very small units, were confronted with unusual problems which had to be solved independently. In order that the purpose and the results of the measures taken by both sides may be understood and appraised correctly as part of the overall operations, the development of the situation of the corps will first be briefly described.

---

[1] The events described in this chapter are part of the Fourth Battle of Kharkov, 3–23 August 1943. On the German side, the Fourth Panzer Army and Armeeabteilung Kempf (Eighth Army) disposed fifteen divisions, only three of them panzer divisions. They faced two Soviet fronts and part of a third, which brought eleven armies to bear against the Germans. Earle Ziemke, *Stalingrad to Berlin: The German Defeat in the East* (Washington, DC: Office of the Chief of Military History, United States Army, 1968), pp. 151–2.

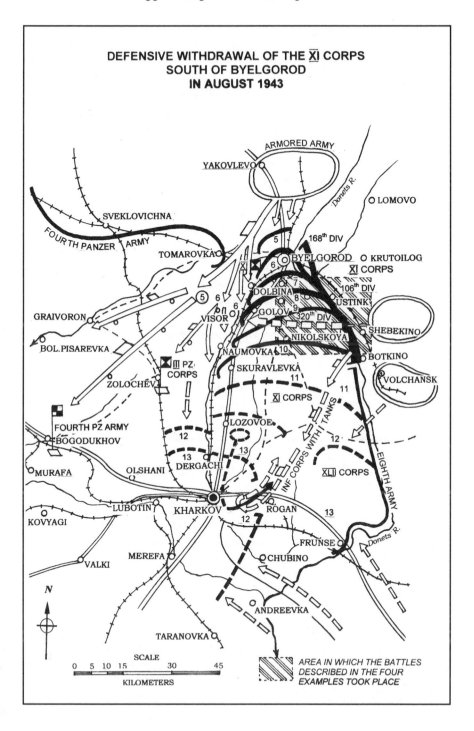

DEFENSIVE WITHDRAWAL OF THE XI CORPS
SOUTH OF BYELGOROD
IN AUGUST 1943

ARMORED ARMY

YAKOVLEVO

LOMOVO

SVEKLOVICHNA

FOURTH PANZER ARMY

TOMAROVKA

168th DIV

BYELGOROD   KRUTOILOG

XI CORPS

DOLBINA

106th DIV

USTINK

GRAIVORON

VISOR

GOLOV

320th DIV

SHEBEKINO

BOL.PISAREVKA

NIKOLSKOYA

NAUMOVKA

BOTKINO

III PZ CORPS

SKURAVLEVKA

VOLCHANSK

ZOLOCHEV

XI CORPS

FOURTH PZ ARMY

LOZOVOE

BOGODUKHOV

XLII CORPS

MURAFA

OLSHANI

DERGACHI

LUBOTIN

KHARKOV

ROGAN

KOVYAGI

FRUNSE

MEREFA

CHUBINO

VALKI

N

ANDREEVKA

TARANOVKA

SCALE

0   5 10 15   30   45

KILOMETERS

Donets R.

EIGHTH ARMY

INF CORPS WITH TANKS

AREA IN WHICH THE BATTLES
DESCRIBED IN THE FOUR
EXAMPLES TOOK PLACE

After the large-scale German pincer attack against Kursk (codename "Zitadelle") started on 5 July 1943 had failed, the positions of all units participating in the attack were again withdrawn to the line of departure, or, at least, close to it. In this process, the four infantry divisions comprising XI Corps,[2] which in the attack had been committed at the southern flank, were returned to their old, well-fortified positions located along the upper Donets River in the area on both sides of Belgorod. In the preceding heavy battles, which had continued for a whole month, the divisions had suffered severe losses. They could not expect to receive any replacements for a long time to come. Their combat strengths were down to 40 to 50 percent of those prescribed in their tables of organization, and in the case of some regiments they were even lower.

The disengagement from the enemy proceeded smoothly. Even the bridgehead at Belgorod, which had been held by XI Corps, the last unit to fight east of the Donets River, was evacuated with ease. The enemy divisions, which had been beaten shortly before, advanced toward the river again very cautiously. They probably did not understand why the Germans were withdrawing voluntarily, and, therefore, were suspicious. Their suspicions were not unjustified, since many a German retirement had been followed by a surprise attack which had wrought havoc on the enemy's forces. This time, however, the withdrawal was genuine, with no trickery intended. It was solely dictated by the desire to intercept, on a shorter fortified line, the expected counterattack of the enemy's strategic reserves, which were still intact.

On 5 August 1943, after the enemy artillery had fired heavily for one hour, the enemy offensive began along the Belgorod–Kursk highway.[3] Its unmistakable aim was to push through the salience of the front around Belgorod at the point where the boundary between two German armies was situated, and thereby to dislocate the defensive line. The enemy completely succeeded in achieving his objective. His heavy barrage hit the German 167th Division,[4] which had taken up positions in a former Russian antitank ditch located a few kilometers in front of the well-fortified line. Within a short time, massed enemy tanks had crossed this ditch; at noon they passed the corps command post and poured into the depth of the German positions, all the while firing on fleeing German trains. On the following morning, after a forced march in the night, their points had reached the surprised headquarters of the Fourth Panzer Army, which was located

---

[2] XI Corps included the 106th, 168th, 198th, and 320th Infantry Divisions under the command of Armeeabteilung Kempf (Eighth Army). Paul Carrell, *Scorched Earth*, p. 304. The 6th Panzer Division had become separated from the rest of III Panzer Corps (commanded by General der Panzertruppen Breith).— Editor.

[3] The Soviet *53rd Army* (commanded by I. M. Mangarov) and the *1st Mechanized Corps* (commanded by General-Lieutenant M. D. Solomatin) were the forces attacking down the Belgorod–Kursk highway. Spreading left of the *53rd Army* were the *69th Army* and *7th Guards* Army. All these armies were subordinated to the *Steppe Front*, commanded by the redoubtable Colonel-General (and later Marshal of the Soviet Union) I. S. Koniev. Coming in on the right flank of the *53rd Army* was P. A. Rotmistrov's *5th Guards Tank Army*. G. Zhukov, *Reminiscences and Reflections*, Vol. 2, p. 202.

[4] The 167th Infantry Division had fought under the Fourth Panzer Army's XLVIII Panzer Corps at Kursk.— Editor.

in Bogodukhov. Since the army had no reserves available to close the ten-kilometer gap in the front between Belgorod and Tomarovka, or to stop the massed enemy tanks which had already broken through to a depth of 100 kilometers, the enemy's advanced elements reached the area northeast of Poltava on 7 August. The map accompanying this study illustrates, more clearly than words, the dangerous situation into which this development thrust XI Corps, which was fighting with its front toward the east.

On the very first day, it was attacked in the rear by enemy armored forces situated 30 kilometers in the depth of its positions. These armored forces simultaneously exerted crushing pressure on its unprotected left flank. In this serious situation, the corps was left to its own devices, and was also hindered by a Führer order, which had arrived at the last minute, saying that Belgorod was to be held under all circumstances.[5]

As far as possible, everything that the situation required was done. It is, however, not the object of this study to describe this in detail. The author, therefore, will confine himself to describing a few incidents which show the unusual tactical skill and improvisation necessary to prevent the threatening catastrophe, and the strain on the mental and physical powers of both officers and men at a time when the enemy also tried to achieve a breakthrough on the Donets River. Only tough fighters experienced in Eastern combat conditions were able to master this difficult situation.

The temptation was to take forces out of the Eastern front along the Donets River and to employ them, with their front reversed, in the Lopan River sector to protect the rear. Since, however, the Donets River front was very long and only thinly manned, it was impracticable to do so without disastrously exposing this sector, against which the enemy was conducting feint and relief attacks. This would have spelled doom to the corps. As a result, only the remnants (500 battle-worn soldiers without artillery and heavy infantry weapons) of the 167th Division, which had been separated from the Fourth Panzer Army during the breakthrough, and the weak 6th Panzer Division,[6] whose men, although they had only ten tanks, possessed a good morale, were available for the defensive withdrawal at the Lopan River for the time being. The corps had immediately assumed command over these two divisions, since they were cut off from communication with their army. During the night of 5 August, the 168th Division on the left of the corps, which was under heavy enemy pressure north of Belgorod, was pivoted 180 degrees around Belgorod and likewise employed to protect the rear after the corps had attached to it one Tiger tank company and one assault gun company, comprising a total of 25

---

[5] A Führer Order was the most dreaded order a senior officer could receive. It forbade any withdrawal under any circumstance, and deprived the commander of the flexibility and maneuver desperately needed in such crises. Hitler had given such an order in the crisis of the retreat before Moscow in December 1941, and it had been the very thing that had stabilized the front and prevented a collapse of the front. Tragically for countless German soldiers, Hitler had fixated on this as a solution to every crisis, which it manifestly was not. The result were huge losses of men and equipment.—Editor.

[6] The incorporation into XI Corps must have given a boost to the morale of the men of the 6th Panzer Division who had served under Raus from 25 November 1941 to 6 February 1943. At this time, the 6th Panzer Division was commanded by Oberst Wilhelm Crisolli (see Appendix 1).—Editor.

armored vehicles. Sustained by their tanks and antitank weapons, the two weak divisions withstood all attacks by the enemy infantry, which was supported by large numbers of ground attack airplanes and by 150 tanks.

South thereof, in the threatened sectors along the Lopan River, it was necessary to rapidly form combat forces from ground organizations of the Luftwaffe and from the combat trains and supply services of the corps. With the aid of 88mm antiaircraft batteries of the Luftwaffe, which were employed solely against tanks in spite of the enemy's continuous air raids, these improvised forces managed to prevent the enemy from pivoting his troops against the Kharkov–Belgorod *Rollbahn* and advancing against the rear of the Donets River front. On the morning of 8 August, enemy armored reinforcements succeeded in breaking through the 168th Division and gaining a foothold on the eastern bank of the Lopan River. An immediate counterattack by the 6th Panzer Division, however, threw the enemy back and eliminated the threat. This time, by a narrow margin, things had gone well.

Enemy armored forces lunging further to the south, however, were able to cross the Lopan River and push toward the *Rollbahn*. By a fortunate coincidence, an assault gun brigade comprising 42 assault guns, which was being moved up from the adjacent corps on the south, was just approaching and was able to attack and destroy, one by one, the enemy armored groups which had crossed the Lopan River. Afterward, the assault gun brigade remained the only mobile tactical reserve of the corps, and continued to render valuable service.

The corps believed that the greatest difficulties lay behind it when, on 9 August, a dangerous crisis arose as a result of the fact that the 168th Division had "vanished suddenly" during the preceding night. The only possible explanation seemed to be that it had been captured by the enemy. Actually, however, it was found three days later in position in an extensive forest north of Kharkov 45 kilometers behind the front, where its commander, who had had a nervous breakdown, had led it without the knowledge of the corps. It was primarily due to the personal initiative of the corps commander that even this most serious of all crises could be overcome that day. On the front line, he assumed command of the critical portion of the sector, and with lightning speed took any measures which were necessary to close the large gap to prevent a withdrawal of adjacent units, and to rearrange the chain of command.

This brief description of combat operations should be kept in mind by the reader and made to agree in time with the following examples. It is only then that the significance of these events will be fully appreciated.

Example 1: The "Swamp Battalion"

The heat of summer was still parching the blood-drenched fields along the banks of the upper Donets River when XI Corps, after the failure of its large-scale offensive against Kursk, returned to the well-fortified positions along the western bank of this river which it had occupied before the attack. The regiments of the 320th Division were situated approximately 30 kilometers south of the town of Belgorod, and those of the 106th Division were situated directly north of them on the hills on both sides of "A" Brook valley, through which a highway ran westward to the big Kharkov *Rollbahn*. An enemy advance through the valley would quickly interrupt this vital communication. It was the responsibility of the battalions employed on both sides of the valley to prevent this.

The enemy was surprised by the sudden withdrawal of the German troops, who had so far been successful. On the second day, he cautiously and hesitantly felt his way forward to the Donets River, the eastern bank of which is much lower than the western. At the junction of "A" Brook with the river, the terrain was swampy and covered with reeds. The river was not fordable at any point. It seemed obvious that it would be very difficult for the enemy to achieve a breakthrough here. During the day, he would probably be able to hide in the maze of trenches remaining from his battered former positions and in the innumerable shell craters, but his troops would be unable to move into the open without being identified and brought under fire by the German defenders. The German weapons, from their well-camouflaged bunker positions, controlled the Donets River valley, which was very level, along its entire extent of three to four kilometers, so that it was impossible for the enemy to prepare an attack during daylight. As a result, a dead silence prevailed in the sun-drenched glittering sand desert on the eastern bank of the Donets River all day long.

At night, on the other hand, there was lively activity. First, enemy scouts looked for convenient crossing sites along the river bank. Later, groups of enemy soldiers appeared on the western bank to reconnoiter German defenses and take prisoners. To this end, they applied a method which they had already frequently used with success on previous occasions. At night, they crept up to German sentries standing in a trench and waited, often for hours at a time, for a suitable moment to overpower them. When they had succeeded in doing so, they immediately gagged the surprised victim, tied his arms and legs with ropes, and made a loop around his ankles, by which he was often dragged over distances of several hundred meters to the nearest enemy trench. This was done in complete silence. Only the tracks discovered the next morning indicated the direction in which the sentry had been taken.

The only possible way of protecting oneself against this inhumane form of kidnapping consisted of increasing the number of security patrols and sentries, having the sentries maintain constant contact with each other, establishing obstacles with alarm devices, laying minefields, and using trained watchdogs which, like setters, immediately indicated every movement in the vicinity of a sentry and attacked the enemy as he crept up or lurked in ambush. The endurance and ingenuity of the Russian soldier was astonishing. If he was unable to realize his intention during the first night, he continued to appear every following night until he was successful. If he became aware that effective countermeasures had been taken, however, he did not fall into the trap, but went in search of a spot which was more appropriate, and he continued to search until he found such a spot. Often he was successful because of the carelessness of a German sentry,

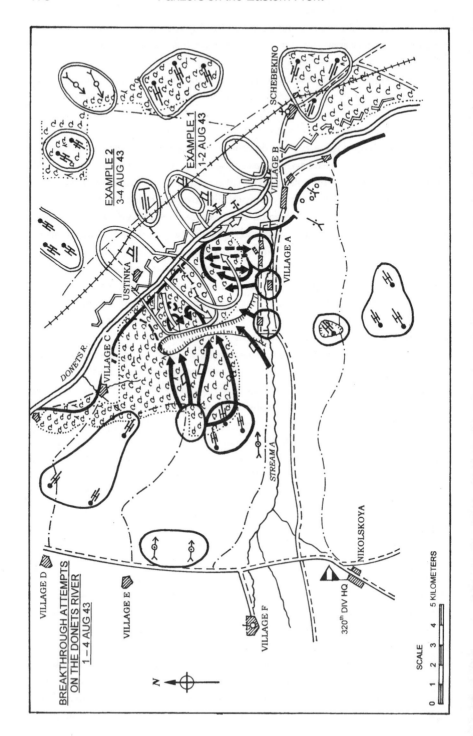

BREAKTHROUGH ATTEMPTS
ON THE DONETS RIVER
1–4 AUG 43

EXAMPLE 1
1-2 AUG 43

EXAMPLE 2
3-4 AUG 43

SCHEBEKINO

VILLAGE B

VILLAGE A

USTINKA

DONETS R.

VILLAGE C

STREAM A

VILLAGE D

VILLAGE E

VILLAGE F

NIKOLSKOYA

320ᵗʰ DIV HQ

N

SCALE

0 1 2 3 4 5 KILOMETERS

which he immediately noticed and exploited. In this strange and brutal manner, the enemy managed, in this example, but on other occasions also, to obtain valuable information concerning details of the defense, which he soon utilized very skillfully. Thus he also found out, for instance, that the German position was thinly manned owing to a shortage of forces, and that this was particularly true of the tree-covered hill sector north of "A" Brook.

It was here, as a result, that the enemy made his first attempt to cross the river. The men of the battalion in positions here, however, were on their guard. They had identified and mined the tracks of enemy scouting parties, and had adjusted their machine guns and mortars on the crossing points used by these parties so that the weapons were ready for night firing. They kept a close watch during the following night. As expected, just before dawn, enemy companies appeared and prepared to cross the Donets River at the three reconnoitered points using emergency equipment. They were taken by complete surprise when suddenly mines exploded and killed the first of their soldiers to land on the western bank, and when the companies still on the eastern bank were caught in the fire from numerous machine guns and mortars, these weapons being greatly feared by the Russians. The companies scattered while sustaining severe losses. The river-crossing equipment left behind was destroyed by German artillery fire at dawn.

It would have been a mistake to think that the Russians would abandon their intention to cross the river after this setback. On the contrary, they repeated their attack on the following night and at the same point, using stronger forces and new equipment. The defense, however, also put up a heavier show of force than during the preceding night by concentrating on this point the fire of all weapons within range. This fire caused terrific losses.

Only one small enemy group managed to escape destruction, by clinging to the steep slope of the western bank, where the fire could not reach it. During the day, however, German combat patrols were able to drive this group into a nearby swamp, where, with the mud reaching up to their chests and with the reeds providing scant cover, it resumed fighting, remaining there all day. To the astonishment of the German defenders, this Russian group still occupied its swamp position on the next day. It was no longer alone, however; at its side one, or two additional swamp companies had taken up positions. This was something which German or other European troops would never had done. The swamp was situated on the western bank, that is, on the German side just in front of the valley position which had been established 300 meters from the western bank of the river because the swamp in front of it made a very good obstacle. No German commander would have thought of placing his men into the swamp so that they would be close to the river. The enemy saw a chance to gain a foothold on the western bank and formed a "swamp bridgehead"—a situation which the German did not envy. It was considered impossible for the enemy to remain in the swamp for any long period of time. An observer stationed on a church tower, who had a very good view of the whole swamp bridgehead, saw the helmet-covered heads of the defenders, concealed by the reeds, show up like corks from the necks of champagne bottles. The Russians rested their rifles in the forks of branches or on boards and were ready to fire. By their side, the frogs of the swamp frolicked and peacefully croaked their monotonous evening song as an accompaniment to the conduct of the enemy, which seemed senseless to the Germans. And yet, the enemy must have had a plan when he took this step. What could his scheme be? It was only the subsequent events that answered the question.

Example 2: An Enemy Battalion
Fights in German Uniforms, 3 and 4 August 1943

Meanwhile, the fighting continued. Thwarted in their latest crossing attempts, the enemy changed both the scene of action and his method of attack. It was plain that he had fared very badly in his latest attempt, otherwise he would not have abandoned his intention after the second attempt. To change or abandon a plan once it had been adopted was not characteristic of the Russian way of thinking, and, if such a thing was done, it always indicated that the Russians had suffered a serious defeat.

The sector of the battalion adjacent on the north now became the objective of the enemy's attacks. The sector was situated in a group of wooded hills in an area where their elevation varied very greatly and afforded only a very limited field of view because of the dense underbrush. The eastern edge of the hills situated on the western bank of the river, which was from 30 to 50 meters high, provided the defender with good visibility and a chance for effective use of his weapons. However, once the enemy managed to gain a foothold in the woods, which were difficult to defend, it would be difficult to dislodge him.

Experience had shown that it was possible to drive the Russians out of a wilderness such as this only by using massed troops or resorting to such extremely radical means as flamethrowers or flamethrowing tanks, or by setting fire to the forest. Often it was necessary to encircle and destroy his forces in close combat, which resulted in severe losses on both sides. His tenacity surpassed anything previously known in other theaters of operation. The danger of becoming involved in combat here was all the greater because the line was thinly manned for lack of sufficient forces (after the preceding heavy battles, the companies were at scarcely half their combat strength), and no adequate reserves were available in the rear. At best, a few well-trained assault patrols and the regimental reserve, comprising a company of 60 men, were all that was at the disposal of the battalion for the elimination of a penetration. To set fire to the young trees with their green leaves was impossible. Hence, the command regarded the future with grave concern. It was necessary to bring about a collapse of the enemy attack in front of the main line of resistance; otherwise, the command risked a loss of the wooded hill zone which the enemy needed as an assembly area for the subsequent thrust it planned. Only the artillery, which was strong and still intact, and the Luftwaffe could thwart the enemy's plan. Both did all they could.

No sooner had the enemy readied his first stream-crossing equipment in the willows and reeds than it was identified and destroyed by artillery fire, in spite of its excellent concealment. Reconnaissance aircraft observed heavily manned trenches in the vicinity of the Donets River. A short time afterward, bomber wings arrived on the scene and in waves smashed the enemy's troop concentrations and his advanced heavy weapons. Thereafter, it was quiet for the rest of the day. Even the enemy batteries, which had previously adjusted their fire to the German positions along the edge of the hills, were silent because they feared the German bombers and, even more, a German 210mm howitzer battery which had accurately determined the location of the enemy batteries by sound and flash-ranging, and which had taken them under effective and precisely adjusted fire before they were able to change their position. The result was a further withdrawal, and great caution on the part of the enemy artillery, both of which served substantially to decrease its effectiveness.

The periodical surprise fire undertaken by the Russian *Stalinorgeln*,[7] however, continued to be very irksome. These rocket launchers changed their location immediately after firing a salvo, and hence could never be taken under fire by the German artillery. It was only after it had been observed that they always took up their position, in irregular succession, at the same three or four points situated at crossroads, that they were silenced by a number of ambush batteries. Each of these batteries had adjusted its fire to one of the rocket-launcher positions so that all the alternate positions were hit simultaneously by a hail of fire as soon as the launchers fired a salvo. The fire from one of the ambush batteries, then, was certain to hit the target directly. Many a rocket launcher was disabled by use of this method. The crews of the others stopped moving their launchers into position openly and firing freely at German targets. The rocket launchers abruptly ceased to constitute a threat. In this instance, too, the old saying that "necessity is the mother of invention" proved true.

Only now did the troops enjoy a period of quiet. It was a pleasant interlude before the storm. The enemy, however, saw that he possessed an advantage during the night, and he knew how to utilize this advantage. German artillery and heavy infantry weapons attempted in vain to interfere, by means of harassing fire, with the new preparations the enemy was making for an attack across the Donets River. This time, he was about to try his luck simultaneously at two points, as indicated by his lively nocturnal activity. Naturally, the first of these two points was where he had suffered defeat on the preceding day. However, few kilometers south of this point, where a highway bridge had formerly crossed the Donets River, lively movement and the dropping of logs and other equipment into place was heard. Here the enemy was preparing to bridge the river, and it was here that his main action was to be expected. The night was full of unrest and tension. The enemy threw new men and *matériel* into the battle, which he meant under all circumstances to decide quickly in his favor. A hard day began.

With the first light of dawn, salvo after salvo was fired, devastating the bunker positions of the northern battalion along the edge of the hills. After all the light batteries

---

[7] *Stalinorgeln* ("Stalin's Organs") were mobile multiple-barrel rocket launchers.

and a large number of heavy trench mortars had joined the fire fight, it assumed the proportion of a regular witches' Sabbath. Concentrated on a small area, this "infernal" fire demolished all the defense installations and shelters in the position. Uprooted and shattered tree trunks covered the ground and made all movement impossible for the remaining men, who resignedly crouched in shell craters and awaited the attack of the enemy's infantry.

At length, after the barrage had continued for almost two hours, the shells whistled over their heads into a position situated in their rear. They had scarcely discerned this shift of fire when the first enemy troops approached. After the paralyzing wait under nerve-racking fire, the chance of becoming active again came as a relief to the infantrymen. Here and there, a volley of fire from a machine gun already hit the advancing enemy, submachine guns began to rattle, and hand grenades burst on every side. But all these sounds were drowned out by the German barrage, which sent mud and columns of water spouting into the air, smashed the enemy stream-crossing equipment, and inflicted heavy casualties on his forces.

Nevertheless, the Russians succeeded in getting several of their companies across the river, since the German defenses were no longer compact. The enemy's preparatory fire had made great gaps in the German defenses, which, to begin with, had been thinly manned. Soon enemy spearheads had penetrated through the wide gaps and had enveloped the pockets of resistance, although these put up a desperate fight. The enemy's cheering troops were heard farther and farther in the rear of the Germans. Yet they (the Germans) held their ground, even in this seemingly hopeless situation. There was still a chance that detachments from adjacent units or reserves would come to their rescue. Until this happened, however, they would have to hold. Each hour seemed an eternity.

Suddenly, however, German machine-gun fire raged in the forest behind them. It was easily recognized by its very high rate of fire. Soon the rattle of submachine guns followed, the bullets whistling past their ears. Volleys of hand grenades exploded, and a rousing "Hurrah!" was heard through the din of the forest combat operations, but ceased as abruptly as it had begun.

"Our reserves are attacking!" the encircled men called out to each other. "They are coming, they are coming!" And their hearts leaped. Soon, a few groups of the enemy were seen in full retreat. Their number kept increasing. Here and there, the fighting flared up at close range, but it soon subsided again. The number of encircling forces decreased. They were caught in the current of the retreat. Close on their heels followed the rescuers.

A heavily armed German combat patrol reached the encircled men first. By noon, the old position was entirely in German hands again. This time, it had still been possible, by using the last local reserves, to eliminate the enemy penetration and to avert calamity. The remnants of the enemy, although they had sustained severe losses, were nevertheless able to cling to a thin strip of terrain on the western bank of the Donets River just outside the German position and to hold this ground, thanks to the very good support they received from their artillery. This indicated clearly that the enemy planned to move up reinforcements and renew his attack. To repulse this new attack, no more reserves were available. The enemy attacked that very afternoon, at a time when the point of main effort of the German artillery and air action was situated in the adjacent regimental sector, likewise seriously threatened.

The Russians managed to achieve a deep penetration, which, after assault guns had been employed, it was possible to stop only on the western edge of a gorge traversing the forest from north to south. The movement of these guns was facilitated by forest roads and narrow lanes through the forest which led to the gorge. The assault guns and the engineers attached to them once more offered good support to the retiring scattered units of the badly battered infantry battalion. The withdrawing soldiers rapidly assembled along the forest gorge, which was a few meters in depth and which was conveniently situated and prepared for defense along its western run. All attempts on the part of the enemy to cross the gorge were frustrated by the new front, which had been reinforced by twelve assault guns and 100 engineers. Every machine gun appearing on the opposite rim of the gorge was then destroyed by a well-adjusted round from an assault gun. With every passing hour, the resistance was strengthened by men returning from furlough and from hospitals, and by soldiers from service units who were usually moved to focal points in critical moments. In addition, the bottom of the gorge itself was rapidly mined, and tree obstacles and alarm devices were set up. These measures also substantially increased the strength of the resistance. Even before darkness, the threat of an enemy breakthrough had been eliminated.

The situation of the battalion adjacent on the south, however, was taking a rather critical turn. The northern flank of this battalion had been caught by the enemy push described above. It was able to oppose the enemy with only a weak, oblique defense line, which the Russians bypassed instead of pivoting heavy forces southward to expel the battalion from its dominating position on the hill. In this manner, the enemy hoped to be able to attack the valley position in the rear, and thus bring about its collapse. The brave battalion, however, repulsed all attacks of the superior enemy forces and continued to hold its tactically important bastion.

All of a sudden, a completely unexpected event occurred. In a gap between the two battalions which were being attacked, soldiers in German uniforms and with German equipment appeared and, in good German, reported the arrival of reinforcements which were to come to the aid of the harassed sector. This news was received with great joy and made its way through the position with lightning speed. Before it was possible, however, to ascertain the origin and strength of this unexpected help, the Russians attacked along the entire front of the battalion. The situation became extremely strained. The defenders were employed in the front line to the last man.

At that moment, the soldiers of the newly arrived companies poured out of the woods in dense columns and opened a murderous hail of fire against the flank and rear of the defenders' forces. In the confusion that followed, there were shouts of "Here are

Germans!"—"Don't fire!"—"Cease fire!"—"Madness!"—"What's going on here!" No one understood the other and no one understood what was happening. The uncertainty and confusion had risen until everything was a hopeless mix-up, when abruptly the fire ceased and the pseudo-Germans attacked the German defenders with earsplitting yells of "Hurrah! Hurrah! Hurrah!" In this bewildering situation, desperate for the German battalion, in the forest everyone now began to fight everyone else. It was impossible to tell friend from enemy. No one seemed to be able to help or disentangle the chaos.

The battalion commander now understood the purpose of the insidious attack and was aware that the one decision possible was to reach the northern edge of "A" Village in order to save his unit and prevent the valley position from being rolled up. He called for the men to gather in the village. This call had the effect of a kindling spark. The voice of the commander was recognized and his order was passed on. Soon, every German soldier knew what to do. The will of the commander asserted itself. The order was not easy to execute; but unless it was carried out, every man and every piece of equipment was lost. The commander was firmly convinced that his officers and his seasoned infantrymen would make it.

Quickly he gathered up a few officers and all the soldiers in his immediate vicinity and formed an assault detachment from them, which he led personally. Holding submachine guns and rifles in front of them ready to fire, or daggers and hand grenades in their clenched fists, they killed the Russians wherever they met them, recognizing them by their Mongolian features whether they wore Russian or German uniforms. In this manner, the commander and his men made their way through the fighting soldiers and, in short bounds, reached the forest edge, from which some depressions and gullies led to the first houses of the village. Imitating this first party, everywhere soldiers banded together to form small detachments under the command of officers or noncommissioned officers and fought their way back to the village. Here the commander immediately organized positions and incorporated in the defense of the village all newly arriving groups, as well as all soldiers of rear services who happened to be present in the village, regardless of the unit to which they belonged. The regimental headquarters, which had been informed immediately, rushed a company and a few assault guns, which had been transferred quickly by trucks from the division, to the gravely distressed battalion.

Favored by the terrain which sloped toward the village and afforded cover from visibility and fire, the battalion, with the exception of some small elements, had assembled and prepared itself for defensive operations by late afternoon. When the enemy appeared on the edge of the forest soon thereafter, he was hit by machine-gun fire and compelled to retire to the protection of the forest. Wherever he repeated his attempt to advance on the village, artillery and assault gunfire thwarted his intentions. Again and again, he was forced to withdraw into the forest after sustaining serious losses. Gradually dark fell. Meanwhile, a number of stragglers were arriving at their units by detours. At night, the battalion had all but reached its full strength again. In view of the severe crises which it had gone through, its losses were very small. The battalion commander's presence of mind and the initiative of the noncommissioned officers saved the battalion from certain doom. The enemy's violation of international law, though resulting in the loss of an important bastion, failed to bring about the collapse of the front.

The speed with which the battalion recovered from the blow which it had received at the end of the day is indicated by the fact that the commander was able, that very night, to plan to recapture the lost position on the following morning, using the same unit, which was still under the influence of the black day it had gone through. And he put his plan into effect at once. At dawn on 4 August, he hoped to hit the enemy (who was certain to try and advance further) so hard by means of a surprise blow that the lost hill position would be recaptured. The plan seemed very reasonable, and it was to be realized.

As soon as there was enough light to permit firing, the enemy artillery and the heavy mortars began to shell the village which was spread out in length. Soon the fire became very intense. With a deafening din, echoed over and over again by the forest, the shells roared and whistled up to and burst in the village and on the other side of the road. Under the protection of this wall of fire, wave after wave of Russians broke out from the rim of the forest and ran down the slope of the *Hutweide*.[8]

The leading elements had already come within storming distance when the German counterattack began. Ground attack and bomber wings appeared over the scene and attacked the enemy on a continuous basis. The assault guns, the number of which had been greatly increased during the night, moved forward against the enemy, all guns firing. These guns and the machine guns being fired from trenches, foxholes and houses, as well as the artillery, antitank guns and antiaircraft artillery, spread such havoc in the ranks of the enemy's forces that their position on the terrain, which afforded no cover whatever, became untenable. Their only chance to escape the hail of fire was to withdraw to the forest.

At the very moment, however, when the enemy first began withdrawing, the German artillery started firing a barrage on the edge of the forest. This inflicted severe losses on the enemy's forces, who were running in all directions looking for a way to save themselves. Only battered remnants managed to find refuge in the forest. But even here the enemy was given no time to assemble his troops and to use them in a renewed defensive effort, because the infantrymen, who were still smarting from the enemy's trickery on the previous day, followed the Russians, tracked them down in the forest and, by pushing forward rapidly, prevented the enemy from gaining a firm footing again in the German hill position. Hardly two hours had passed since the beginning of the attack when the leading elements of the German infantrymen again reached the defense position they had occupied on the previous day. Soon afterward, the important bastion was back in German hands.

The treacherous attack of the previous day had indeed brought about a rather critical situation, but his day's counterattack had nullified the enemy's unfairly gained success.

---

[8] A meadow not shown on the attached map.

Heavy losses in men and equipment were the result of this operation. Those who died that day included the majority of the Russians who had worn German uniforms.

Example 3: Tanks Cross a River
on Top of Other Tanks, 5 August 1943

It has already been mentioned that on the night of 2 August, the enemy also made preparations to cross the Donets River south of the junction of "A" Brook with the Donets. Here, too, an incident took place which astonished the German troops, even though they were accustomed to unusual situations. They had never seen the like of it before.

Soon after dark, as has already been mentioned, a noise was heard from the floodplains lining the eastern bank of the river. This noise unmistakably indicated that the enemy was planning to build a bridge there in order to be able to cross the Donets River rapidly with heavy equipment. A short time later, sawing and hammering was heard in the clear, quiet night: construction of the bridge, it seemed, had already begun. The enemy shells which occasionally whistled toward a ridge jutting out far eastward were unable altogether to drown out the noise of the work. For a while, the enemy was allowed to proceed, but then he was hit all the harder. This could easily be done since the fire of the artillery and other heavy weapons on the hill position had been adjusted on the old bridge site and was ready to be used at night.

The ridge forming a salient which afforded good possibilities for cover had been converted into an invincible bastion months ago. Shell-proof dugouts and tunnels and bunkers constructed several meters below ground level protected the men stationed in this position from even heavy artillery fire. In tunnels running far forward, the apertures of which were so well-concealed during the day that they were invisible, contained the very dangerous "ambush" machine guns, which were silent during the day and independently opened a devastating fire only at critical moments. They were tremendously effective against the most important points and approach routes of the enemy. They dominated both banks of the river and flanked the enemy swamp bridgehead which formed a salient aimed in the direction of the church of "A" Village. All firing data for the points mentioned had been worked out and checked. During the night, small searchlights illuminated the immediate outpost area. Their limited range was a help only to the infantry weapons. Even the employment of these weapons was permitted only on special orders or in cases of emergency. The enemy was absolutely unaware of these special measures, since so far no use had been made of them. Now they were about to play their part. But their hour had not yet come.

First, a surprise fire attack by several batteries was to multiply at one blow the progress made in the construction of the bridge. At the exact time set, just before midnight, a hurricane of fire was unleashed against the bridge site. It stopped as abruptly as it had begun. In the flickering light of a fire, which had flared up next to the bridge site, the outlines of a crisscross maze of beams and piles were observed. The half-finished bridge had been smashed to pieces, wounded men groaned, and the shadows of figures flitting about seemed to be those of men coming to their aid. They were not disturbed.

Scarcely half an hour later, activity was resumed at the identical place. The hammering went on, so that it was necessary to repeat the concentration after midnight. The result was the same as before. Then all was quiet. A few ammunition dumps burned and exploded after having been hit. Soon these fires were extinguished. As was to be expected, after a while, the enemy resumed his efforts to build a bridge at that same point. He was trying to have it finished by dawn.

To prevent him, without wasting too much ammunition, from realizing this intention, the Germans now started a slow, harassing fire with a 210mm howitzer battery. This battery had carefully adjusted its fire on the bridge site, and, as a result, heavy shells were sent over one by one at irregular intervals and, insofar as it was possible to observe in the flash of each detonation, they either hit the target or fell in the immediate vicinity. In the course of an hour, the effect after each impact could be deduced from the enemy's behavior. If a heavy shell did major damage, a prolonged intermission occurred in the work, but, if the effect was limited, the hammering was resumed at once. Thus, the danger existed that the enemy might be able to complete the construction of the bridge by dawn in spite of the harassing fire.

In order to prevent this, the Germans gave a few ambush machine guns the mission of raking the construction site with fire at short intervals. The exceedingly accurate and rapid fire of these weapons had a devastating effect. This could be deduced from the screams of victims and the fact that the work was immediately suspended. In spite of the losses inflicted on the enemy by this procedure, he attempted to continue his work; but after a while, his energy flagged and finally he discontinued his work entirely.

At intervals, however, the German howitzers continued the harassing fire in order to discourage a resumption of the work on the part of the enemy, and to complete the destruction. Only when day broke was it possible to obtain a full view of the result of the night's firing. It was a horrible picture that offered itself to the observers. A maze of splintered timbers stuck up into the air, and in the interstices were the mutilated bodies of the Russians who, scorning death, had tried to complete the structure. A still greater number of mangled bodies covered the area around the bridge site, while others half emerged from the marsh pools made by howitzer shells, where they had taken final refuge. The vicinity was strewn with disabled vehicles, dead horses, and a wide variety of ammunition and equipment. Death had taken a heavy toll.

The enemy had disappeared, and his plan had failed. After this complete fiasco, the Germans believed that they would no longer have anything to fear at this point, especially since the Russians had managed, on that very day, to achieve successes against the regiment adjacent on the north—successes which they would probably seek to expand. If, however, the enemy engineers had succeeded in completing the construction of the bridge, which would have given the enemy command a chance to launch a simultaneous thrust in the valley, this sector of the front would have been threatened with collapse.

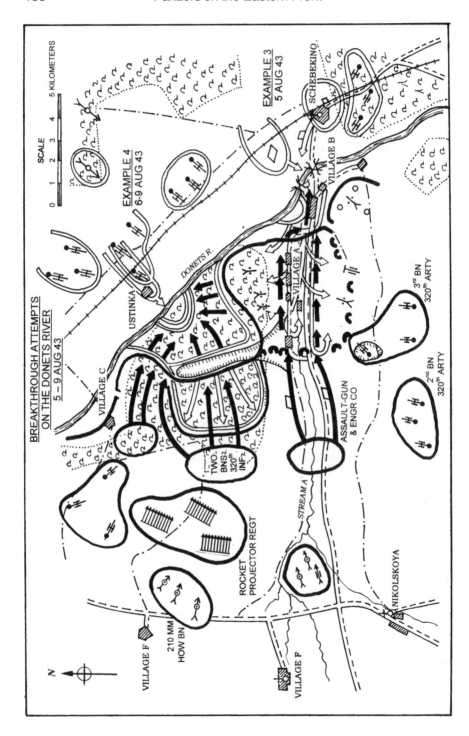

BREAKTHROUGH ATTEMPTS
ON THE DONETS RIVER
5 – 9 AUG 43

SCALE

0 1 2 3 4 5 KILOMETERS

EXAMPLE 4
6-9 AUG 43

EXAMPLE 3
5 AUG 43

N

DONETS R.

VILLAGE C

USTINKA

VILLAGE A

VILLAGE B

SCHEBEKINO

TWO-
BNS²
320ᵗʰ
INF²

ROCKET
PROJECTOR REGT

210 MM
HOW BN

VILLAGE F

VILLAGE F

STREAM A

ASSAULT-GUN
& ENGR CO

2ⁿᵈ BN
320ᵗʰ ARTY

3ʳᵈ BN
320ᵗʰ ARTY

NIKOLSKOYA

In the valley sector, all was quiet during that day. As soon as darkness fell, however, the enemy repeated his attempts to effect a crossing at the same place as on the preceding night, using new men and equipment. The Germans had not expected this. Nevertheless, they were prepared for defense, and they utilized the experience gained on the preceding night. Immediately, bursts of machine-gun fire sounded and the howitzers began to fire, just as they had at the end of the defensive action on the previous night. The machine guns turned out to be by far the most dangerous weapon for all live targets, and the howitzers were the most accurate and effective means of destroying vehicles and equipment. This night, the enemy again was not discouraged from continuing his efforts, in spite of extremely heavy losses. Before midnight, however, he broke off his hopeless undertaking. Judging from the movements of track-laying vehicles, which could be heard immediately afterward, he had moved up caterpillar tractors in order to haul off his machinery, his supply stocks, and the bridge-building equipment which was still intact, thus saving them from complete destruction.

This time, however, the conclusions drawn from the observations were erroneous. To the great surprise of German commanders and local units, the noise of the track-laying vehicles did not cease as dawn drew near; on the contrary, it came closer and closer! The caterpillar tractors turned out to be tanks which had already crossed the Donets River and the points of which, at the break of dawn, had reached the area in front of "B" Village. They were already firing their first shots against the fortified edge of the village. This was the signal for a general attack. The enemy artillery opened fire against the village. An even more formidable hail of the enemy's light and heavy shells hit the hills on both sides of the valley, since it was the enemy's intention to neutralize these dominating bastions of the German defense. Now, life also began to stir in the swamp bridgehead. A general attack along the entire valley front and against the strongpoints on the adjoining hills was intended to bring these, as well as "A" Village, into the enemy's hands and to facilitate the planned attack aimed at the Kharkov–Belgorod *Rollbahn*.

At once, the Germans began to lay a barrage in front of the hill positions and in front of "A" Village. This barrage, as well as the large number of obstacles and minefields, stopped the enemy until there was sufficient light to permit accurate firing. It then became possible to bring the defense weapons fully to bear. Only then was there a chance of obtaining an accurate idea of the situation. The leading enemy tanks had already overcome the roadblock situated in front of "A" Village, and were pushing forward to the center of the village, followed by infantry echeloned in depth. Other tanks veered from the rear toward the fortified edge of the village, and gradually overcame the German strongpoints and pockets of resistance. In this process, they were joined by elements of the "Swamp Battalion." Soon they had reached the church and the northern edge of the village. They did not venture beyond it, however, since lively antitank and machine-gun fire was aimed at them from the hill opposite.

Fighting for every single farmhouse, the German defenders of the village retired westward step by step. The enemy, who meanwhile was also under accurate and effective artillery fire from the southern hills, became more cautious as his open flanks increased in length. He waited in vain for help from adjacent forces, which were still tied down in front of the German defenses on the hills. During the morning, it was only hesitantly that a few tanks and, close behind them, a few small combat patrols advanced to the last houses of the mile-long village. The majority of the Russian infantry, in a strength of two to three battalions, veered toward both sides, from which it received lively machine-gun and artillery fire.

A German ambush battery, which had established itself in complete concealment in a forested depression forming a salient, suddenly fired point-blank into the rear of the "Swamp Battalion." The battalion had been trying, this time from the south, to capture the southern elevated strongpoint with which it was already familiar, and had been tied down, with its front facing north, by machine-gun fire. As a result, the battalion was caught by fire from two sides, which was unbearable even by Russian standards and which wore out the resistance of this battle-toughened enemy.

By noon, the Russian general attack had been stopped everywhere. The enemy had been trapped in a deep, but very narrow pocket, in which he could move neither forward nor backward without sustaining heavy losses. His situation became more and more unpleasant, since all attempts on his part to bring up reserves in order to force a breakthrough were thwarted by the formidable German defensive fire from the flank and rear. Only when it was dark would it be possible for the Russians to move up sufficient numbers of troops to give the offensive a new impulse. This constituted a grave threat to the German defenders, who had already been obliged to employ their last man and their last weapon to stop the enemy advance. And yet, on that same day, it was imperative to find a way to throw back across the Donets River the enemy forces which had achieved the penetration. A way to do this had been found during the morning, and had already been put into effect.

Nine assault guns and one engineer company were quickly moved from the northern forest sector and were expected to arrive any moment. The men in the company were stalwart fellows, "prepared to kidnap the devil from hell!" Very familiar with the assault guns, well-versed in teamwork, and supported by additional flanking weapons (machine guns, antitank guns, and antiaircraft guns) which they had brought along, the engineers and assault gun crews started a frontal counterattack on both sides of the village street even before 1300 hours. Their mere appearance infused new hope in the men fighting in the threatened sector of the front. Since the men operating the flanking weapons saw the village lying in front of them as if it were situated on a raised table, ideal cooperation with the combat force was insured. A few ground attack airplanes also participated in the operation.

The engineers were eager, above all else, to reach the Donets River and find out how the enemy had managed to cross the river, and to do so with a large number of tanks, in spite of the fact that he had been prevented from building his bridge. This was the question which was uppermost in the minds of all participants in the battle, and one which greatly puzzled even the command, since the latter in particular had been fully familiar with the Donets River for months and, having had its depth measured, knew it to be an absolute tank obstacle, which in the preceding offensive even German Tiger tanks and assault guns had been able to cross only after a 70-ton bridge had been constructed. Yet, from the hill on the south, the tracks of tanks which led to the eastern bank of the river and continued on the western bank were plainly visible. Hence, the Germans concluded that the tanks which had appeared so suddenly must have been amphibians. There was only one among the commanders present, however, who had ever met with amphibious tanks in the East before. This was the corps commander himself, whose former armored unit in July 1941 had encountered six light amphibious tanks, which the United States had furnished to Russia,[9] and had disabled all six of them on the Szilnia Stream south of the village of Novoselye, situated on the large *Rollbahn* to Leningrad. In size, these amphibious tanks, however, compared to the T-34, which undoubtedly was involved here, as David compared to Goliath. As a result, it was impossible for the Russian tanks which crossed the Donets River without a bridge to have been amphibious tanks.

How then did the enemy tanks, whose characteristics were well-known, manage to make their way across the river, the depth of which had shortly before been sounded and found to be three meters? Although the T-34 had the greatest cross-country mobility of all tanks on the continent, and had often accomplished astonishing feats, all the men were unanimously of the opinion that the T-34 could not get across the Donets River here.

It was only after many more hours of heavy fighting that it was possible to solve the riddle. First, it was necessary to reach the river. This required time, since the enemy offered very stubborn resistance. Each house had to be wrested from him in close-in fighting. His infantry even clung to the ruins as long as his tanks were visible in the vicinity. The tanks now constituted the backbone of the defense, just as they had furnished momentum for the attack in the morning. All weapons were firing at them from all sides. This had little effect, unless an armor-piercing weapon scored a direct hit and set one of them ablaze. The assault guns, which here were the most dangerous weapon for the T-34s, had a difficult mission to fulfill. The excellent enemy tanks, which were numerically superior, stubbornly held their ground and allowed the assault guns to approach. Many of the latter had had to suffer a few direct hits on their reinforced front armor before they had been able to incapacitate a T-34. One or the other's plate of front armor was smashed in the process, relegating the assault gun concerned to a secondary place in the rear of those of its fellows whose front armor was still intact.

Despite all difficulties, the assault guns gradually made headway. After the duel had lasted for over an hour, five enemy tanks were burning, whereas but a few assault guns had sustained light damage, and all remained in operation. By the time the center of the

---

[9] Reviewer's Note (1952): "The author had only a fleeting glance at these vehicles, and assumed them to be of U.S. manufacture. Since he did not again encounter tanks of this type, he now believes they were test models of Soviet origin. The U.S. did not have vehicles of this type in production in 1941."

village had been reached, further losses by the enemy had gradually brought about a balance of power. The resistance put up by the enemy infantry stiffened in the valley, as a result of the fact that more and more units were caught in their flank by the German advance and were obliged to veer to the valley front. It was only after ground attack aircraft had become available again to attack these units with bombs and their armament in continual sorties, and after the fire into their rear from the hills on both sides had assumed unbearable proportions, that their will to fight decreased notably. The tanks, however, still continued to offer extremely heavy resistance. Their crews knew that a withdrawal was certain to result in defeat. Their refusal to yield, though unable to prevent the German victory, delayed it considerably. It was only in the late afternoon that the last enemy tank had become a victim of the few assault guns. Thereupon, enemy resistance collapsed.

When darkness fell, the Germans had again reached their old positions on the western edge of "A" Village. The long-range observer returned to his "eagle's nest" at the top of the church tower, which he had left that morning. In the last glow of twilight, assault guns and engineer patrols following the defeated enemy reached the point of the river where the enemy tanks had effected their crossing in the morning mist. Even at very close range, no sign of a bridge could be detected. It was only when the depth of the water was sounded that the riddle was solved. At a depth of half a meter the engineers came upon a submarine bridge. The enemy had built such bridges on various other occasions in order to shield river crossings from German air observation and to save them from destruction. Consequently, the bridge as such did not cause as much astonishment as the fact that it obviously had been built in an incredibly short time, in spite of devastating gunfire. Only upon a closer inspection of the foundation on which the bridge rested the mystery was unraveled. Two rows of undamaged tanks were discovered, which had been driven into the water one behind the other and which served as supports for the improvised submarine bridge. Planking had been hastily placed on top of them and attached to them with ropes. Thereafter, the venture of letting tanks cross the river on top of other tanks was immediately undertaken. It mattered little to the Russians that a few tanks overturned had plunged into the water in the process; the main thing was that a majority of the tanks managed to reach the other bank. The German assault guns saved them the necessity of returning over this strange bridge.

The crossing was a one-time improvisation which, however, served its purpose in spite of its great shortcomings. The enemy had hoped to be able, after a successful completion of his operation, to retrieve his tanks from the water and use them again. As matters stood, however, they were blasted by German engineers and went where others of their kind had gone before them in the course of the day—to the "tank graveyard." This constituted the last activity at the end of a day of heavy combat. Now the silence of night drew "a veil of peace over the scene."

Once again, an utterly unusual step on the part of the enemy had resulted in surprising success, which had been of grave concern to the German commanders. Their countermeasures, which have been described in detail, and the courageous bearing of the troops, however, nullified even this enemy success. The success of the counterattack undertaken by so small a combat group as nine assault guns and about 80 engineers was primarily due to the employment of a large number of automatic weapons, the fire from which was excellently coordinated and which hit the enemy with annihilating effect. This success was typical, since it was the result of employing a minimum number of excellently trained men, but supporting them with the most effective weapons.

Example 4: The Bridgehead Within a Bridgehead, 6–9 August 1943

In view of the large-scale development of events at the corps, as outlined at the beginning of this study, it is understandable that the situation in the Donets River sector with which this study has been dealing so far did not quiet down. The enemy's endeavor to achieve a decisive success here, at all costs, made him adopt unusual methods. In this connection, it may be well to describe one peculiar event which occurred in the final stage of these battles.

At the end of all the operations narrated on the preceding pages, only one bridgehead remained in the hands of the enemy. How this bridgehead originated has already been described in Example 2. The enemy had managed, at the time, to push the southern flank battalion of the 106th Infantry Division back to a gorge in the forest called *Totenschlucht*, or "Gorge of the Dead" and to capture the eastern edge of this gorge. During the subsequent fighting in the area south thereof, all had remained relatively quiet in this sector. After the enemy's armored attack in the valley sector which has been described in the preceding Example 3 had failed, however, it seemed certain that the enemy would try to mount his next offensive in the *Totenschlucht*, in spite of all the difficulties which this gorge would necessarily offer to any attempts to cross it. And that is what happened.

After two days, a new Russian attack actually started at this point. It coincided in time with the most difficult fighting of the corps against the armored and infantry units which were attacking deep in its rear in the Lopan sector with a view to encircling and destroying XI Corps from here. Hence, it was necessary to do everything to prevent a further advance of the enemy across the Donets River, since this might lead to the destruction of the entire corps.

As yet, however, the forces which had been made available on the quiet southern flank by employing recruits and replacement units there had not arrived on the scene. It was a great risk to employ these young troops, inexperienced in battle as they were, side by side on a broad front. But the situation compelled the Germans to accept the risk; the first day of fighting showed that it had been imperative to do so. At length, the enemy managed, after his assaults had been repulsed several times, to cross the minefields by means of an unsparing employment of his men. The method he used in this process was very simple. He continued to drive his men into the heavily mined gorge in front of his lines until even the last mines had been detonated, so that in the end "fields of bodies" had replaced the minefields. Then the next waves of attack were able to step over these bodies and climb the western edge of the gorge.

Every attempt to break over the edge, however, was thwarted by the devastating defensive fire of the German machine guns. This fire took an ever-increasing bloody toll among the enemy's men, until finally an unbroken line of dead lay at the edge of the gorge. Many a brave Russian soldier still held his rifle in firing position, while his head, pierced by bullets, rested on his weapon. The enemy was intent on forcing a breakthrough at all costs. Again and again, new waves of attack stepped into battle over the dead, until German resistance finally began to break as a result of the losses suffered and a lack of ammunition.

After the struggle for the *Totenschlucht* had lasted several hours, the German infantry was obliged to withdraw step by step. It was able, however, to maintain its possession of the hotly contested western edge of the forest zone until evening, when help was already approaching from behind the forest. The enemy had captured a large part of the forest, thereby substantially expanding his bridgehead on the western bank of the Donets River. His efforts to achieve a breakthrough, however, had failed. During the night, he moved up additional battalions in order to gain a complete success the next day.

The German reinforcements, however, had also arrived and prepared themselves for a counterattack. Two battalions taken from the 320th Infantry Division in the previously described manner and one battalion of the 106th Division, reinforced by a few assault guns, had the mission of regaining the forest in a concentric attack and of throwing the enemy back across the Donets River. This attack was to be preceded by fire from most of the corps artillery, reinforced by a rocket-launcher regiment and several 88mm antiaircraft batteries. The Luftwaffe, unfortunately, was prevented from joining in the attack since it was needed in its entirety in the sector of the Fourth Panzer Army, where the enemy had achieved a penetration and where it had not yet been possible to destroy the masses of tanks employed. The absence of the Luftwaffe from the scene of the present attack was offset in part by the fact that the enemy, too, employed a majority of his aircraft in the other zone where he was trying to bring about a major decision.

Assembly for the counterattack proceeded smoothly. At the prescribed hour, the launchers of the rocket-launcher regiment and the artillery of two divisions began to fire. Causing a terrific din, the shells detonated amid the massed troops which the enemy had concentrated for the attack he, too, was planning to undertake, smashing them. In between, heavy howitzer shells came roaring over into the *Totenschlucht* and, with a formidable impact, detonated in the midst of the troops and staffs, which had prepared themselves for the attack there. The danger that the German barrage in the forest might hit the German front line was eliminated by a systematic retirement immediately before the beginning of the preparatory fire. This brief retiring movement had been scheduled precisely according to the clock. It went as far as the rear edge of the forest. It had been preceded by infantry fire, which was to simulate an attack on the enemy. Simultaneously with the preparatory fire, which began with a terrific surprise concentration on the enemy front line, the infantry attack started. Gradually, the concentration was moved eastward as far as the *Totenschlucht*, which, being under fire as it was from the north, south and west, was once more turned into a mass grave for Russian soldiers and Russian hopes. The combined fire of all arms not only had a high moral effect, but also did great material damage, so that the German attack made rapid headway. With assault guns and strong combat patrols forming the point, the German forces reached the *Totenschlucht* before noon and crossed a short while afterward. The gorge offered a ghastly picture of death and ruin.

The battalion of the 106th Division, which was attacking from the north with assault-gun support, also advanced rapidly and pushed more and more deeply into the enemy's flank. Even the battalion which had so often been in distress and had over and over again tried to establish a firm hold of the strongpoint on the hill situated north of the church of "A" Village, now joined the battle from the south with gunfire and combat patrols. Everywhere the enemy was in full retreat. By noon, the concentrically attacking battalions had gained direct contact with one another in all sectors. In spite of all defensive efforts on the part of the enemy, the iron ring around his decimated forces was being drawn tighter. The plan was to encircle and destroy the enemy's forces, even before they reached the river. By the early hours of the afternoon, the area which the Russians still held on the western side of the Donets had become so small that considerable elements of the attacking forces, including most of the assault guns, had had to be withdrawn from the front for lack of space. It seemed that it would be no more than a matter of a few hours before the enemy's defeat was complete, and the whole western bank would be in German hands. All of a sudden, however, enemy resistance stiffened again.

The German spearheads quite unexpectedly encountered heavily mined tree branch obstacles tied together with barbed wire, which proved impossible to overcome. Attempts to blast the obstacles showed that, behind the leading obstacles, there were rows and rows of others which were even more difficult to remove and which were covered by heavy defensive fire. For the first time that day, a lively artillery barrage started, which, as it was reinforced by heavy trench mortar fire, made any further advance impossible. Soon it became evident that, during the preceding days, the enemy had established a heavily fortified area on the western bank of the Donets River. In the event of a reverse—which he considered possible in the light of his most recent experience—he had intended to hold this area under all circumstances. The area was a kind of "emergency bridgehead" which was intended to save the enemy another costly crossing of the river if the worst came.

Indeed, all attempts by the Germans to eliminate this thorn in their own side failed. The assault guns could not keep abreast of the other troops in the very uneven and wooded terrain. As a result, their valuable support was lacking, as was that of the formidable concentrations of the entire artillery and the rocket-launcher regiment, which were unable to "soften up" this small area a few hundred meters in diameter. On the other hand, however, their hail of fire dislodged the tree obstacles, tore gaps in the minefields, and battered the woods. It was still impossible, however, for even a single combat patrol to break through. Even the flamethrowers were unable to make an impression on the enemy, since his men crouched in small dugouts and bunkers, against which even this terrible weapon was ineffective. Although a few bunkers were destroyed and a number of dugouts buried under falling earth, enough remained on either side and in the rear of them to prevent any attempt to advance.

As we subsequently ascertained in interrogations of prisoners of war, this fortified area was occupied by a "security garrison" which had been taken from a choice unit commanded by commissars, and which had not taken part in the preceding battles. These men were faced with the alternative of holding their positions to the last man or being shot in the neck. Another part of their mission, however, which they failed to fulfill, was to stop the retreating battalions as long as they were still on the western bank of the river. These battalions had been so greatly battered by the impact of the German fire and by the drive of the brave German infantry that they eluded the grasp of their commanders. In this terrain, with its very much limited visibility, neither the draconian measures of the Russian officers and commissars nor the fire opened on the troops by the security garrison of the small bridgehead were of any use. They served only to increase the bewilderment of the panic-stricken troops and add to their losses.

Nevertheless, the enemy's unusual measure of building a small, heavily fortified "defensive bridgehead" within a large "offensive bridgehead" during an offensive operation repaid the effort, for it was owing to this inner bridgehead that the enemy, in spite of all the adversities he had encountered during the past days, still had one foot on the western bank of the river which had caused him so many difficulties and sacrifices.

The "bridgehead within a bridgehead" remained a thorn in the side of the Germans and a ray of hope to the enemy. It may also have made it easier for many a Russian commander to transmit the bad news of the newly sustained heavy defeat to higher headquarters. The Germans sealed off the bridgehead and stopped attacking it in order to avoid unnecessary bloodshed. Since the Russians, who needed time to get over the severe reverse they had suffered, also refrained from action, there was a brief rest, during which both opponents had a chance to recover.

In the meantime, the situation in the rear of the Donets front had greatly deteriorated as a result of the rapid withdrawal of the army adjacent on the west. Russian armored units on the Lopan River pushed deeper and deeper in their efforts to envelop the corps and made necessary a phased withdrawal of the northern salient of the front and, as a result, the withdrawal of further units from the Donets River front. At the last minute, the enemy tried to push forward from his small bridgehead in order to attack the corps in its rear. Once again, he managed to reach the *Totenschlucht*. Only rearguards, however, were left to face him. When, a few hours later, he started his decisive attack, he pushed into a void. The rearguards, which had simulated the presence of a defensive front to the enemy, had to follow the division, which meanwhile, without enemy interference, had been moved from the Donets River line to the northern front. Thus, the enemy's last hope of rupturing the vital artery of the German XI Corps had been shattered.

The peculiar measures of the enemy on the Donets River front had caused a great deal of surprise and grave concern to the local German commanders, and had taken their bloody toll from the troops. The fact that the Russians did not achieve the aims which these measures were designed to serve must be attributed solely to the presence of mind and the flexibility of the German commanders and to the courage of their troops. These qualities helped them master all unusual situations.

Chapter 5

The Pomeranian Battle and the Command in the East

Discussion with Reichsführer SS Himmler and Report to the Führer

Topic 1: First Discussion with Reichsführer SS Himmler

Toward the end of the disastrous operation in East Prussia, the staff of the Third Panzer Army and I were relieved from assignment, and during 8–10 February 1945 we were transferred by boat and rail to Rummelsburg (Pomerania). There we were attached to Army Group Weichsel (Reichsführer SS Himmler), but were not yet committed.

I immediately established personal contact with the corps on the right of the 11th SS Panzer Army (Lieutenant-General Steiner) and the corps on the left wing of the Second Army (General Weiss), both of which were engaged in bitter defensive fighting to the south of my headquarters. It was intended for the time being that these corps be subordinated to my command as a new Army sector.

Shortly after arriving in Rummelsburg, I requested to be presented to the Army Group Commander, Reichsführer SS [Heinrich] Himmler, and be permitted to make my report to him. My appointment was made for 13 February 1945.

Late in the afternoon of 13 February, several technical staff officers and I arrived at Himmler's headquarters in a camp in the woods southwest of Prenzlau. There I was given a thorough report on the situation and plans by the Army Group G-3 (Operations Officer), and then, by orders from Himmler, I was invited to have dinner with him (Himmler) and his closest assistants at 2000 hours. Himmler appeared promptly, received me, and introduced me to his associates. He was obviously in good spirits and carried on a lively conversation, touching upon no official matters. As he talked, he evinced a marked interest in the arts and sciences. The meal was simple but well prepared and served perfectly. Since guests were present, an exception was made and everyone at the table was served one glass of red wine. Himmler himself drank only mineral water. An hour later, Himmler rose from the table and arranged to meet me for a discussion at 2230 in the office at his quarters. I was with Himmler at the appointed hour, and there I met his Chief of Staff, SS Obergruppenführer Lammerding. The conference, originally planned for only half an hour, was prolonged by Himmler to 0300 because of my lengthy report, and thus lasted four and one-half hours. Lammerding was present only until about midnight, and then, because of the heavy air raid at Dresden, he received permission from Himmler to leave and visit his family residing there. Consequently, from approximately midnight to the end of the discussion, I was alone with Himmler.

To this very day, I remember in detail the conversation given below. Also I am still able to repeat word for word Himmler's main remarks and questions, as well as my replies. It is all the more simple for me, since, on returning to Rummelsburg, I immediately informed my Chief of Staff, Brigadier General Mueller-Hillebrand, about the conversation, and also because later I often discussed the outcome of the conversation with others.

Himmler: As you have been informed by my G-3, the 11th Panzer Army, together with other SS panzer divisions and SS panzergrenadiers which have been brought up, will break through to the south from the area southwest of Stargard the day after tomorrow and attack the Soviet armies flanking Küstrin from the rear and annihilate them. The Führer expects decisive results for the outcome of the war from this attack. Originally, I had planned to place you, an experienced armored-force commander, in charge of this mission. Unfortunately it was not possible to obtain your release from East Prussia in time. My suggestion of postponing the attack so that assembly of forces could be completed, and that you and your staff might still be integrated, was reflected upon by the Führer. Give me your honest opinion as to the course of action and the chances of success in this offensive.

Raus: A comparison of strength of both sides (our *one* reinforced panzer army as opposed to the three Russian tank armies and three to four infantry armies) is sufficient to conclude that the attack can lead only to failure. By achieving better coordination of our own units and by selecting a shorter route for the attack by your panzer divisions, perhaps some ground may be gained at one point or another, but then they will come to a standstill. *Under no circumstances, however, can a decisive result be expected.*

Himmler: [Visibly affected by this adverse opinion, asked me to be just as frank in telling him what I would do in his place.]

Raus: Do not attack, but hold the panzer units which have been moved up in readiness to definitely repulse the impending enemy attack. After the attack has been warded off successfully, I would improve the contour of our line through a counterattack, so that we would be able to hold our position against all future enemy attacks. [Additional reasons were cited in a lengthy discussion on this point.]

Himmler: That is out of the question. The Führer has given orders for the attack and will not change his mind. *For that reason, the attack will be launched under any circumstances.* I intend to discuss your proposals as to a more efficient execution of the attack with Guderian.[1] [Himmler then summoned General Guderian by telephone to come to him from Zossen immediately.]

---

[1] Generaloberst (Colonel-General) Heinz Guderian (1888–1954) was Chief of the General Staff of the Germany Army (Oberkommando des Heeres, or OKH) from 1944 to 1945.—Editor.

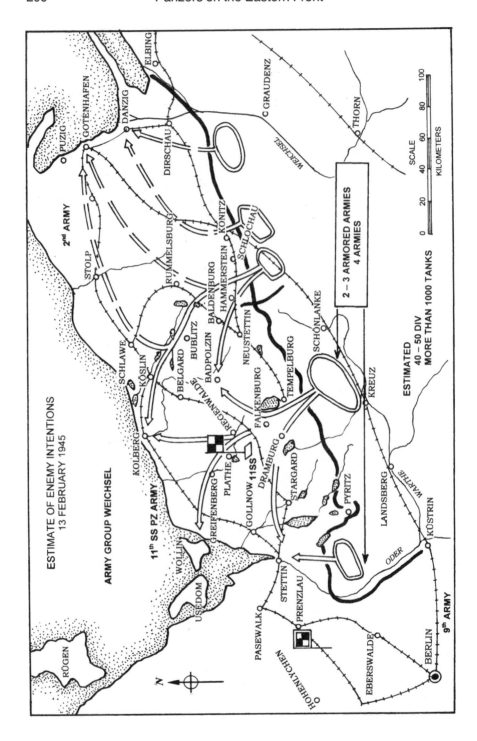

ESTIMATE OF ENEMY INTENTIONS
13 FEBRUARY 1945

Raus: [After I had again given reasons for my opinion and very firmly suggested not to carry out the attack] I am convinced that the attack will have come to a standstill by the second day. In that event, I recommend that you no longer fight uselessly but halt the attack immediately and withdraw strong reserves for the defense against the Soviet counterattack, which can definitely be expected. *However, under no circumstances can these reserves be transferred to another theater before the defense against the counterattack has succeeded, since that would bring about the collapse of your army group.* [Detailed dialogue. Himmler was convinced by this evaluation.]

Himmler: [Then, apparently to arouse my enthusiasm, told me confidentially that at approximately the same time Army Group South, together with the 6th SS Panzer Army and other forces flanking Lake Balaton, would launch a large-scale attack against the Soviet Armies, poised for an assault on Vienna, and recapture Budapest.]

Raus: [Judging from my experience, I did not encourage him in any expectations of success even in this assault, because our forces were too weak and the 6th SS Panzer Army would be exposed to the danger of being cut off and annihilated at Lake Balaton. I also recommended that the same procedure be followed in this case that I had advised for Pomerania, and added that success could be gained only if it were possible to weld the 6th SS Panzer Army *and* the 11th SS Panzer Army, as well as all other available forces, into one force and use it in *one* of the two sectors.]

Himmler: [In the course of quite lengthy discussion, he pointed out that the overall situation would not permit such a concentration of forces, and clung to his belief that these two offensives would decide the outcome of the war.]

Raus: [When the conversation turned to the subject of the overall situation, I seized the opportunity of speaking about the serious miscalculations made by the Supreme Command and their consequences. About this time, there was a short pause while Lammerding left for Dresden for the reasons mentioned above. The discussion continued now only between Himmler and me.] Herr Reichsführer, permit me to make use of this first opportunity of being able to speak to you, the most influential individual in the nation next to the Führer, in order to tell you in all frankness what I think about the manner in which the war has been conducted during the last few years and the situation as a result thereof. I know that my statements could take me to the Moabit Prison and perhaps even to the gallows, but I shall not be able to vindicate myself before God and the German people if I remain silent on the subject.

Himmler: [Seriously] Proceed.

Raus: Since Stalingrad, our conduct of operations has created serious doubts in the minds of commanders of all grades and during the last months cannot be understood at all.

From the standpoint of space alone, it is clear that the advance of the German Army as far as the Volga and the Caucasus, and the resulting defensive operations along a 3000 kilometer-long front, exceeded the capacity of the German Armed Forces and the German allied forces. *The bow was strained to the utmost and had to break.* The strength-consuming fighting around Stalingrad and on the Don, and the ramifications of these actions, led to a military defeat of gigantic proportions. Two-thirds of the Eastern front began to totter, the allied forces were crushed and swept away, and a complete collapse of the front became apparent. The catastrophe was prevented only by the miraculous courage and tenacity of the German commanders and troops and by the exertion of the every ounce of strength.

The Supreme Command did not deduct the inevitable inferences from these facts, but issued orders with increasing obstinacy and stubbornness, which led to the elimination and destruction of numerous large and very large units. This unsystematic robbery gnawed at the very marrow of German combat strength, and has brought us to the edge of the abyss into which we are in danger of being hurled, unless those miracles occur which our people have been led to expect. The Supreme Command has lost all concept for time and space, and the relationship with military strength, and is leading the subordinate Army commanders by the nose in such a way that *they are able to issue orders only with hands tied and a rope dangling above their heads,* since they have to carry out orders under penalty of death, and in return are driven away in shame and condemned as traitors to their country if the result of the battle is unfavorable. [I paused here in expectation of a contradictory utterance from Himmler or my immediate arrest. Neither of these two took place.]

Himmler: [Unmoved, looked me squarely in the eyes and said:] Continue.

Raus: [Now began to substantiate my views with examples.]

a. Instead of organizing an *aggressive strategic defense* in suitable sectors selected well in advance, the Command was unwilling to surrender as much as one kilometer of space.

b. Every reserve which had become available anywhere was immediately committed in local offensive operations, which failed because they were carried out with inadequate resources and, as a result, in addition to loss of ground, employment of these forces was without gain. [Reference is made to the pincer attack against Kursk, July 1943, to the counterattack against Kiev, and to the plans in Pomerania and Hungary.]

c. *Construction of rear positions has been prohibited for a long time,* since allegedly units looked toward the rear and consequently did not present strong enough resistance. The result was exactly the opposite. Example: During the withdrawal to the Dnieper, even hastily prepared positions were of enormous value. However, on the Dnieper, almost no preparations had been made, and consequently the enemy reached the opposite bank within a short period and neutralized this water barrier. Troops felt bitter disappointment, and their misgivings toward the Supreme Command grew. To be sure, there were considerable preparations in East Prussia; however, the badly debilitated army no longer had enough strength to occupy and hold the positions.

d. Local strongpoints and so-called *"centers of resistance" were emergency measures* which, however, through stubborn resistance even in a hopeless situation, led not only to the loss of the places, but also to the loss of the unit and its confidence in the Command.

e. Improperly integrated or encircled and strength-consuming sectors had to be held at any cost, and ate up troop units or led to their loss.

f. Entire armies were left to the defense of areas until they were encircled, and for that reason did not play a role in the main theater of war (Caucasus, Crimea,[2] Army Group North in Courland,[3] and the Fourth Army in East Prussia). The same catastrophic situation is in store in the case of Pomerania and Hungary if the planned operation is carried out.[4]

g. The *new units*, constantly coming from nowhere, are not given adequate training or equipment and lack time to mould themselves into a team. Of necessity, they are *thrown into gaps*, and, in the course of large-scale fighting to which they are not accustomed, melt like snow in the heat of the sun.

h. *Enemy air action* is inflicting such enormous damage at home that very important war material does not reach the front at all, or only in extremely inadequate amounts. [I referred to the repeated difficulties concerning chiefly ammunition, machine guns, rifles, antitank guns, tanks, assault guns, and spare parts, as well as fuel for motor vehicles, etc.]

[I concluded the report by once more calling attention to the fact that, in conducting the war in such manner, men, equipment and terrain were lost to such an extent that Germany was in very grave danger. *With this threatening situation on all fronts, decisive results are expected by the nation's government.* I now

---

[2] Hitler refused to evacuate the Seventeenth Army in Crimea before it was cut off by the Soviet offensive that threw the Germans back to the Dnieper River. Hitler's argument for maintaining the Seventeenth Army there was to prevent the peninsula from being used as a Soviet "aircraft carrier" to attack the Rumanian oilfields. Starting in early April 1944, the Red Army eliminated the Seventeenth Army in one month. Of 230,000 men, 151,000 were evacuated and the rest killed or missing. Although a majority of the troops were saved, 80,000 lives and all the army's equipment were lost. Additionally, the Germans lost the use of an entire army between late October 1943, when it was cut off, and early April 1944, when the Red Army attacked. Alfred Seaton, *The Russo-German War*, p. 431.

[3] In October 1944, the Red Army cut off Army Group North and isolated it in the Courland peninsula of Latvia. Hitler refused to evacuate the army group, consisting of the Sixteenth and Eighteenth Armies, with the specious logic that they were tying down large Soviet forces. They were not. Two veteran armies would have been of immense help in shoring up the collapsing Eastern front.—Editor.

[4] The German attack in the Lake Balaton area of Hungary in March 1945 turned out to be just the disaster the author predicted at this meeting with Himmler.—Editor.

	remained silent as we looked at one another for a while without uttering a word.]
Himmler:	[Then moved closer to me, bent over and spoke slowly in a subdued voice enunciating every word:] *I agree with you.* [Himmler was silent again then.]
Raus:	[Surprised by this reply, and, after drawing a long breath, asked:] *Why did you not inform the Führer then?*
Himmler:	[After a short pause:] I expected this question. [Another pause, then he continued:] *I have already told the Führer all of these things.*
Raus:	*And what did the Führer say?*
Himmler:	[Pointing his finger, replies after a short time in a raised voice:] The Führer replied most violently: "You are a defeatist, too!" And in a fit of rage showed me the door.
Raus:	[This incident was confirmed some time later by Major-General Kienzel, the last military expert detailed to Himmler by OKH,[5] who was present during that discussion between Himmler and Hitler.]
Himmler:	[Then described the difficulties at his front and the bitter fighting for the "centers of resistance" Marienburg and Schneidenmühl. He was particularly worried about the latter, since the loss of Schneidenmühl—bitterly contested—was imminent, and because he knew Colonel Remlinger, the local commander, personally. Remlinger had only several hundred men left and scarcely any ammunition. Hitler did not reply to Remlinger's request for permission to break out with the remainder of the garrison.]
Raus:	[Once more brought the conversation to the subject of the great danger which presently threatened Army Group Weichsel, and brought out a map indicating the following enemy intentions on the Pomeranian Front.

At the outset, the enemy will probably break through the front at its weakest point toward the Second Army and, in an assault via Koeslin, cut off contact with the Second Army in order to isolate it. Then strong breakthrough attacks on one flank toward Danzig and on the other flank toward Stettin via Stargard have to be taken into account. Both attacks will attempt to split up and annihilate the armies in this area.

[These statements were interrupted by an urgent telephone call from the G-3 of the Army Group. A radio message from Colonel Remlinger to Himmler was relayed concerning a successful breakout in a northerly direction toward his own front on the part of Remlinger and the remainder of his garrison. The breakout was made on Hemlinger's own initiative, since, up to this time, he had waited in vain for the requested permission.]

---

[5] The OKH (Oberkommando des Heeres, or General Staff of the Germany Army) was responsible for all operations on the Eastern front. The High Command of the Armed Forces (Oberkommando der Wehrmacht, OKW) was responsible for operations in all other theaters.—Editor.

Himmler: [Listened intently, then placed down the receiver, jumped up, and with joyful enthusiasm paced back and forth as he repeatedly shouted to me:] *Did you hear that? Remlinger made it! Remlinger made it! He did exactly right! I say he did exactly right!*

Raus: [Agreed with Remlinger's independent decision and voiced the hope that a large number of these courageous men—favored by the densely wooded terrain—would be able to reach our own lines. While we were still talking at length regarding the possibilities of aiding the unit which had broken out, the telephone rang again. I listened in on the order from Hitler, transmitted through OKH, ordering Remlinger, together with his garrison, to return to the "center of resistance" immediately and continue its defense.]

Himmler: *You are absolutely right. I shall not forward this order.*

Raus: [This incident confirmed my belief that Himmler was not tricking me, but that he was serious when he agreed with my contentions.]

Topic 2: Second Discussion with Reichsführer SS Himmler, 7 March 1945

A short time after my first discussion with Reichsführer SS Himmler, the Eleventh Panzer Army launched the offensive as ordered by the Führer. After achieving insignificant initial success, it came to a standstill on the second day, with the loss of many of our tanks.

In spite of my emphatic warning (see First Discussion with Himmler), all of the SS Panzer divisions and SS panzergrenadier divisions which had been moved up for this offensive were drawn out of the front and transferred to the Silesia–Saxony area of operations, regardless of the fact that far superior Soviet forces were ready to launch a counteroffensive.

When the front had been unjustifiably weakened by this measure, I received the order from Army Group "W" to relieve the commander in chief of the 11th SS Panzer Army (SS Lieutenant-General [Obergruppenführer] Steiner),[6] and, together with my staff (Third Panzer Army), take over the command of the remaining weak forces for the defense of the wide sector.

On 22 February—2400 hours after assuming command—the Soviet Armies, in overpowering strength, launched the expected counteroffensive. This attack sealed the fate of Pomerania.

After the crumbled line had been reestablished on the Oder, despite very heavy losses and thanks to the unequaled courage of the troops, I was again summoned to a conference with Himmler on 7 March. It took place in the Hohenlychen Sanatorium (northeast of Berlin), where Himmler lay ill with angina. Accompanied by his aide, I arrived there at approximately 3 o'clock in the afternoon. On entering, Himmler raised

---

[6] Felix Steiner (1896–1966). Hitler was to recall this remarkable soldier on 24 April 1945 and order him to relieve Berlin; however, the forces were so inadequate that he chose to move west to surrender to the British. Mark M. Boatner, *The Biographical Dictionary of World War II* (Novato, CA: Presidio Press, 1999), p. 536.

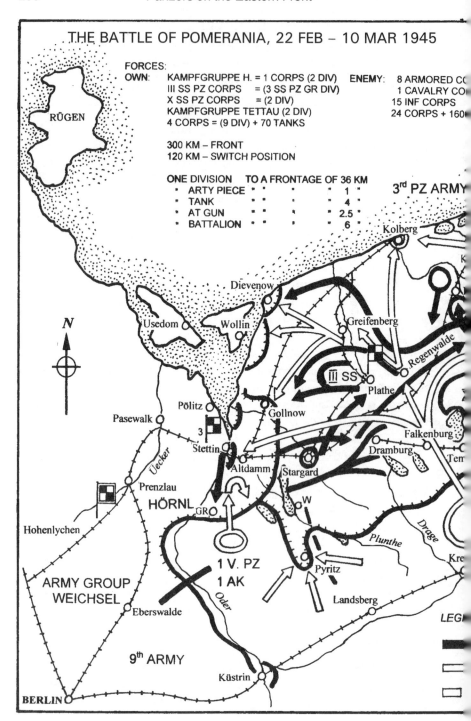

THE BATTLE OF POMERANIA, 22 FEB – 10 MAR 1945

FORCES:
OWN: KAMPFGRUPPE H. = 1 CORPS (2 DIV)   ENEMY: 8 ARMORED CC
        III SS PZ CORPS   = (3 SS PZ GR DIV)   1 CAVALRY CO
        X SS PZ CORPS   = (2 DIV)   15 INF CORPS
        KAMPFGRUPPE TETTAU (2 DIV)   24 CORPS + 160
        4 CORPS = (9 DIV) + 70 TANKS

        300 KM – FRONT
        120 KM – SWITCH POSITION

        ONE DIVISION   TO A FRONTAGE OF 36 KM
          " ARTY PIECE " "   "   " 1 "   3ʳᵈ PZ ARMY
          " TANK   " "   "   " 4 "
          " AT GUN " "   "   " 2.5 "
          " BATTALION " "   "   " 6 "

RÜGEN

N

Kolberg

Dievenow

Usedom   Wollin   Greifenberg

Regenwalde

III SS

Pölitz   Plathe

Pasewalk   3   Gollnow

Stettin   Falkenburg
                      Dramburg   Ten
     Altdamm Stargard

Prenzlau   W

HÖRNL
    GR

Hohenlychen   Plunthe   Kre
                             Pyritz   Drage

ARMY GROUP   1 V. PZ
WEICHSEL   1 AK   Landsberg
      Eberswalde

               Oder   LEG

9ᵗʰ ARMY

          Küstrin

BERLIN

Uecker

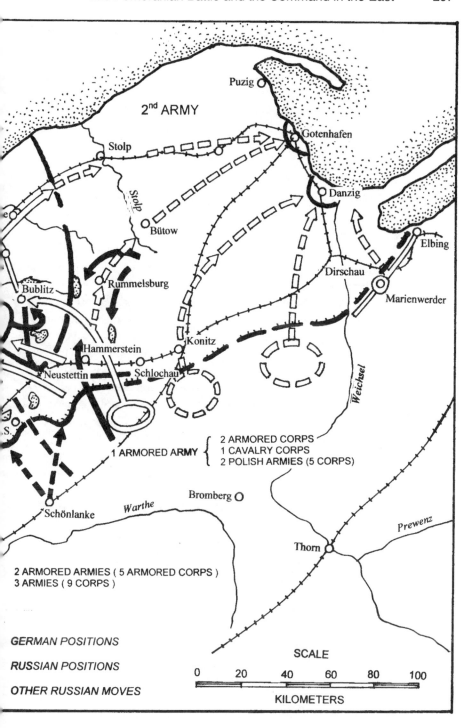

2nd ARMY

Puzig

Gotenhafen

Stolp

Danzig

Stolp

Bütow

Elbing

Dirschau

Rummelsburg

Bublitz

Marienwerder

Hammerstein

Konitz

Weichsel

Neustettin

Schlochau

1 ARMORED ARMY { 2 ARMORED CORPS
                 1 CAVALRY CORPS
                 2 POLISH ARMIES (5 CORPS)

Bromberg O

Warthe

Prewenz

Schönlanke

2 ARMORED ARMIES (5 ARMORED CORPS)
3 ARMIES (9 CORPS)

Thorn

GERMAN POSITIONS

RUSSIAN POSITIONS

OTHER RUSSIAN MOVES

SCALE

0   20   40   60   80   100

KILOMETERS

up partially in bed, greeted me in a friendly manner and offered me a chair near his bed. His aide left the room and we were alone. The following conversation lasted over an hour.

Himmler: You have passed through some very difficult days, but in spite of all obstacles you have again stabilized the front.

Raus: [Reported on the course of the fighting and constantly referred to the fact that, in the face of my recommendations, all reserves were withdrawn and transferred from the front. Consequently, the front, now weakened to the utmost, was attacked and smashed by the enemy's counteroffensive as expected.]

Moreover, in the course of the enemy offensive, you repeatedly issued orders which prevented me from acting along lines demanded by the situation. For example, you forbade the withdrawal of protruding sectors to favorably located and well-prepared positions along shorter lines at the lakes. In that way, unnecessary losses could have been avoided and forces could have been released for the creation of reserves. (Puritz, Stargard and Neustettin.) These forces would have been adequate to seal off the initial penetrations. But the enemy achieved deep penetrations at Neustettin and in the area east of Stargard, and we found ourselves short of troops required to contain the pressure. The one reserve unit (Panzergrenadier Division "Holstein"), which I organized by weakening even the attacked sectors of the front, had to be committed in accordance with your orders toward Rummelsburg via Bublitz, with the hopeless task of establishing contact with the Second Army; and, in so doing, the unit was needlessly exhausted. Later, it was unavailable at the point of main effort east of Stargard, where the 5th Jäger Division was overpowered and split after waging an extremely courageous defensive battle against superior armored units in the ratio of 20 to 1. The bulk of X SS Panzer Corps and Corps Tettau, which were fighting in the area between the two points of penetration, were thus in danger of being encircled and annihilated. With respect to this constantly increasing danger, I requested permission during a period of five days, each day more urgently, finally imploring you to grant my request to pull the forces out of this threatened area at the nighttime to prevent their encirclement, since they would otherwise be sacrificed to no purpose. Even then, you did not agree [to] the withdrawal, but instead you added special emphasis to the disapproval by threatening a court-martial action against all key officers. As a result, both corps, with the exception of a few elements of Corps Tettau, which may still be able to fight their way back, were captured on the fifth day. These staggering events led to the rapid loss of Pomerania as far as the Oder, where the remnants of the Army were again able to organize into a unit and occupy positions for successful defense. Effectively supported by navy and air force units fighting on the ground, it also became possible for the infantry to hold on to a series of important bridgeheads on the east bank of the Oder.

Since the two corps were already encircled, the 10th SS Panzer Division "Frundsberg," ordered to return from Silesia at the time, was now to reestablish contact with Second Army squeezed within a small area in the Danzig–Gotenhafen district by attacking across Pomerania, which was already occupied by a number of enemy armored and infantry armies. It was altogether impossible to carry out this mission, and served to demonstrate to what extent you and the Supreme Commander had misjudged the existing situation. Even the fact that Army Group neglected to have someone establish personal contact with the Third Panzer Army, which was struggling in a desperate situation, cannot make it clear why that command, by issuing rigidly binding orders and threats, made demands that could not be complied with and crippled the command of the Army.

Himmler: [Listens to these remarks in a serious and attentive manner and then replies:] I know that you understood the actual danger in the Pomeranian front and predicted these events in advance.

Raus: It is not a question of prediction. I am thoroughly convinced that every other experienced army commander would have evaluated the situations in precisely the same manner and would have made the same recommendations to you.

Himmler: I have supported your proposals every time and have forwarded them to the OKH because the Führer has reserved the right to make every decision himself. The Führer, however, always rejected these proposals very emphatically and reproved me severely.

Raus: As you admitted yourself during our first discussion, such action is really contrary to the interests of our people for which we are all fighting, and to whom *the Führer, too, is responsible.*

Himmler: You are right, but the Führer is convinced that he is doing the right thing, and for that reason demands, with unrelenting harshness, the execution of his orders. He tolerates no opposition, and as a result rejects every recommendation which does not conform to his way of thinking.

Raus: [In a raised voice:] But you should not accept a refusal if your convictions differ. Otherwise such action will lead to a disastrous end.

Himmler: Calm down. There will be a turning point soon. *We shall win the war.*

Raus: That does not make sense to me. I do not follow you.

Himmler: [Ends the conversation there and orders two cups of tea and rolls. Then he asked me to describe such actions to him which would show that the unit fought courageously and carried out the orders to the letter. Both the Führer and he placed extremely high value on these points. The tactical reports did not reveal these facts to any degree and are much too cut and dried.]

Raus: [Describes a number of incidents, most from personal experience in the Pomeranian operation, which revealed conclusively the courage and sacrifice displayed by the troops.[7]]

Himmler: [Listened with close attention and showed great excitement. After finishing my description of the fighting, Himmler sat up in bed, pressed my hand and enthusiastically exclaimed:] That was excellent. You should report that to the Führer personally! Are you prepared to do so?

Raus: Very much so. I was about to ask your permission to report personally to the Führer on the heavy fateful battle for Pomerania.

Himmler: [In my presence, immediately called the Führer's headquarters and asked to be connected with the Führer. After only two or three minutes, Hitler answered. His voice sounded monotonous and weary, but could be heard plainly.] My Führer, the commander of the Third Panzer Army is here beside me and has just now reported in detail on the Pomeranian battle. The report was very interesting—you ought to hear it yourself. May I send the General to you?

Hitler: Yes, have him come tomorrow. I am having a conference tomorrow afternoon, which will also be attended by all my principal staff members. They can listen to him at the same time.

Himmler: Very good. When shall he come?

Hitler: He is to be here at the bunker tomorrow afternoon at 4 o'clock. He will deliver his report after the conference.

Himmler: Good. The General will be there punctually. [That ended the conversation between Himmler and Hitler, and also my discussion with Himmler.]

Topic 3: Report to the Führer, 8 March 1945
(Written from memory)
Introduction

As agreed by telephone between Reichsführer SS Himmler and the Führer on the occasion of my second discussion with Himmler in Hohenlychen, I arrived on 8 March from my command post in Stettin (Artillery Barracks). I arrived at the Reich Chancellery by car at 1600 to deliver my report on the Battle of Pomerania. The report was made in the Führer's Bunker, located in a small garden in the grounds near the Reich Chancellery.

After repeatedly checking my identification, an SS officer escorted me down a long stairway into the spacious hall, deep underground, of the bunker. On both sides of the hall, doors opened into the various conference and workrooms. All the rooms were tiled in white and olive green, well-lit and simply furnished. At the moment, a number of generals who had arrived for the conference were gathering in front of the Führer's door. I was speaking with several of the men with whom I was acquainted, when an SS

---

[7] These incidents are contained in my report to the Führer of 8 March 1945.

Lieutenant-Colonel stepped up to me and asked me to come with him for a moment. He led me into an adjoining room and courteously informed me that he would have to search me thoroughly. He did not accept my objection that I was the Commanding General of the Third Panzer Army, who had been ordered here by the Führer, and that I had already established my identity more than once. He searched my pockets and clothing thoroughly. I was permitted to go then, and I was free to return to the hall, where I again joined the general officers who had come for the conference.

General Conference

As the officers of the Führer's Staff were invited into the adjoining Führer's room for the conference soon afterward, I joined other officers who did not participate in it, as a listener. The conference revolved around the events of the past days, which were reported on with the aid of maps, first on the Western front and then on the Eastern front, by the respective chiefs of staff. The Führer sat at a table, bent over the maps, and followed the review of the operations. Most of the others present remained standing as they listened to the report. Hitler raised brief objections only now and then, and did not enlarge technical details until later. However, to my knowledge, no deliberations were engaged in, no recommendations were made, and no decisions were made, in spite of the grave tactical situation at that time in the west (crossing of the Rhine) and in the east (Soviets advancing into Silesia and Hungary).

After this conference, the Führer, together with the chiefs of the various components of the armed forces and his inner circle, remained in the conference chamber. All the others left. A short time later, I was summoned to this chamber for the report to the Führer.

Report to the Führer

Aside from Hitler, those present were: Reichsmarshal Hermann Goering, Feldmarschall Keitel, Grossadmiral Dönitz, Generaloberst Jodl, Generaloberst Guderian, Reichsleiter Bormann, and General der Infanterie Burgdorf, and their chiefs of staff. They sat around a long table covered with maps. I stepped up to the Führer, greeted him and handed him two situation maps. The first one, of 13 February 1945 of the Eleventh SS Panzer Army (SS Obergruppenführer Steiner), indicated the estimate of enemy intention, as cited during my first discussion with Himmler, and the second showed the actual development of the all-out Russian offensive against the sector of the above-mentioned army, over which, together with the staff of the Third Panzer Army, I had assumed command.

The Führer glanced distrustfully at me over his glasses, and muttered something to himself which sounded like: "That should not have happened." He then took the maps into his very trembling hands and, comparing them, contemplated first one situation and then the other, which essentially were the same. I faced a physically broken-down, embittered and suspicious man whom I scarcely recognized. The knowledge that Adolf Hitler—now only a human wreck—held the fate of the German people in his hands alone was a deep shock to me.

Without returning my greeting, and visibly angry, he said, "Proceed!"

Preparation of the Defense

In my introduction, I pointed out that I took over the command of the sector of the Eleventh SS Panzer Army from Obergruppenführer Steiner only *twenty-four hours before* the all-out Soviet attack was launched, and for that reason had no opportunity to make any kind of decisive changes in the inadequate defensive scheme. I was even more handicapped because when I took over the command, it *did not have any reserves* at its disposal as all of the panzer divisions, having been withdrawn from the front after Steiner's frustrated offensive, had been transferred to another theater. However, even during those few hours, it was still possible for me to regroup the 5th Jäger Division (a unit with the highest degree of offensive capabilities) along a narrow front disposed in depth in the sector east of Stargard, where the major actions would probably be fought, and employ it in such a manner that, with the support of tanks, antitank defense and the bulk of artillery, deployed in depth, it would be able to temporarily hold its ground, even in the face of a powerful enemy attack.

Moreover, even before I took over command, I had issued orders for the construction of a dense network of tank obstacles in the army rear area, which abounded in wooded areas and bodies of water and thus lent itself well for this purpose. In a few days, with the energetic cooperation of party members and local inhabitants, obstacles sprang up on all bridges, village entrances, and bypasses, as well as at highway and road entrances leading into woods or swampy terrain. These barriers were guarded by stout-hearted members of the Volkssturm,[8] who had been trained in the use of the Panzerfaust.[9] Moreover, men equipped with antitank weapons were held in readiness with bicycles and motorcycles for mobile employment and for establishment of strongpoints. The entire civilian telephone network was put into service for the purpose of issuing tank warnings and to maintain communication between the blocked zones and with the military authorities. Never before had an area been transformed into such a tightly meshed antitank obstacle within so short a period of time as had been accomplished in Pomerania. The aim of this measure was to prevent enemy tanks which had broken through from carrying out a surprise advance, or at least to delay it.

These precautions turned out very satisfactorily, as I will describe in detail by enumerating several incidents later on. These measures, however, represented only a fraction of the precautionary measures which would have been required in order to offer successful resistance against the large-scale enemy attack.

---

[8] "In October 1944 Hitler had activated the *Volksturm*—a home guard—under party leadership, composed of men aged 16 to 60 otherwise draft-exempt. The members were to be put into Army uniforms, if available; if not, they were to wear the party uniform or civilian clothes." Earl F. Ziemke, *Stalingrad to Berlin: The German Defeat in the East*, p. 413. See also Erhard Raus's extensive treatment of the Volksturm in Rauss, *The Anvil of War*, pp. 113–17.

[9] The Panzerfaust was a recoilless antitank grenade and launcher, both expendable.

Situation and Forces

At the time my headquarters assumed command of the Eleventh SS Panzer Army, the army consisted of III SS Panzer Corps with three SS panzergrenadier divisions. These had been considerably weakened a short time before in an unsuccessful attack. In addition, it controlled X SS Panzer Corps, with two army infantry divisions in the center of the front; Corps "Hoernlein," with replacement troops from the military district of Stettin and one air force field division (fighting as ground force with the Army) on the right flank; and Corps "Tettau," with Division "Baerwalde" formed from the school units from the Grossborn and Hammerstein training centers on the left flank. The second division, "Pomerania" in Corps "Tettau," was composed of Volksgrenadier battalions[10] and improvised units which were hastily organized from construction and survey battalions as well as supply units of all three components of the armed forces. This division contained neither a signal battalion nor artillery nor antitank weapons. Several recently formed regiments and battalions, in fact, lacked regimental and battalion commanders, which I assigned from troops returning from leave to Army Group Courland as they passed by me on the highway. I immediately sent them in my car to the units already engaged in fighting as their commanders. Division "Pomerania" occupied a switch position which extended along the left boundary of the army perpendicularly to the front (old Pomerania position against the Poles). Altogether, eight divisions with 70 tanks occupied a defensive front of 240 kilometers. Accordingly, each division had to hold an average frontage of 36 kilometers.

To every kilometer of frontage, there were one artillery piece, one heavy machine gun, two light machine guns and forty men. At every two and one-half kilometers there was one antitank gun. At every four kilometers there was one tank, and at every six kilometers there was one battalion. Facing this line, the enemy had concentrated three tank armies comprising eight tank corps, five infantry armies comprising fifteen corps, and one cavalry corps. My army of four corps and 70 tanks consequently faced a total of eight enemy armies of 24 corps and 1,600 tanks.

Here the Führer interrupted me in a reproachful voice with the words: "The enemy does not have 1,600 tanks but only 1,400." I pointed out that ,aside from the eight newly constituted Russian armored corps, at almost full strength, there were also separate armored units operating in conjunction with the Cavalry Corps. Hitler acknowledged by a nod of his head that he would not dispute my objection.

Course of Battle

Now I began the review of the tactical operations of the "Pomeranian battle." From the orientation given me by my predecessor about the enemy, and from observations during the last twenty-four hours, I concluded that an all-out enemy offensive was imminent.

---

[10] Volksgrenadier was a term first applied in autumn 1944 to infantry divisions reorganized on a reduced T/O with an increased ratio of automatic weapons.

Initially, preparations for an attack were observed in two places (on the boundary toward the Second Army, and in the area east of Stargard), and later also at a point south of Stettin (Greifenhagen). Particularly extensive concentrations of tanks and infantry units were determined east of Stargard. During the last few days, southeast of Neustettin, close to the boundary of the Second Army, the enemy had conducted aggressive reconnaissance in force, which stopped later on. During these actions, the first prisoners of the First Polish Army under Russian command were brought in. This fact, together with the comparative calm, led to the conclusion that a large-scale attack was not to be expected at this point. The neighboring forces to the left (Second Army) also did not observe any disturbing enemy activity to the front of their right wing.

By *noon of 22 February*, however, I suddenly received a message from my left wing that the enemy had broken through in the area of the adjoining division ("Charlemagne"[11]) of the Second Army, and that enemy tanks were rapidly driving toward northwest by way of Stegers. During the afternoon, approximately fifteen Russian tanks coming from the area of the Second Army actually appeared at the outskirts of Baldenburg. This was 35 kilometers to the rear of my army's left wing. They were stopped at the tank barriers by elements of the Pomeranian Division after three tanks were knocked out. After being considerably reinforced during the night of 23 February, the enemy again attacked Baldenburg the next morning with approximately 35 to 40 tanks and one or two battalions of motorized infantry. These enemy forces overpowered the garrison there of 60 construction engineers and naval surveying personnel, broke through the switch position, and pushed cautiously forward in the direction of Bublitz. The weak local garrison there (service troops of the Pomeranian Division) assigned to man the tank barriers, together with mobile tank destroyers, moved up from the surrounding woods and successfully attacked the enemy. Consequently, his action was confined to keeping the railway station under fire, but he did not attempt an attack against the town. Not until 24 February, and after bitter fighting, did the enemy enter the north section of the town and occupy the railway station. In the course of this action, sixteen tanks were destroyed by Panzerfausts. In the meantime, powerful forces had been moved up in support of this enemy spearhead and forced the remnants of the penetrated adjacent wing (Division "Charlemagne" and the 15th Latvian SS Division) into my army sector, where they caused unrest among the improvised units of the Pomeranian Division, whose morale was low anyway. Moreover, Russian troops who had followed the treks of German

---

[11] " 'Charlemagne' (Puaud), a French infantry contingent elevated in the Autumn of 1944, to the status of an SS Waffen grenadier division, originated in a pre-existing volunteer regiment known as the Légion Volontaires Françaises (LVF). Incorporated into the German Army as 638th Regiment (7th Infantry Division), the LVF served [in] Fourth Army in the battle of Moscow ... before seeing action against partisans on the same Central Front in 1942–3. Reconstituted in 1944 as an SS division, some 7,000 French volunteers served briefly in two battle groups—one under Army Group Weichsel, surrounded in Pomerania and virtually destroyed there, the other including survivors from Pomerania defended Hitler in the Reichs Chancellery until forced to capitulate on 2 May 1945." Roger Edwards, *Panzer: A Revolution in Warfare, 1939–1945* (London: Arms and Armour Press, 1989) p. 69.

refugees had penetrated Neustettin and had occupied the railway station of the city (approximately 20 kilometers in the rear of our own front). They could only be dislodged from the city after severe street fighting.

Since the Second Army, together with the forces (7th Panzer Division and infantry) which had been moved up via Rummelsburg, had failed in their effort to block off the penetration on their front at Stegers, more and more enemy units advanced deep into the flanks of my army. My own flank thus became enveloped, and was pushed back toward Neustettin. Enemy pressure also became constantly stronger in the area between this town and Bublitz. Contact with the Second Army was completely cut off by the armored assault which had pushed forward from Bublitz toward the heights east of Koeslin. The ordered attempt to reestablish contact with the Second Army by employing the SS Panzergrenadier Division "Holstein," which had just been drawn out of the line south of Stargard and moved into reserve in an attack from the area south of Bublitz toward Rummelsburg, did not succeed, since the division was too weak and the terrain too difficult due to its vegetation. After minor initial success, the division was gradually forced back by superior enemy forces. It remained tied down, nevertheless, in my east flank, and, being the only reserve unit, it was later unavailable in the defense against the *enemy's main attack which was launched east of Stargard about 1 March.*

At that point, after a terrific artillery concentration, a sizable enemy tank force penetrated the front of the 5th Jäger Division on a line four kilometers wide and six kilometers deep. However, the courageous division, deployed in depth, was able to block the drive for the time being with its own strength, without breaking contact to the right or left. But, during the next day, enemy tanks attacked in such great strength that the sector of the 5th Jäger Division between Falkenburg and Drammburg was penetrated, and the left flank of III SS Panzer Corps and the right flank of X SS Panzer Corps joining the division sector were rolled back. The front was thus cracked open. The enemy tanks had freedom of movement and pushed ahead. On the next day, spearheads already appeared at Regenswalde eight kilometers east of my army's command post, which, however, continued to remain there. Strong infantry units followed and widened the gap. The enemy also gained ground daily in the direction of Bad Polzin. Neustettin had been taken. Only on the west flank of the army was it possible to repulse all enemy attacks against Greifenhagen and Pyritz, which was encircled on several occasions. In the north, nevertheless, Koeslin was lost after several days of fighting, and tank spearheads pushed forward in the direction of Kolberg. Tanks from the south also attempted to reach the city, which had been designated a "center of resistance." Enemy pressure increased daily on the extended flanks of the corps whose sector had been penetrated.

The Führer, who until now had followed my report on a map, suddenly looked up and interrupted me, now in a hesitant but calm voice, with the words: "We have been acquainted with the further course of the operation from the tactical reports submitted by you and the Army Group. Now tell us how the commanders and the troops behaved in battle."

Hitler as well as the invited listeners apparently were well aware that I was now about to touch upon the encirclement and annihilation of X SS Panzer Corps and elements of Corps "Tettau," and would give the reasons for these developments. (See report of my second discussion with Himmler.)

Since this disaster can only be traced to his orders, which were forwarded by Himmler and were contrary to all proposals made by my army, he, by this interruption of the report, prevented me from speaking freely on the subject and offer his own orders as evidence. This assumption is substantiated by the fact that the part of my report up to this point dealing with the tactical developments of the Pomeranian battle must have been just as familiar to him from the army reports as that portion which would clearly show the dramatic effects of his personal orders.

After this unexpected change in my report, I described a number of small combat events which well illustrated the behavior of troops and commanders. They seemed the most appropriate as a reply to Hitler's question, "How the commanders and troops behaved in battle."

Examples of Valor

1. After the breakthrough on 22 February 1945 south of Stegers, enemy tanks suddenly appeared at the outskirts of Baldenburg. The antitank barriers on both ends of town, which extended over a considerable distance, were kept open for the normal through traffic. Suddenly, the guard at the barrier at the southern exit of the town saw a Russian tank approaching at full speed. He quickly attempted to place one of the heavy wooden horizontal bars into position. He did not succeed, however, and the leading enemy tank drove through, firing at the roadblock, and pushed into the city. A second and a third T-34 followed closely behind and also attempted to pass through the barrier. However, at the last moment, the alerted guards (three men) still managed to get the crossbar in place in spite of tank fire. Nevertheless, the leading tank still tried to get into the town and consequently attempted to quickly ram the obstacles, but in so doing was set on fire by a Panzerfaust. A rifleman firing a second shot hit the next tank and put it out of action as well. In the meantime, another soldier from the construction engineer unit also destroyed with a Panzerfaust the lead tank, which had advanced into the town. When the tank unit became aware of the fate of its lead tanks, it stopped, widely scattered, in a small patch of woods close by and halted its advance for the day. As a result, a few 50-year-old soldiers, through their calm, courageous action, were able to bring the initial penetration of fifteen tanks to a halt, and thus enabled the weak local holding force to defend, unaided, the village until the following day. The successful Panzerfaust men had seen enemy tanks for the first time in their lives and had put them out of action. For their valor, they were awarded the Iron Cross, Second Class.

2. The tank unit referred to above, after having been substantially reinforced near Baldenburg, broke through the switch position. The very weak holding force of the Pomeranian Division maintained its position against all the attacks of the enemy's motorized units, and thus only the tanks were able to open a very narrow gap along the front, which was closed a number of times by the defending forces. As a result, the momentum of the tank attack aiming at Bublitz had been crippled. That was one of the main reasons for lack of aggressiveness displayed by the unit as it reached the gates of the city, where it remained for two days. The other reason was the unit's insecure position in the woods, where it was continually surprised by mobile tank destroyers. On one day alone, it lost sixteen tanks, and on the following day twelve more were knocked out by tank destroyers which went after them in the woods. In this manner, the tank assault against Koeslin was delayed. Maps showing the future plans of the tank unit were found in one of the wrecked tanks.

3. In order to widen the gap and protect the south flank of the enemy tank unit which had penetrated at Baldenburg, an enemy infantry unit supported by three T-34s turned off toward the southwest, took the village of Bisohofthum, and advanced toward Kasimirshof. This town was held by a small detachment of approximately twenty construction engineers under the command of a line NCO who, having been badly wounded, had temporarily been placed in charge of highway construction workers. Besides rifles, the detachment had only one machine gun, and the NCO was armed with two Panzerfausts. When he noticed the enemy approaching, he deliberately and very calmly issued the order: "Everyone take cover in the foxholes here on the outskirts of the village and permit the leading three tanks to roll by without firing on them. I will take care of these. Fire on the infantry following them at a range of 500 meters and prevent their entrance into the village. I shall station myself behind this house on the main street of the village and wait for the tanks." A few minutes later, one by one and carefully maintaining intervals, the tanks rolled into the village. The NCO knocked out the last tank with one Panzerfaust, whereupon the second tank turned toward the group of houses, firing in movement toward the spot where he presumed resistance came from. But, using bushes as cover, the NCO had already crept up close to the tank, and from only a short distance had knocked out this tank as well with the last Panzerfaust. When the lead tank saw the other two go up in flames, he pulled out of this sinister town by a sidestreet and started on his way back. In so doing, he pulled the enemy infantry pinned down by the defensive fire of the detachment along with him. Immediately, the courageous NCO, together with his men, took up the pursuit, and during the counterattack also recaptured the village which had been lost earlier. The NCO was again badly wounded during this action. So much for the description by his battalion commander, to whom I spoke personally at the main aid station in the presence of wounded participants of that action.

4. On 25 February, air force reported another unit of 22 tanks in a place 25 kilometers southeast of Koeslin. A detachment of antitank fighters of about 60 men, which had immediately started out in that direction, stalked through the woods near the village. At night, a strong reconnaissance patrol was dispatched to the village under cover of darkness and was to locate the tanks. During their reconnaissance, the patrol noticed a light in a house and Russian officers were observed as they sat at their evening meal. The window was ripped open in one quick movement, and at the same moment a hand grenade was thrown into the room. At this signal, the antitank fighters rushed into the village, firing rapidly as they came, and thus threw the surprised tank unit into utter turmoil. After brief fighting, a number of tanks were knocked out and set ablaze. In the ensuing confusion, the remaining tanks quickly evacuated the village, which remained in our possession two days longer. Shortly thereafter, I was able to contact the courageous antitank fighters myself over the telephone from Koeslin.

5. For three days, the reconnaissance battalion of the 10th SS Panzer Division "Frundsberg," having been moved up recently, had brought strong enemy tank columns to a stop with their assault guns at Regenswalde and Plathe and thus rendered the westward evacuation of long columns of vehicles and carts from Kolberg possible. Subsequently, in action at Greifenberg, the battalion prevented a turning maneuver and the further advance of enemy tank units aiming at Stettiner Haff by offering stubborn resistance until it became completely encircled. Through the exertion of its last ounce of strength, the battalion blasted its way out of the tank encirclement and broke through to its own lines.

6. During early March 1945, a tank unit suddenly appeared at one end of the autobahn running from Stettin to the east, with the obvious intention of advancing rapidly toward Stettin on the best possible road. This was prevented by setting up a barrier at that point, which was guarded by a weak covering force. The small detachment of valiant soldiers was surrounded and fired upon from all sides by enemy tanks. By using Panzerfausts and an antitank gun which was knocked out later, the detachment prevented the tanks from entering the autobahn. In this effort, the detachment dwindled to only a few men. Finally, after two or three hours of this unbalanced struggle, the enemy abandoned his plan when some of our own Tiger tanks approached. Six enemy tanks which had been set ablaze were the price the enemy had to pay in this effort. The autobahn remained in our hands.

7. In order to prevent the establishment of a bridgehead east of Altdamm, tank units attempted to strike from the north via Gollnow into the rear of III SS Panzer Corps, which was engaged in bitter fighting along both sides of the Stargard–Stettin highway and railroad line. This was prevented by a reinforced armored infantry regiment located in the area of Gollnow after fighting bitterly for the town and railway station. For more than a day the struggle surged back and forth. Numerous enemy tanks were destroyed, but our own forces also suffered heavy losses. Enemy tanks, initially focusing their efforts on the railroad station, drove into the area of our own artillery, which fought to the last round but was finally subdued. Two batteries were destroyed in the course of this heroic struggle. These sacrifices, however, saved the corps from a much worse fate.

8. Encircled by the enemy, elements of Corps "Tettau" were fighting in the rear of the enemy near Regenswalde, and greatly harassed his operations. Recently, the army had

reestablished radio contact with this force and had ordered it to turn northward and attempt to reach the coast west of Kolberg, so that it might fight its way forward along the coast to the Divenow bridgehead. This unit reached the coast yesterday. Instructions as well as orders were transmitted to this force by means of a liaison plane [Fieseler Storch], which had to detour far out over the sea. The unit should arrive in Divenow in a few days.[12]

9. Yesterday (7 March), an enemy unit with 34 tanks, in an attempt to reach the large bridge, broke through the Divenow bridgehead, which was being defended by young naval personnel. The navy troops, well-trained in the use of the Panzerfausts and under the command of Army's antitank officer, had neither antitank guns nor artillery, but were solely equipped with rifles and a few machine guns, besides many types of Panzerfausts. Armed with only these weapons, they took up a fierce pursuit and knocked out 33 of the 34 tanks which had broken through. One enemy tank which had already reached the bridge across a tributary was blown up, together with the bridge.

10. And, just before coming in, my chief of staff reported to me that an enemy tank attack was again carried out today against the same bridgehead held by the navy troops. The enemy, however, never reached our positions because the young navy troops, greatly impressed by the previous day's victory, did not wait for the attack of the 36 advancing enemy tanks echeloned in width and depth. On the contrary, the navy troops, disposed along a broad front, jumped off and in disorganized fashion attacked the rapidly firing tank unit from all sides, and, regardless of their own heavy losses, forged ahead toward the tanks until they were within effective Panzerfaust range. In a short time, all 36 tanks were knocked out. Their death-defying courage in relying on the Panzerfaust brought about a complete victory. This unsurpassed heroism will someday go down in the annals of German history.

Conclusion

"My Führer, the report should clearly indicate that the commanders of both large and small units, as well as the troops and the individual soldiers, have done everything in their power to withstand the vastly superior enemy forces. They lacked neither ability, willingness, nor courage, but they did not possess superhuman strength. They all fought bravely and tenaciously, even when the situation was hopeless, since no one wanted to be guilty for the loss of German territory. In spite of being outnumbered from 6 to 20 times in manpower and equipment, the command and troops endured the utmost hardships in trying to avert a complete collapse of the front.

"It can be explained only in this way—that in spite of all the existing needs, the front has been firmly reestablished in bridgeheads east of the Oder, even to the extent of being able to launch a successful counterattack at the southern wing, where yesterday 86 enemy

---

[12] As a matter of fact, Group "Tettau" arrived at the bridgehead on 12 March, *after* the report to the Führer. It brought with it about 20,000 soldiers of various units and approximately 30,000 refugees who, with their vehicles and carts, had attached themselves to this movement.

tanks were knocked out, and ground suitable for further stabilization of a defensive front was gained.

"As a peculiarity of the Pomeranian battle, I can report that of the 580 enemy tanks which have been knocked out up to this time, 380, or two-thirds, were destroyed by the Panzerfaust—that is, by the courage of the individual soldier. Never before has an army achieved so much success with the Panzerfaust.

"Therefore, I can only express my complete appreciation to my commanders and all the troops of the army for the great courage and self-denial shown in the unbalanced struggle for Pomerania."

Final Observation

The Führer and the others present were obviously impressed by my remarks, but did not utter a word. I was dismissed by a trembling nod of Hitler's head.

My successor arrived the next day at my headquarters in Stettin with a Führer order, and, in accordance, I had to turn over command of the army to him and was transferred to the officers' reserve pool. *That was the end of my 40-year tour of service.*[13] A few days later, Reichsführer SS Himmler was also relieved of his command as Commanding General Army Group "Weichsel."

---

[13] Raus's replacement was General der Panzertruppen Hasso von Manteufel, who had ridden to well-deserved fame as commander of the elite Panzergrenadier Division Grossdeutschland. Himmler's replacement was Generaloberst Gotthard Heinrici.—Editor.

Appendices

Appendix 1: 6th Panzer Division History and Order of Battle

The 6th Panzer Division earned on the battlefields of World War II one of the finest combat records of any division in the war, fighting in the invasion of Poland in 1939 to the defense of Vienna in 1945. For much of that time it was commanded by one of Germany's most gifted practitioners of the art of armored warfare and a superb leader— Generaloberst Erhard Raus. It could be said that wherever there was crisis to be mastered, the 6th Panzer Division was called—and it did not disappoint.

The 6th Panzer Division traced its origin to one of the first armored divisions in the German Army. Its parent formation was formed in on 12 October 1937 in Wuppertal (Rhineland-Westphalia), Wehrkreis VI, as the 1st Leichte Brigade (Light Brigade). In 1938 it was upgraded to division size and redesignated the 1st Leichten Division (Light Division). It had become, in essence (though not in name), a panzer division with the addition of the 11th Panzer Regiment. At this time the division's main subordinate formations included the 11th Panzer Regiment, the 4th Mechanized Cavalry Regiment, the 76th Motorized Artillery Regiment, the 41st Antitank Battalion, the 57th Engineer Battalion, and the 82nd Signal Battalion. The 65th Panzer Battalion was temporarily attached to the division in 1938 in anticipation of the invasion of Czecholslovakia over the Sudeten Crisis; the attachment was made permanent the following year. After the German takeover of Czechoslovakia, the division was issued Czech 35T tanks, which, at the time, were superior to all German tanks but the Mark III. The 4th Battalion of the 4th Mechanized Cavalry Regiment was converted to the 6th Motorcycle Battalion on 1 April 1939.[1]

The division was mobilized for the Polish Campaign in September 1939, subordinated to XIV Motorized Corps. At that time, it had the organization given in Table A1. On 18 October 1939, the 1st Leichten Division was converted into the 6th Panzer Division under the command of Generalmajor Werner Kempf. The division's infantry element was reorganized under a new 6th Motorized Infantry Brigade (Schützenbrigade 6) in 1940. The 4th Mechanized Cavalry Regiment was converted into the 4th Motorized Infantry Regiment (Schützenregiment 4). Its new organization (see Table A2) was in preparation for the Battle of France.

---

[1] Michum, Samuel W., Jr., *The Panzer Legions: A Guide to the German Army Tank Divisions of World War II and their Commanders* (Westport, CT: Greenwood Press, 2001), p. 71

TABLE A1: ORGANIZATION, INVASION OF POLAND, 1939

4th Motorized Infantry Regiment (3 battalions)	Schützenregiment 4
6th Motorcycle Battalion (reconnaissance)	Kradschutz Abteilung 6
11th Panzer Regiment (2 battalions)	Panzerregiment 11
65th Panzer Battalion	Panzer Abteilung 65
76th Motorized Artillery Regiment (3 battalions)	Panzer Artillerieregiment 76
6th Motorcycle Battalion	Kradschutz Abteilung 6
41st Antitank Battalion	Panzer Abwehr Abteilung 41
57th Engineer Battalion	PionierAbteilung 57
82nd Signal Battalion	Nachtrichtungs Abteilung 82
57th Service Command	Division Einheit 57

TABLE A2: ORGANIZATION, CAMPAIGN IN THE WEST, 1940

Division HQ	
6th Motorized Infantry Brigade	Schützenbrigade 6
4th Motorized Infantry Regiment (3 battalions)	Schützenregiment 4
6th Motorcycle Battalion (reconnaissance)	Kradschutz Abteilung 6
11th Panzer Regiment (2 battalions)	Panzerregiment 11
65th Panzer Battalion	Panzer Abteilung 65
76th Artillery Regiment (2 battalions)	Panzer Artillerieregiment 76
41st Antitank Battalion	Panzerjäger Abteilung 41
57th Engineer Battalion	Pionier Abteilung 57
82nd Signal Battalion	Nachtrichtungs Abteilung 82
57th Service Command	Versorgungsdienst 57

The division fought in the campaign in France in 1940 under XLI Panzer Corps, commanded by Generalleutnant Georg Hans Reinhardt. The division attacked through Belgium, crossing the Meuse as part of Panzer Group von Kleist, the vanguard of Army Group A, and played an important part of the [2] drive that closed on Dunkirk from the south, moving 217 miles in nine days to overrun and capture the British 145th Brigade at Cassel. It then took part in the drive to the south that broke the French, traveling from the Aisne to the Swiss border.[3]

A victorious 6th Panzer Division returned to Germany in July and surrendered large cadres to form the 16th Panzer Division. It also underwent another reorganization. The 6th Motorized Infantry Brigade joined by the addition of the 114th Motorized Infantry Regiment (Schützenregiment 114, formerly the 234rd Infantry Regiment of the 60th Infantry Division). A third artillery battalion was added to the 76th Artillery. In August the division moved to East Prussia where it was subordinated to the Eighteenth Army.

---

[2] Michum, *op. cit.*, p. 72.
[3] Michum, *op. cit.*, p. 72.

TABLE A3: ORGANIZATION, OPERATION BARBAROSSA, 1941

Division HQ

6th Motorized Infantry Brigade	Schützenbrigade 6
4th Motorized Infantry Regiment (2 battalions)	Schützenregiment 4
114th Motorized Infantry Regiment (2 battalions)	Schützenregiment 114
6th Motorcycle Battalion (reconnaissance)	Kradschutz Abteilung 6
11th Panzer Regiment (2 battalions)	Panzerregiment 11
65th Panzer Battalion	Panzer Abteilung 65
76th Artillery Regiment (3 battalions)	Panzerartillerieregiment 76
41st Antitank Battalion	Panzerjäger Abteilung 41
57th Engineer Battalion	Pionier Abteilung 57
82nd Signal Battalion	Nachtrichtungs Abteilung 82
57th Service Command	Versorgungsdienst 57

The 6th Panzer Division's organization immediately prior to the invasion of the Soviet Union in Operation Barbarossa was as shown in Table A3. Each of the motorized infantry regiments consisted of two battalions and a support company with six 75mm infantry guns. By this time, only the 6th Company, 114th Motorized Infantry Regiment, had received the half-track armored personnel carrier (SPW, or Mittler Schützen-panzerwagen—SdKfz 251/1).

The separate 65th Panzer Battalion essentially formed a third battalion for the 11th Panzer Regiment. Each panzer battalion had two companies equipped with light tanks and one with mediums. The panzer regiment's establishment totaled 220 tanks. The most modern were the 42 Mark IV (mediums) with short-barrelled 75mm guns. "The low muzzle velocity of this gun (420 meters per second and a high-angled trajectory) allowed a maximum armor penetration of only 41mm." The largest number of the division's tanks were 105 Czech 35Ts with a 37mm gun. "These tanks became useless below freezing-point, since their power and steering controls were pneumatic. They had been out of production since 1938 and, although extremely reliable, were at the edge of their system-life and had been declared 'no longer suitale for combat' some months before. However, owing to the low tank production in Germany, no replacement tanks were available." The remainder of the tank force consisted of 73 Mark II models (PzKpfw II, or SdKfz 121), armed with a puny 20mm weapon. The 6th Panzer Division was the only panzer division with such a motley collection of types, which forced it to fight "from the very beginning in mixed combat groups," according to General Kilmansegg, a division staff officer at the time of the invasion of the Soviet Union.[4]

The 41st Antitank Battalion was also badly underarmed, with twelve 50mm and twenty-four 37mm antitank guns. The latter were clearly obsolete by 1941 and had earned the nickname "door knocker" among the troops. The 76th Artillery Regiment

---

[4] Helmut Ritgen, "6th Panzer Division Operations," *The Initial Period of War on the Eastern Front, 22 June–August 1941. Proceedings of the Fourth Art of War Symposium, Garmisch, FRG, October 1987*, Colonel David M. Glantz, ed. (London: Frank Cass, 1993), pp. 108–10.

had two battalions of light artillery (twenty-four 105mm howitzers) and a medium battery of eight 150mm howitzers and four 105mm cannons.

Colonel Helmut Ritgen, Adjutant of the 2nd Battalion, 11th Panzer Regiment, at the time, stated some 46 years later: "In retrospect, the armament and vehicles of the 6th Panzer Division were really poor. It was a miracle that the division reached the outskirts of Leningrad and Moscow, in spite of an enemy superior in numbers and material. This achievement was the result of supreme leadership combined with excellent morale and training."[5]

The 6th Panzer Division crossed the Soviet border on 22 June 1941 as part of Operation "Barbarossa." It fought under the command of Generalmajor Franz Landgraf in the drive on Leningrad by Army Group North. Oberst (Colonel) Erhard Raus commanded the 6th Motorized Brigade. The division was part of XLI Panzer Corps (commanded by Reinhardt), along with the 1st Panzer Division and the 36th Motorized Division. XLI Panzer Corps and LVI Panzer Corps, commanded by General der Infanterie Erich von Manstein, formed the 4th Panzergruppe, commanded by Generaloberst Erich Höpner.

Barely two days into the invasion, the 6th Panzer Division was engaged in the first great tank battle and encirclement operation of "Barbarossa." The Soviet *3rd Mechanized Corps* launched a powerful counterattack at the 6th Panzer Division near the town of Rossienie in Lithuania. For the first time, the Germans encountered the heavy and seemingly impervious KV-1 and KV-2 heavy tanks. One column of trucks of the 114th Motorized Regiment was overrun and crushed by these monsters. Then the division attacked, skillfully employing its weapons against the superior Soviet tanks, while the other elements of the corps encircled the Soviets. The enemy's *3rd Mechanized Corps* had been crushed, leaving over 200 tanks on the field (see Chapter 1).

Within three weeks XLI Panzer Corps had advanced 750 kilometers. On 2 July, the 6th Panzer Division reached the Stalin Line, the line of fortifications that guarded the old Soviet border before the Baltic States and eastern Poland had been gobbled up by Stalin in 1939–40. In four days of heavy combat, the 6th Panzer Division was the first German unit to fight through the Soviet defenses. By 10 July the corps was within 100 kilometers of Leningrad. According to Raus, the situation became even more desperate:

> On 11 July, shortly before reaching Porkhov, the Kampfgruppe suddenly had to wheel northwestward at a 90-degree angle in order to come to the assistance of the 1st Panzer Division (XLI Panzer Corps) which was locked in desperate fighting on the Leningrad *Rollbahn*, and then had to establish a bridgehead at Lyady. After extremely difficult and time-consuming marches and battles, it was possible, by launching a sudden attack, to capture the bridge over the Plyussa River and occupy Lyady.

Upon completing this mission, the corps commander personally ordered Raus to turn northward and seize two bridgeheads over the Luga River. Kampfgruppe Raus fell upon

---

[5] Ritgen, *op. cit.*, p. 110.

both bridgeheads and seized them before the Red Army guards knew what was happening. But the Soviets reacted quickly and desperately, throwing everything they could at the Germans to break Raus's grip on the bridgeheads. For ten days, in a classic defensive operation, Raus fought off superior forces and inflicted hugely disproportionate casualties. (See Chapter 2, Example 1).

In September, the 6th Panzer Division broke through the Leningrad Line south of the great metropolis and attacked the strong Soviet position at Krasnogvardyesk from the rear. This position had held up several German infantry corps. A Soviet tank counterattack threatened to overrun the division, four unit commanders were killed, and the situation boiled to a crisis when the 6th Panzer counterattacked and smashed the enemy attack. In breaking through the Leningrad Line, the division encountered and overcame the most sophisticated defense seen on the Eastern Front. In reducing the Soviet fortifications, bunker by bunker, the Germans encountered some of the bitterest fighting of "Barbarossa." Raus concluded:

> With that, the most tenacious Russian defensive battles of 1941, between Kransogvardeysk and Leningrad came to an end. Only the flexible leadership of battle-tested armored forces, attacking with elan, made it possible to overcome the defense zones which had been set up in al all-out effort of the latest Russian defense technique. Within a week, the German 6th Panzer Division had had to break though and roll up twelve positions, repel several counterattacks, and take more than 300 heavily defended bunkers.[6]

Only days after the victory at Krasnogvardyesk, the division and XLI Panzer Corps were transferred to the 3rd Panzergruppe in Army Group Center's attack on Moscow in Operation "Typhoon." "On 10 October 1941, the first day of the offensive, its 260 tanks made a deep penetration into the enemy lines near Vyazma. Ten days later the Russians were encircled and the mission was accomplished" in the great encirclement at Vyazma which took 600,000 Soviet prisoners.[7]

The recently promoted Generalmajor Raus assumed command of the division on 25 November 1941. As part of XLI Corps, it led the Army Group's subsequent attack on Moscow, reaching within 25 miles of the Soviet capital before strong resistance and exhaustion brought the entire operation to a halt. Then the full force of the Russian winter struck. By 3 January, the number of moderate and severe frostbite cases had risen to 800 a day. Raus was to write:

> The 6th Panzer Division was then to lead the attack on Moscow and take the city. Its spearheads were approaching the objective when nature suddenly put a protective wall around the Russian capital. The autumn mud brought the blitzkrieg to a sudden end. It swallowed the most valuable equipment. The cold winter continued the terrible destruction. Then came the German withdrawal, during which every tank, every antitank gun, and almost every artillery piece of the division had to be sacrificed. Enemy attacks and cold weather caused innumerable casualties during rearguard actions. When the once-proud

---

[6] Rauss, *Fighting in Hell*, p. 82.
[7] Rauss, *The Anvil of War*, p. 33.

6th Panzer Division finally assembled its forces in January 1942, all that remained were 57 riflemen, 20 engineers, and three guns.[8]

In the meantime, Raus had to save the survivors. He ordered the engineers to use the large amounts of explosives that had recently been delivered to blow craters in the frozen ground and covered with lumber. The frostbite rate immediately dropped to four a day. Ten days later, when that front had to be abandoned, he was able to pull the remnants forty miles to the rear to reconstitute his division. Survivors kept trickling in. Still the division did not have enough men to provide cadres for alert units to attempt to block the major Soviet offensive that was gearing up in January to encircle the two broken armies of Army Group Center (Fourth and Ninth Armies). Raus intercepted every straggler and broken fragment of a unit within reach and formed improvised alert units. Men started to return from leave and hospital, and these Raus formed into a provisional motorcycle company. Within ten days, similar actions along the army group front had filled in the gaps. The division had lost virtually every motor vehicle and had to make due with 1,000 Russian panje wagons. The men now referred to the division as the "6th Panzer of Foot". By early February, it became necessary to attack because the *Rollbahn* and supporting railroad were just behind the front and dangerously vulnerable. This "Snail Offensive," in which time was not important, rolled back the Soviets in a series of small-unit actions that fought for tiny villages and strongpoints. By the end of March along the front, the Red Army was pushed out of 200 villages and into marshy ground.[9] (See Chapter 2, Examples 2 and 3 for Raus's detailed description of these operations).

Losses in the division eventually forced the consolidation of the two motorized infantry regiments into two battalions and the panzer regiment into one battalion, fighting as infantry during the winter of early 1942. Even in this reduced state, the 6th Panzer Division continued to perform its combat missions superbly against great odds. Reduced as it was, the division tied down far larger numbers and kept the initiative.

In April 1942, the division was withdrawn and transferred to northwestern France. Virtually the entire division was furloughed. Large numbers of replacements filled the empty ranks. The division absorbed the survivors of the 22nd Panzer Division. As the ranks swelled, new equipment flowed in. In June, the 65th Panzer Battalion was folded into the 11th Panzer Regiment, which was reduced to two battalions. At this time, the 298th Army Antiaircraft Battalion (Heeres Flakartillerie Abteilung 298) and the 41st Tank Hunter Battalion (based on the 41st Antitank Battalion) were added to the division. The 6th Motorized Infantry Brigade HQ was abolished; its two regiments would now report directly to the division commander. On 5 July 1942 every motorized infantry regiment (Schützenregiment) in panzer formations was redesignated as Panzergrenadier, reporting directly to division. The 11th Panzer Regiment received 160 Mark III (PzKpfw

---

[8] *Ibid.*, pp 33–4.
[9] *Ibid.*, pp.34–40, 51–2; Michum, *op. cit.*, p. 73.

TABLE A4: ORGANIZATION, RELIEF OF STALINGRAD, LATE 1942

Division HQ

4th Panzergrenadier Regiment (2 battalions)	Panzergrenadier Regiment 4
114th Panzergrenadier Regiment (2 battalions)	Panzergrenadier Regiment 114
11th Panzer Regiment (2 battalions)	Panzerregiment 11
6th Reconnaissance Battalion	Panzeraufklärungs Abteilung 6*
76th Panzer Artillery Regiment (3 battalions)	Panzer Artillerieregiment 76
41st Tank Hunter Battalion	Panzerjäger Abteilung 41
57th Engineer Battalion	Pionier Abteilung 57
82nd Signal Battalion	Nachtrichtungs Abteilung 82
57th Service Command	Versorgungsdienst 57

III) tanks with a 50mm long-barreled gun. The 76th Panzer Artillery Regiment retained its structure of three battalions, two with twelve 105mm howitzers each and the third with a dozen 150mm howitzers The regiment would be truck-towed until the next year. .A vital addition was made to the division with the appointment in July of Oberst Walter von Hünersdorff as commander of the 11th Panzer Regiment. Von Hünersdorff was "seen as a rising star of the army", but, as a dedicated anti-Nazi, was a secret member of the anti-Hitler conspiracy.[10] It was in this form and with such commanders that the division would fight at Stalingrad (see Table A4).

During the next six months Raus thoroughly trained the division, based on experiences in 1941–42 in Russia. In the middle of November, the division received orders to return to Russia as part of LVII Panzer Corps in a desperate bid to break the encirclement of the 6th Army in Stalingrad. Arriving on 28 November, the 6th Panzer Division's lead elements went straight into battle to stop the continuing Soviet advance. In the next month, the division fought its way to within 33 kilometers of the encircled army, inflicting heavy casualties on the opposing *51st* and *2nd Guards Armies* and the *4th Cavalry Corps*. Raus had assembled his division for the last lunge to break the encirclement on 23 December when a counterorder diverted his division to another sector to staunch the collapse of the Germans' Rumanian allies north of Stalingrad. Although LVII Panzer Corps also contained the 17th and 23rd Panzer Divisions, both divisions together did not equal the combat power of the fully restored 6th Panzer Division, which Raus described as 10 to 20 percent overstrength by the time it went into battle.[11]

It was a testament to the fighting qualities of the German soldier, brought out, tempered, and sharpened by the hard training Raus had given the division. Wielding this lethal weapon of modern war, his inspired leadership drove the division so deeply through the Red Army's frantic defenses that Stalin personally allocated his best army, the *2nd Guards Army*, to stop the 6th Panzer Division. That army broke itself in a great

[10] Michum, *op. cit.*, pp. 73, 77.
[11] Rauss, *Fighting in Hell*, p. 83.

attack on 19 December. The division's success was also a testament to the uniformly high level of leadership in the division as well, typified by the commander of the 11th Panzer Regiment, Oberst Walter von Hünersdorff, whose ability as a noted tank expert earned him a mention in the memoirs of Feldmarschall Erich von Manstein.[12] All throughout the drive to relieve Stalingrad, von Hünersdorff was in the thick of the action. Raus and he formed one of the most effective command teams in the German Army. In the effort to relieve Stalingrad, Raus was to claim that 400 Soviet tanks were destroyed. It was no fault of the 6th Panzer Division that it was never able to try for the final thrust to relieve the Sixth Army trapped in Stalingrad. The orders to attack on 24 December were rescinded at the last minute as the division was quickly shifted to shore up a collapse of the front in another area. Given the drubbing that the 6th Panzer Division and LVII Panzer Corps had given two Soviet armies, a determined breakout attempt by the Sixth Army trapped in Stalingrad might have had a reasonable chance for success.

After the debacle of Stalingrad, the German front was pushed all the way back to the Dnieper River. On 7 February, Generalleutnant Raus passed command of the division to von Hünersdorff. He was not to have the luxury of a leisurely transition. The Soviets had raced after the retreating Germans and seized Kharkov on 12 February. The situation reached a crisis when von Manstein counterattacked, trapping the Soviet spearheads of the *Southwest Front* on 22 February between two armored pincers, II SS Panzer Corps and the 6th and 17th Panzer Divisions, LVII Panzer Corps' cutting edge. As the Germans fought their way into Kharkov, the 6th Panzer Division, with its SS counterparts, linked up again in a second encirclement, this time of Kharkov itself, on 14 March. With the loss of Kharkov, the great Soviet counteroffensive following Stalingrad collapsed.

After Kharkov, the division had the opportunity to rest and refit. In April, the 2nd Battalion, 11th Panzer Regiment, returned to Germany to be reequipped with the new Panther Mark V tanks.[13] It was thus with one panzer battalion of Mark IV tanks that the 6th Panzer Division fought in the Battle of Kursk that July. At that time, the division was organized as shown in Table A5.

Leading from the front, the brave von Hünersdorff was wounded twice on 14 July and died three days later in a field hospital, tended by a nurse who was his own wife. At the climax of the battle, in the struggle between the Soviet 5th Tank Corps and the II SS Panzer Corps at "Prochorowka," the 6th Panzer Division played a critical role. "On the SS right, III Panzer Corps (Breith)—6th Panzer Division (Hünersdorff) especially—attacking northwards in support of the SS by taking Rotmistrov in the left flank, pushed hard against determined opposition, an 11th Panzer Regimental (Oppeln) battle group winning a Donets crossing at Rschavetz, pointing the way to Prochorowka and contact with the SS armour. But the 6th Panzer Division was stopped."[15] Following the

---

[12] Manstein, *Lost Victories*, p. 330.
[13] Michum, *op. cit.*, p. 74.

TABLE A5: ORGANIZATION, KURSK AND BEYOND, 1943

Division HQ
Division Staff
    57th Mapping Detachment (motorized)
Panzerregiment 11
    2 panzer battalions[14]
Panzergrenadier Regiment 4
    2 panzergrenadier battalions(motorized)
Panzergrenadier Regiment 114
    1 panzergrenadier battalion (motorized)
    1 panzergrenadier battalion (half-track)
    1 infantry gun company
Panzeraufklärungs Abteilung 6
    1 armored car company
    1 armored car platoon
    2 motorcycle companies
    1 heavy recon company (motorized)
    1 light recon company (motorized)
Artillerieregiment 76
    1 medium battalion
    1 heavy battalion
    1 medium battery (motorized)
    1 observation battery (motorized)
Heeres Flakartillerie Abteilung 298
    2 heavy flak batteries
    1 light flak battery
    1 flak battery (self-propelled)
    1 light flak column (motorized)
Panzerjäger Abteilung 41
    1 panzerjäger company (motorized)
    1 panzerjäger company (self-propelled)
Pionier Abteilung 57
    2 pioneer companies (half-track)
    1 pioneer company (motorized)
    1 Brüko K bridging column
    1 light pioneer supply column (motorized)
Nachtrichtungs Abteilung 82
    1 panzer telephone company
    1 panzer radio company
    1 light signals supply column
Feldersatz Abteilung 57
    4 companies
Versogungsdienst 57

---

[14] The 2nd Battalion, 11th Panzer Regiment, was absent at Kursk.

wounding of von Hünersdorff, Oberst Wilhelm Cirsoli assumed temporary command
of the division.

The Fourth Battle of Kharkov soon followed in August as the German armies
staggered back from defeat at Kursk with the Red Army in close pursuit. In the
confusion, the 6th Panzer Division became separated from III Panzer Corps. Retreating
south toward Kharkov, the division passed into the area defended by its former
commander, now commanding XI Corps. Raus immediately placed the division under
his command and assigned it a sector on the corps left. In this case, the left was the
position of danger because it was up in the air, and the Soviets were heading straight for
it. With Raus in overall command, the men of the 6th Panzer Division must have felt
their luck had returned (see Chapter 4). Then events may have made them reconsider.
On 9 August, the 168th Infantry Division on the 6th Panzer Division's right simply
disappeared. Its commander had had a nervous breakdown and ordered his command
to the rear. As Raus sorted the situation out, the 6th Panzer Division had to extend its
front to cover the gap. As Raus was to recount:

> The 6th Panzer Division on the left flank faced a difficult situation when, in addition to
> its own sector, it had to take over the one previously held by the missing 168th Division.
> The enemy exerted heavy pressure and the panzer division requested immediate antitank
> support. The corps commander dispatched twelve antitank guns and arranged for an air
> strike on the Russian tank column advancing east of the Lopan River. These combined
> efforts prevented the immediate collapse of the German flank cover.[16]

When the wayward 168th was located and put back into line, Raus gave the 6th
Panzer Division a well-deserved rest as corps reserve. The German front was
conducting a withdrawal to backup positions at this time, when the Soviets smashed a
new German regiment of the neighboring right-hand corps. The Soviet tanks ran over
the survivors and pressed XI Corps' rear and into Kharkov itself, and occupied the big
tractor plant. Raus then threw the 6th Panzer Division at them, and in tough fighting
they drove the Soviets out, destroyed their tanks and dispersed the remnants.[17] Despite
the drubbing Raus gave to the Soviet armies attacking his defenses around Kharkov,
their superior numbers threatened to encircle the city, which finally had to be
abandoned. But the Fourth Battle of Kharkov had marked another fine chapter in the
6th Panzer Division's combat record—one in which its score of destroyed tanks in the
war climbed to 1,500.[18]

The day before the city fell, command of the division passed to Generalmajor Rudolf
Freiherr (Baron) von Waldenfels. The new commander was no stranger to the division.
He had commanded the 4th Motorized Infantry Regiment from 1941 to 1942, and, after
commanding the Panzer School near Paris, he was returned to his division just as it was

---

[15] Edwards, *Panzer*, p. 182.
[16] Rauss, *The Anvil of War*, p. 193.
[17] *Ibid.*, p. 194.
[18] Michum, *op. cit.*, p. 74.

evacuating Kharkov. Save for a few short absences, he would command the division until the end of the war.

Nothing but desperate defensive fighting followed for the 6th Panzer Division across the Eastern front in the remainder of 1943 and 1944. As part of Breith's III Panzer Corps (1st Panzer Army), the 6th Panzer helped break open an escape route for the two German corps trapped in the Cherkassy (Korsun) pocket in north Ukraine in February 1944. Von Manstein reinforced the division: to the 11th Panzer Regiment were added the 503rd Heavy Panzer Battalion, equipped with 34 Tiger tanks, and the 2nd Battalion of the 23rd Panzer Regiment. The combined force was called Heavy Panzer Regiment "Baake," after the 11th Panzer Regiment's commander, Oberst Franze Baake. Against an endless number of Soviet tanks and alternating thawing and freezing weather, the relief ground its way forward until, strength exhausted, it reached the village of Lisyanka. In three weeks, the Tiger battalion alone had knocked out 400 Soviet tanks; but it was down to only six of its own.[19] Most of the forces in the pocket fought their way to the III Corps salient. Had Baake's corps' spearhead not penetrated as far as it did through the belts of Soviet armies, the forces in the pocket would never have been able to escape.

Encircled with the rest of the First Panzer Army by the March Soviet offensive, the 6th Panzer Division fought its way to safety in the panzer army's vast moving pocket. Again it was called upon to be the spearhead. The First Panzer Army commander, Generaloberst Hans Hube, threw Panzerkampfgruppe "Baake" at the encircling Soviets. Baake's tanks shattered the enemy and allowed the pocket to link up with the German front at Buczacz on 7 April. In this operation, its tank strength had slipped to a handful of vehicles; it also lost all the heavy guns of the 2nd Battalion, Panzer Artillery Regiment 76. Thereafter, the 6th Panzer Division and III Panzer Corps fought unsuccessfully to stem the Soviet offensive against Army Group South , south of the Carpathians.

Finally, the division was pulled out of the line in May and sent back to Germany to rest and reequip. The attached Panther and Tiger tank units were reassigned, and the division organization was pruned by 2,000 men to meet the more austere table of organization of "Panzer Division 44." Tank companies were reduced from 21 to 17 tanks. Armored personnel carriers were issued to the 2nd Battalion, 114th Panzergrenadier Regiment, and the regimental staff. As with so many German units which had fought on the Eastern front, the 6th Panzer Division had acquired local volunteers—a Cossack squadron, which it had brought back to Germany unofficially as the 3rd Battalion of the 114th.[20]

The Soviets, as usual, would not allow the rest to last very long. On 22 June, they launched Operation "Bagration," which was to lead to the destruction of Army Group Center. The 6th Panzer Division quickly found itself trying to stem the spreading catastrophe, as Soviet spearheads were racing toward the Baltic near the border of East

---

[19] Ziemke, *Stalingrad to Berlin*, p. 233. Michum states that the "6th Panzer Division then launched a violent counterattack, destroying 268 Soviet tanks and 156 guns in a single thrust." Michum, *op. cit.*, p. 74.
[20] Michum, *op. cit.*, p. 75.

Prussia, to cut off Army Group North through the open flank left by the collapse of Army Group Center. Flung into the gap, the 6th Panzer Division held an escape route open for 5,000 German soldiers fleeing from Vilna in neighboring Lithuania. Later in August, the division moved south to the Narew River line to cover the southern border of East Prussia. In these battles, its score of tank kills reached the amazing number of 2,400.[21]

In December 1944, the 6th Panzer Division was fighting as part in the defense of Budapest. Hitler assumed direct command of tactical operations from his headquarters in Berlin, with tragic consequences.

> 3 and 6 Panzer Divisions . . . were ordered to leave all tanks, assault guns, armoured personnel carries and self-propelled artillery in the Balaton Margareten line area, while the dismounted infantry, separated from their tanks, vehicles and gun support, were to be committed to the north of Budapest against Kravchenko's tank army, this remarkable order coming . . . by word of mouth of Guderian, the expert on armoured warfare. So it came about that when 4 Guards Army and 46 Army attacked 3 Panzer Corps a few days afterwards, using large numbers of infantry formations to cross the wet and ditch-intercoursed ground, they had no difficulty in sweeping around the flanks to the rear. 3 Panzer Corps, without infantry, could not stop them.[22]

A subsequent attack by III Panzer Corps south of Budapest penetrated only four miles, with the loss of 68 of 80 tanks.

One more mighty convulsion awaited the 6th Panzer Division in 1945. Hitler had concentrated the last of his panzer forces for a great counterattack in Hungary. The attack ground forward against increasing Soviet resistance, until the army group commander committed the 6th Panzer Division as his remaining panzer reserve on 14 March. With 200 tanks and assault guns, the 6th Panzer slugged it out with the *27th Army* for two days until the Soviet counteroffensive began. With that, the German position in Hungary collapsed. Surrounded many times in its escape, the 6th Panzer Division repeatedly fought its way out.

The 6th Panzer Division retreated into Austria in order, and with enough of its combat power left to still be lethal. Raus could not help referring to the spirit of his old division when he wrote for the US Army:

> Russian armored forces always incurred severe losses wherever they encountered German armor still organized in units of any appreciable strength. Thus, as late as April 1945, the battle-weary German 6th Panzer Division succeeded, in what was probably the last tank battle, in repulsing vastly superior Russian tank forces in the plains of the lower March River, and in knocking out 80 tanks.[23]

The division fought its last battle in defense of the ancient Hapsburg capital of Vienna, holding open the Reichsbrücke over the Danube for the escape of countless

---

[21] Michum, *op. cit.*, p. 75.

[22] Seaton, *The Russo-German War*, p. 499.

[23] Rauss, *Fighting in Hell*, p. 72.

DIVISION COMMANDERS, 1941-1945

GenMaj Erich Höpner	12 Oct. 1937–31 Jul. 1938
GenMaj Wilhelm von Löpner	1 Aug. 1938–9 Oct. 1939
GenMaj Werner Kemp	10 Oct. 1939–5 Jan. 1941
GenMaj Franz Landgraf	6 Jan. 1941–25 Nov, 1941
GenMaj Erhard Raus	25 Nov. 1941–6 Feb. 1943
GenMaj Walther von Hünersdorff	7 Feb. 1943–13 Jul. 1943
Oberst Wilhelm Crisolli	25 Jul. 1941–21 Aug. 1943
Oberst Frhr von Waldenfel	22 Aug. 1943–7 Feb. 1944
Oberst Werner Marcks	8 Feb. 1944–20 Feb. 1944
GenMaj Rudolf Frhr von Waldenfels	21 Feb. 1944–12 Mar. 1944
Oberst Walter Denkert	13 Mar. 1944–24 Mar. 1944
GenMaj Rudolf Frhr von Waldenfels	25 Mar. 1944–22 Nov. 1944
Oberstlt Friedrich Wilhelm Jurgens	23 Nov. 1944–19 Jan. 1944
GenLt Rudolf Frhr von Waldenfels	20 Jan. 1945–8 May 1945

German soldiers and civilians. After the fall of that city on 14 April, the remnants of the 6th Panzer Division moved to Brünn (now Brno) in Czechoslovakia, where they surrendered to Patton's US Third Army, which, under orders, turned their prisoners over to the Soviets in early May. As with most German POWs in Soviet hands, those who survived captivity only returned to Germany ten years later.

Perhaps the best epitaph for the 6th Panzer Division is the simple statistics cited by Samuel Michuim in his book *The Panzer Legions*: "During the war, this excellent division suffered very heavy losses: 7,068 killed, 24,342 wounded, and 4,230 missing—36,640 casualties in all. Its maximum strength never exceeded 17,00 men and was usually considerably less."[24]

It would be hard to find a panzer division—any division for that matter—with as distinguished a combat record as the 6th Panzer. None could claim its unique honors—to have fought in the first and last armored battles of the *Russland Krieg*, the Russia War (at Rossienie in Lithuania in June 1941 and on the Lower March in Austria in April 1945)—and to have been the victor in both.

---

[24] Michum, *op. cit.*, p. 75.

Appendix 2: The Other Side of the Hill

S. L. A. Marshall Gets the Ball Rolling

At the end of World War II, the US Army embarked on an unprecedented effort to find out what had actually happened on the European battlefields, and, more importantly, why events played out as they did. Most modern armies write postmortems from their own records, but this one was dramatically unique. It sought to include, for the first time, "the other side of the hill." In other wars, the enemy's side of the story had never been systematically exploited. Memoirs and official accounts had come out over time and been used, but the passage of time and the defense of reputations had dulled their usefulness.

The American effort was based on the unprecedented opportunity that lay in total victory. Most of the enemy's senior officers who had opposed the American armed forces were in captivity. As with most unorthodox ideas, the concept was not an institutional product. In this case, the need was matched to the resource by the then Colonel S. L. A. Marshall of the Army Historical Division, one of the senior Army historians in the European Theater of Operations (ETO). Marshall had become famous for an innovative and effective form of immediate post-combat interview with the troops that would capture their experiences before they became lost to memory:

> ... my official duties required me to get a full and final accounting of what had happened on that field.
>
> It was done by assembling the survivors of every unit that had fought, interviewing them as a group, and recording their experiences personal and in common from the beginning of movement till the end of fighting.
>
> The method of reconstructing what develops in combat, relating cause to effect, and eliminating the fog, is my own. . . . It works because it is simple, and because what one man remembers will stir recall in another. The one inviolable rule, if each group interviewing is to get valid results, is that the question-and-answer routine must be in sequence step-by-step from first to last.[1]

Now that the war had just ended in Europe, this same energetic and innovative mind was again working outside the normal, approved groove:

> For months my head had buzzed with the idea that I had to find a way to enfold the German high commanders and their main staff officers in our operation, or else we would never know more than half of what had happened to our forces from Normandy on. The Germans would never do their history. We had captured most of the records, but the records were not enough. We needed to know the reasons for decisions, and we could only get them from live witnesses. Failing that, our story would show only one side of the hill.[2]

Marshall's efforts to prod the Army into doing the obviously right thing then took on the aspects of a conspiracy produced by Machiavelli and Puck. Marshall had several things going for him that the similarly perceptive Fuller and Liddell Hart did not a

---

[1] S. L. A. Marshall, *The Fields of Bamboo* (New York: The Dial Press, 1971) p. 1.
[2] S. L. A. Marshall, *Bringing Up the Rear* (San Rafael, CA: Presidio Press, 1979), p. 153.

generation before. For one, Marshall had the knack of being "one of the boys" with officers far senior to himself. Already at this date, he had many friends in high places disposed to be helpful. For another, he was skillful at navigating the military bureaucracy, and had a fine touch at knowing exactly how much audacity the system would bear and a sense of timing to maximize its effect. He also knew that the approval of a few key individuals would smooth the way for him:

> My superiors were at first skeptical of this approach and tended either to laugh it off or oppose it directly; there was, however, a deep understanding of the need among my opposite numbers at the War Department. I could well understand why the idea was little favored our own side of the fence. It was radical. Nothing of the sort had ever been done before. There were no regulations to cover it. Nor was the fact that we were confronted with a wholly new situation requiring original methods enough to combat normal administrative prejudice successfully.[3]

His first step was to do his homework. No amount of approval from on high would help if the German generals were not disposed to cooperate. He flew to London to interview the grand old man of the German Army, Field Marshal Gerd von Rundstedt, then a British POW. Von Rundstedt was cordial but admitted the subject was out of his field. He did recommend that Marshall ask General Warlimont, former chief of operations of OKW. If Warlimont agreed, the rest would follow. Marshall flew back to Germany and immediately interviewed Warlimont, who was so excited he said, "Oberst Marshall, I am so certain it will work that I would volunteer right now for your operation if you would have me."

Marshall's first test of the official waters was not encouraging. At the next regular staff meeting of the higher headquarters responsible for the German officers, Marshall raised the subject and was met by gales of laughter from everyone else. He would have to bide his time.

Then Marshall attached one of his key officers, Major Kenneth Hechler, to the staff of a visiting American historian interviewing captured Nazi officials on wartime economics. Hechler was to sound out a broader range of German officers on the idea. At the same time, Marshall sent a team on his own authority into the German POW camps to explore in detail the "conditions we had fixed upon the enemy high commanders." Upon Hechler's return with a positive report of the willingness of many German officers to cooperate, Marshall ordered him to sign four German officers out of the Oberursel POW camp and bring them to the I. G. Farben Building in Frankfurt for a one-day interrogation. They were Generals Fritz Bayerlein, Heinrich von Lüttwitz, and Heinz Kokott, and Colonel Meinhard von Lauchert, the main German commanders in the Battle of Bastogne. In Frankfurt, Marshall ordered Hechler to spirit all four Germans to the Historical Division's new facility in the Chateau Hennemont in France. When Hechler's orderly mind gasped out the word "kidnapping," Marshall was not

---

[3] S. L. A. Marshall, "Introduction," in Albert Kesselring, *Kesselring: A Soldier's Record* (New York: William Morrow & Company, 1954) p. v.

perturbed. He knew that the military bureaucracy would not miss the Germans for at least three weeks, and by then he would have his pilot project hammered out and the results ready to display. One never thinks that military historians can work by the SAS motto, "Who dares wins."

Immediately upon arriving at Hennemont, Marshall found himself breaking more new ground. He directed that the Germans would be escorted to the officers' mess and brazened out the objections from a few of the American officers. As he expected, human nature quickly reversed opinions. There were no leaks to *Stars and Stripes* or official complaints up the chain of command. Marshall's request among the officers for tobacco, candy, and small luxuries for the Germans was cheerfully filled. "We also tried to get word to their families that they were still alive, a boon which had previously been denied them."[4] Unknowingly, Marshall had extended the first hand of friendship and respect to the German officer corps, a gesture that would later repeat itself and create a close relationship with the German Army when it was reborn in 1956.

Marshall immediately began with his four German officers on the Bastogne pilot project. It had the advantage of being a fairly small operation, and one with which he was quite familiar. Marshall quickly had his eyes opened to the world of German military politics as old animosities broke to the surface.

> Bayerlein, who had served under Rommel before commanding Panzer Lehr Division, was the spark plug of the group. A terrierlike individual, then age fifty, he fairly vibrated when he spoke. His contempt for von Lüttwitz, who as corps commander in the attack on Bastogne had been his superior, was my first tipoff that in a POW situation, rank, even among Germans, no longer had the privilege of imposing its view. Thus, by getting staff officers grouped with their commanders as we went along, we would elicit corrective and more dependable information.[5]

Marshall also quickly discovered that, among his German charges, captivity stripped rank of its deference:

When von Lüttwitz rambled in his conversation, Bayerlein would wave a hand in his face and snarl, "Not important! Not important!" And when the somewhat paunchy Junker tried to strike a pompous pose (he still wore a monocle), Bayerlein would turn him livid by howling, "Nuts! Nuts!" It was Lüttwitz who at Bastogne had received Tony McAuliffe's four-letter reply heard around the world. Bayerlein believed that von Lüttwitz had made the worst fumbles at Bastogne, though the record showed that Bayerlein's individual actions and estimates had cost the corps some of its finest opportunities. About those mistakes, and the mistakes of others, he was brutally frank. They became almost a mania with him. When confronted with his own gross blunders, he would put his head back and laugh with abandon. At times he seemed more than a little bit unhinged, but still thoroughly likeable.[6]

---

[4] S. L. A. Marshall, *Kesselring*, p. vi.
[5] S. L. A. Marshall, *Bringing Up the Rear*, pp. 156–7.
[6] *Ibid.*

The pilot project was a success. At the next staff meeting, Marshall raised the subject again:

> There followed the longest wait of the day. The chief of staff turned about to speak softly with General Lee. With that exception, there wasn't a whisper in the room during the prolonged two-way conversation.
>
> Then quick as a wink the tension lifted as the chief looked up to say to me. "I agree with you completely. I take it that you already have your formula. Bring it to me tomorrow morning and I will act."[7]

With that, Marshall and the Germans were in business. By the next week, thirty German generals were transferred from the Oberursel POW camp to Chateau Hennemont. Another twenty generals were transferred to a separate historical shop within the Oberursel camp itself. At Hennemont, Marshall dismissed the guards on the Germans' compound and gave them the freedom of the estate. When the change of policy sank in, the Germans bolted for the door, poured out through the compound gate and disappeared, into the estate's surrounding forest. They were all back for the evening meal. Not one, then or later, was to violate the parole and leave the grounds.

After working with the Germans, Marshall categorized them into three groups: (1) the professionals who were keen to work because it interested them; (2) the 'apple-polishers'; and (3) the Nazi diehards. The first group was no problem; the second was a fact of life; but the third, even the most intractable, after a while began to come around and cooperate, including Hitler's personal adjutant, Major Buchs.[8] The subsequent Chief Historian for Headquarters, US Army, Europe, Colonel W. S. Nye, would have a slightly different and perhaps more official perspective:

> In the initial phases of the program all of the contributors were prisoners of war or internees; participation, however, was always voluntary. While participants were reimbursed for their work, they have been motivated mainly by professional interest and by the desire to promote western solidarity and mutual defense.[9]

Marshall's Brainchild Becomes an Institution

The program continued and expanded after Marshall's departure from Europe in 1946. As Colonel Nye observed:

> Originally the mission of the program was only to obtain information on enemy operations in the European Theater for use in the preparation of an official history of the U.S. Army in World War II. In 1946 the program was broadened to include the Mediterranean and Russian war theaters. Beginning in 1947, emphasis was placed on the preparation of operational studies for use by U.S. Army planning and training agencies and service schools.[10]

---

[7] *Ibid.*, p. 157.
[8] *Ibid.*, p. 159.
[9] *Guide to Foreign Military Studies*, p. iii.
[10] *Ibid.*, pp. iii–iv.

Eventually, over 200 German general officers and senior staff officers were gathered together at a new facility at Allendorf (later Neustadt) in Germany in early 1946 to begin the thorough exploitation of their experiences, a process that continued well into the 1960s, employing none other than the former Chief of OKH, Generaloberst Franz Halder, as the head of the program for fifteen years. The three monographs included in *The Anvil of War* were only a small part of the number that grew into the hundreds. By mid-August 1946, the German group had been thoroughly organized and was fully engaged in writing narrative histories of German operations units which opposed American troops under the command of SHAEF (Supreme Headquarters Allied Expeditionary Force).

When the Americans concentrated so many German general officers and staff officers, they were, perhaps, not quite prepared for the replay of wartime rivalries and animosities among their guests. In addition to the direction of the overall research effort, they hoped that Generalobersts Franz Halder and Heinz Guderian would jointly lead a special project on an organizational history of OKH to facilitate an understanding of the problems involved in the proposed merger of the United States armed forces. Halder and Guderian, as former chiefs of OKH (1938–42 and 1944–45, respectively) were the two officers most qualified to lead this unprecedented historical research effort. Unfortunately, the Americans were to be disappointed:

> Of the two, Halder had more experience in OKH, and any idea of placing Guderian in charge of the OKH project was rendered completely academic by his angry refusal to begin work unless officially assured that he would not be tried for war crimes.[11]

He also feared the more chilling prospect of being turned over to the Poles or Soviets. Furthermore, Guderian and Halder had become so alienated that they were not on speaking terms. The leadership of this great coordination effort then fell naturally into the hands of the more scholarly and less flamboyant Halder. At the highpoint of the work, his staff included twelve lieutenant-generals, four major-generals, nine brigadier-generals, nine colonels, and four lieutenant-colonels.[12]

By the middle of 1947, Guderian had emerged from his cocoon. He had been told on 18 June, his birthday, that he would not be prosecuted, and it now seemed in his best interest to cooperate. By then, the work of the historical research group was firmly in Halder's hands, and Guderian contented himself with commenting and writing on projects only in which he had a special expertise. However, Guderian did contribute to the OKH project which had become Halder's special effort. Halder had conceived of the OKH project as a trilogy—OKH "as it was," OKH "as it should have been," and OKH "as it should be." Halder essentially completed the first two parts. Guderian— who had just agreed to cooperate at last—and Kurt Zeitzler (Chief, OKH, 1942–44)

---

[11] Heinz Guderian, *Unification or Coordination—The Armed Forces Problem* (Historical Division, Special Staff, US Army, February 1949) p. v.
[12] *Ibid.*

were asked to write commentaries on Halder's first two parts. The third part was taken out of Halder's hands and specifically given to Guderian.[13] Guderian's authoritative biographer, Kenneth Macksey, observed:

> As much for the insight they gave into his way of thinking as in the nature of their contribution to the matters with which he dealt, his commentaries are valuable reading: prejudices and pride are intermingled with caustic shafts which won him a special recognition among the Americans.[14]

The cost of Guderian's talent for invective to the overall effort was high. Cliques formed around the two great men. As might be expected, the conservatives championed Halder and the progressives rallied around Guderian. So bitter did the factionalism become that certain officers, such as Field Marshals von Blomberg and Milch (the real builder of the Luftwaffe), who associated openly with Guderian, became guilty by association with Guderian in the mind of Halder. Such was the feeling, that Halder refused even to shake hands with Milch, and even Guderian's attempts to resolve the issue were rebuffed. Those who find such behavior unlikely among men who have held such enormous responsibilities should remember the hammer-and-tongs recriminations and animosities among the defeated Confederate generals after the American Civil War. The venomous feud between Generals Longstreet and Early come easily to mind. Macksey recounts one such incident, in which Guderian's overbearing attitude convulsed the research effort:

> In this military university the members of rival academic factions, in the process of relieving the tedium of captivity, hurled verbal darts at each other while they refought— on paper—the battles of the past. A passage at arms with General der Infantrie Edgar Roehricht provides a good example of Guderian's invective when roused. Roehricht, in a paper describing, somewhat inaccurately from memory, the training organization of OKH, had seen fit to criticize the methods employed by the Panzer Command, and to resurrect the infantry's fundamental distastes for the tank men. As an opening retort Guderian wrote: "This study shows that the author had just as little peacetime training experience as wartime combat experience"—a tart piece of defamation since Roehricht had much experience in many capacities, as Guderian should have known. Guderian went on to object to remarks such as, "The arbitrary manners of the armoured forces from the very beginning..." and summarized his views (to the satisfaction of the American editors, who deleted Roehricht's offending passages) with "The contributor... also knows nothing about the Inspector General of the Panzer Troops. Who was 'disturbed' by the Inspector General? The work of the Inspector General did not lead to any 'duplication of effort' nor did it cause any lack of uniformity in tactical views. It certainly had no 'fatal consequences'."[15]

Halder and Guderian continued to openly hammer each other. It did not help that some of Halder's comments on Guderian's work on unified command were on the mark

---

[13] *Ibid.*

[14] Kenneth Macksey, *Guderian: Creator of the Blitzkrieg* (London: MacDonald and Janes, 1975), p. 240; (London: Greenhill Books; 1992), p. 206.

[15] *Ibid.*, pp. 240–1.

and constructive; the scathing nature of those comments set the two men figuratively at daggers' points. Halder intimated that Guderian was shallow, while Guderian stated that Halder was a man of little substance. It was an unworthy spectacle, which did no credit to either man, as Macksey again noted: "Halder, the cool intellectual with a schoolmasterly manner, and Guderian, the dynamic man of ideas and action, were worthy of better things." In the end, the problem departed with Guderian, who was released from captivity on his 60th birthday in 1948.[16] The Army Historical Division must have been secretly relieved to see such a forceful personality depart. The short biography written by the Historical Division Staff in the preface of his favorite monograph, *Unification or Coordination—The Armed Forces Problem*, betrayed an enormous respect liberally laced with exasperation:

> The military career of Heinz Guderian is in itself enough to establish his ability as an organizer, a theorist, and an aggressive field commander. Even in an American prisoner-of-war enclosure, he retained his exceptional intellectual integrity, his firm and uncompromising attitude, his untactfulness under stress, and his alloy of courtliness and acid humor. He is a man who writes what he thinks and who does not alter his opinions to suit his audience.[17]

After Guderian's departure, Halder's position was secure. He continued to serve as leader of the Military History Program and a civilian employee of the US Army until 1961. At his retirement he was awarded, in recognition for his work, the highest decoration offered to civilian employees by the US Government—the Meritorious Civilian Service Award.[18]

History Marches On

More characteristic of the senior German officers was Field Marshal Albert Kesselring:

> I was taken away with Field Marshals List and von Weichs and a junior officer in a magnificent car to the American Historical Division's camp, Allendorf. Our escort was an officer and a gentleman, his kindness making us feel that we were among people of our own kind. The officers of the Historical Division, under their excellent Colonel Potter, went to great trouble to alleviate the customary hardships of camp life. At Allendorf I began to persuade a number of generals and General Staff officers to participate in the compilation of a history of the war. As my main argument I pointed out that this was our only chance of paying a tribute to our soldiers and at the same time influencing Allied historians in the interests of the truth—recording of our experiences being a secondary purpose. Our chief difficulties lay in the lack of documentary material. All the same, our work, in my opinion, has been useful evidence for any final account of the period. I cannot name all the officers of the Historical Division who deserve my thanks for their understanding of our situation and that of our families—there were too many. Almost

---

[16] *Ibid.*, p. 241.

[17] Guderian, *Unification or Coordination*.

[18] Franz Halder, *The Halder War Diary*, Charles Burdick and Hans-Adolf Jacobsen, eds. (London: Greenhill Books, 1988), p. 10.

without exception they were, and are still, the ambassadors of good will and "fraternization."[19]

Kesselring was as good as his word. He proved to be one of the most prolific authors, writing thirty-five separate monographs. Other major contributors were Generals Fritz Bayerlein, Günther Blumentritt, Rudolf von Gersdorff, Franz Halder, Friedrich Koechling, Fritz Krämer, Heinrich von Lüttwitz, Burkhart Müller-Hildebrand, Lothar Rendulic, Alfred Toppe, Walter Warlimont, Carl Gustav Wagener, and Siegfried Westphal.[20]

Generaloberst Raus was also a major contributor to the series. He was by far one of the best writers. Unfortunately, his excellent prose and gift for drama were sometimes hamhandedly edited for publication in the German Report Series of Department of the Army pamphlets. Official American military writing tends, unfortunately, to the pedestrian—there is the odd impression in the US Army that colorful and dramatic prose is not objective and professional.

Of the first fourteen manuscripts published in this series, Raus was the author of four. They included *Military Improvisations during the Russian Campaign* (DA Pam 20-201, 1951), *German Defense Tactics against Russian Breakthroughs* (DA Pam 20-233, 1951), *Russian Combat Methods* (DA Pam 20-230, 1950), and *The Effects of Climate on Combat in European Russia* (DA Pam 20-291, 1952). The first two monographs were included in Greenhill Books' *The Anvil of War: German Generalship in Defense on the Eastern Front* (1994), along with *Operations of Encircled Forces* (DA Pam 20-234, 1952) by Generalleutnant Oldwig von Natzmer. The second two of Raus's monographs were included in Greenhill Books' *Fighting in Hell: The German Ordeal on the Eastern Front* (1995); this book also contained *Warfare in the Far North* (DA Pam 20-292, 1951) by General der Infantrie Dr Waldemar Erfurth and *Combat in Russian Forests and Swamps* (DA Pam 20-231, 1951) by Geneal der Infanterie Hans von Greiffenberg. Other unpublished monographs by Raus which are included in this book included *The Pomeranian Battle and the Command in the East* (D-189, 1947), and *Small Unit Tactics—Unusual Situations* (P-060g, Part I [1952], Part II [1952], Part III [1953], and Part IV [1954]).[21]

By 1948, most of the German contributors had returned to civilian life, which allowed a change in the tempo and administrative organization of the research program. Contributors could now work on their projects in their own homes, supervised by a small control group of selected former high-ranking officers, headed by Halder. As the number of manuscripts grew into the hundreds, the creation of a thorough index became necessary to make the program's contents accessible. This project was assumed in September 1951 by General der Artillerie Friedrich von Boetticher, German military attaché in Washington (1933–41), and completed by the following spring. At that time,

[19] Albert Kesselring, *The Memoirs of Field Marshal Kesselring* (London and New York, 1953; London: Greenhill Books, 1988), p. 296.
[20] *Guide to Foreign Military Studies*, pp. 242–51.
[21] *Ibid.*, p. 248.

another index was undertaken to evaluate all the manuscripts in the collection according to historical, operational, and technical interest.[22]

Other German officers, such as General der Artillerie Walter Warlimont, Deputy Chief of the Operations Staff of OKW, continued to work on the project from prison cells, where they were serving sentences for war crimes. Warlimont's superior at OKW, Generaloberst Alfred Jodl, consented to work on manuscripts during his trial, as did a number of other men tried as war criminals such as Hermann Goering, Albert Speer, Wilhelm Keitel, Sepp Dietrich, and Joachim Peiper. The contributions of Goering, Jodl, and Keitel, however, were cut short by their subsequent convictions—and, in the case of Goering, suicide, and of the others, hangings. Warlimont was serving a life sentence in Landsberg Prison in Bavaria (Hitler's prison where he wrote *Mein Kampf* after the 1921 putsch) when he was asked to review the study of the organization and functioning of the German Armed Forces High Command, prepared by his successor at OKW. His summary of an armed forces high command 'as it should be,' the *Unification Problem: Some Lessons from the German Experience*, was published in 1950 as part of the German Report Series, only one of twenty-four studies he prepared.[23] No doubt the research done by a number of the officers in the program advanced the cause of the German military memoir. S. L. A. Marshall discovered years later, with some amusement, that one of his 'guests' at Hennemont, Generalleutnant Hasso von Mellenthin, had used his time there to research his own well-received memoirs, *Panzer Battles.*[24]

As the advent of the Cold War made the enmity of the Soviet Union toward the Western allies unmistakable, the accounts of the German officers assumed more than a purely historical value. Many of these officers had recent and exhaustive experience in fighting the armed forces of the Soviet Union. That knowledge would be of great help to the US Army, if properly analyzed and disseminated. In June of 1950, with the invasion of South Korea, the value of these works increased significantly. The United States believed that Korea was only a diversion, and that the main blow would soon fall in Europe. For that reason, the build-up of forces in Europe was greater than that in Korea itself. It was no accident that all fourteen pamphlets were published as part of the German Report Series at the height of the Korean War and clearly addressed situations that already had been experienced in Korea and were anticipated in fighting in Europe.

By 1954, the number of Germans who had been involved in the project numbered 730, of whom 642 were officers. The latter figure broke down by rank as follows:

Reichsmarschall (no British/American equivalent)	1
Generalfeldmarschall (Field Marshal/General of the Army)	5
Generaloberst (General)	21

---

[22] *Ibid.*, pp. iii–iv.
[23] Walter Warlimont, *The Unification Problem: Some Lessons From the German Experience*, Department of the Army, Office of the Chief of Military History, April 1950, p. ii.
[24] Marshall, *Bringing Up the Rear*, p. 159.

General der Panzertruppen, etc. (Lieutenant General)	134
Generalleutnant (Major-General)	160
Generalmajor (Brigadier-General)	180
Oberst (Colonel)	78
Oberstleutnant (Lieutenant-Colonel)	34
Major	23
Hauptmann/Rittmeister (Captain)	7

Although not an officer, Reichminister Albert Speer, the architect of the German war industries production was also a member of this project.

In the end, 501 Army, Waffen-SS, and Luftwaffe generals and another eleven Navy admirals were drawn into the program, in addition to hundreds of other specialists. The more prominent officers are practically a "who's who" of the German armed forces in World War II:

Arnim, Generaloberst Hans-Jürgen
Bayerlein, Generalleutnant Fritz
Beck,Generaloberst Ludwig
Bittrich, General der W-SS Wilhelm
Blaskowitz, Generaloberst Johannes
Blumentritt, General der Infantrie Günther
Brandenberger, General der Panzertruppen Erich
Breith, General der Panzertruppen Hermann
Choltitz, General der Infantrie Dietrich von
Dietrich, Generaloberst (W-SS), Jospeh ("Sepp")
Dönitz, Grossadmiral Karl
Erfurth, General der Infantrie Dr Waldemar
Geyr von Schweppenburg, General der Panzertruppen Leo Freiherr
Goering, Reichsmarschall Hermann
Guderian, Generaloberst Heinz
Halder, Generaloberst Franz
Hausser, Generaloberst (W-SS) Paul
Heinrici, Generaloberst Gotthard
Heydte, Oberst Friedrich Frhr. von der
Hollidt, Generaloberst Karl
Hube, General der Panzertruppen Hans
Jodl, Generaloberst Alfred
Keitel, Generalfeldmarschall Wilhelm
Kesselring, Generalfeldmarschall Albert
Leeb, Generalfeldmarschall Wilhelm Ritter von
List, Generalfeldmarschall Wilhelm

Lüttwitz, General der Panzertruppen Heinrich Frhr. von

Lüttwitz, General der Panzertruppen Smilo Frhr. von

Mackensen, Generaloberst Eberhard von

Manteuffel, General der Panzertruppen Hasso-Eccard von

Meindl, General der Fallschirmtruppen Eugen

Mellenthin, Generalmajor Friedrich von

Natzmer, Generaloberst Oldwig von

Nehring, General der Panzertruppen Walter

Peiper, Oberst (W-SS) Joachim

Pemsel, Generalleutnant Max Joseph

Raus, Generaloberst Erhard

Rendulic, Generaloberst Dr Lothar

Ruge, Vizeadmiral Friedrich

Rundstedt, Generalfeldmarschall Gerd von

Salmuth, Generaloberst Hans von

Seidemann, General der Flieger Hans

Senger und Etterlin, General der Panzertruppen Fridolin von

Skorzeny, Oberstleutnant (W-SS) Otto

Speer, Reichsminister Dr Albert

Speidel, Generalleutnant Dr Hans

Steiner, General der Waffen-SS Felix

Strachwitz, Generalleutnant Hyazinth Graf

Student, Generaloberst Kurt

Tippelskirch, Genral der Infanterie Kurt von

Vietinghoff-Scheel, Generaloberst Heinrich von

Warlimont, General der Artillerie Walter

Wenck, General der Panzertruppen Walter

Westphal, General der Kavallerie Sigfried

Zeitzler, Generaloberst Kurt

With these figures in mind, it was perhaps an understatement by Colonel Nye when he wrote in 1954 that "The program represents an unusual degree of collaboration between officers of nations recently at war."[25] But it was much more than that. Strangely, it was an American officer who spent his life documenting the exploits of his own American troops, S. L. A. Marshall, who helped the Germans remember their own fallen comrades. It was, as Field Marshal Kesselring said, the German general officer corps' "only chance of paying a tribute to our soldiers . . ." In the end, it was simply a matter of keeping faith.

---

[25] *Guide to Foreign Military Studies*, p. iv.

Recommended Reading

Boatner, Mark M., *The Biographical Dictionary of World War II* (Novato, CA: Presidio Press, 1996).

Carrell, Paul, *Hitler Moves East, 1941–1943* (Boston: Little, Brown and Company, 1963).

————, *Scorched Earth: The Russo-German War, 1941–1943* (Boston: Little, Brown and Company, 1970).

Clark, Alan, *Barbarossa: The Russian-German Conflict, 1941–1945* (New York: Macmillan, 1985).

Craig, William, *Enemy at the Gates: The Battle for Stalingrad* (New York: Bantam Books, 1982).

Edwards, Roger, *Panzer: A Revolution in Warfare, 1939–1945* (London: Arms and Armour Press, 1989).

Erickson, John, *The Road to Stalingrad: Stalin's War with Germany*, Vol. 1 (New York: Harper & Row, 1974).

Glantz, David M. (ed.), *The Initial Period of War on the Eastern Front, 22 June–August 1941*, Proceedings of the Fourth Art of War Symposium, Garmisch, FRG, October 1987 (London: Frank Cass, 1993).

Guderian, Heinz, *Panzer Leader* (New York: E. P. Dutton & Company, 1957).

Manstein, Erich von, *Lost Victories: The War Memoirs of Hitler's Most Brilliant General* (Novvato, CA: Presidio Press, 1982).

Mellenthin, F. W. von, *Panzer Battles: A Study in the Employment of Armor in the Second World War* (Norman, OK: University of Oklahoma Press, 1956).

Mitchum, Samuel W., Jr, *The Panzer Legions: A Guide to the German Army Tank Divisions of World War II and Their Commanders* (Westport, CT: Greenwood Press, 2001).

Piekalkiewicz, Janusz. *Operation Citadel: Kursk and Orel, the Greatest Tank Battle in History* (Novato, CA: 1985).

Poirier, Robert G., and Conner, Albert Z., *The Red Army Order of Battle in the Great Patriotic War* (Novato, CA: Presidio Press, 1985).

Rauss, Erhard, et al., *Fighting in Hell: The German Ordeal on the Eastern Front* (Peter G. Tsouras, ed.) (London: Greenhill Books, 1995).

————, *The Anvil of War: German Generalship in Defense on the Eastern Front* (Peter G. Tsouras, ed.) (London: Greenhill Books, 1994).

Rabe von Pappenheim, Freidrich-Carl, *Generaloberst Erhard Raus (1889–1956). Ein Truppenführer in Osfeldzug* (Osnabrück, 1988).

Rotundo, Louis C., (ed.), *Battle for Stalingrad: The 1943 Soviet General Staff Study* (Washington, DC: Pergamon-Brassey's, 1989).

Seaton, Albert, *The Russo-German War, 1941–1945* (Novato, CA: Presidio Press, 1993).

Senger und Etterlin, Frido von, *Neither Hope Nor Fear: The Wartime Memoirs of the German Defender of Monte Cassino* (Novato, CA: Presidio Press, 1989).

Scheibert, Horst von, and Erlfrath, Ulrich, *Panzer in Russland: Die deutschen gepanzerten Verbände im Russland-Feldzug, 1941–1944* (Dorheim: Podzun Verlag, 1971).

Sheibert, *Relief Operation Stalingrad* (Neckargemund, 1956).

Zaloga, Steven J., and Grandsen, James, *Soviet Tanks and Combat Vehicles of World War Two* (London: Arms and Armour Press, 1984).

Ziemke, Earl F., *Stalingrad to Berlin: The German Defeat in the East* (Washington, DC: Office of the Chief of Military History, United States Army, 1968).

Zhukov, G., *Reminiscences and Reflections* (2 vols) (Moscow: Progress Publishsers, 1985).

Index